LABOR'S END

THE WORKING CLASS
IN AMERICAN HISTORY

Editorial Advisors
James R. Barrett, Julie Greene,
William P. Jones, Alice Kessler-Harris,
and Nelson Lichtenstein

*A list of books in the series appears
at the end of this book.*

LABOR'S END

*How the Promise of Automation
Degraded Work*

JASON RESNIKOFF

**UNIVERSITY OF
ILLINOIS PRESS**
Urbana, Chicago, and Springfield

Library of Congress Cataloging-in-Publication Data
Names: Resnikoff, Jason, author.
Title: Labor's end : how the promise of automation degraded
    work / Jason Resnikoff.
Description: Urbana : University of Illinois Press, [2021] |
    Series: The working class in American history | Includes
    bibliographical references and index.
Identifiers: LCCN 2021028061 (print) | LCCN 2021028062
    (ebook) | ISBN 9780252044250 (cloth) | ISBN 9780252086298
    (paperback) | ISBN 9780252053214 (ebook)
Subjects: LCSH: Labor supply—Effect of automation on—
    United States. | Occupational training—United States. |
    Automation—Social aspects. | Labor—United States—
    History.
Classification: LCC HD6331.2.U5 R45 2021 (print) | LCC
    HD6331.2.U5 (ebook) | DDC 303.48/340973—dc23
LC record available at https://lccn.loc.gov/2021028061
LC ebook record available at https://lccn.loc.gov/2021028062

Contents

Acknowledgments

I am indebted to the archivists who offered invaluable assistance at the Harvard Business School's Baker Library, the Schlesinger Library of Harvard University, the John F. Kennedy Presidential Library, the National Archives and Records Administration at College Park, New York University's Tamiment Library and Robert F. Wagner Labor Archive, and the Walter P. Reuther Library at Wayne State University. The Baker Library's Alfred D. Chandler Travel Fellowship, an Exploratory Research Grant from the Hagley Museum and Library, and a travel grant from Columbia University's American Studies Department provided research support. I am grateful to Todd Gitlin, who granted me an interview and allowed me the extraordinary privilege of taking home files from his personal papers. I am likewise grateful to Karen Nussbaum and Margery Davies, both of whom took time to sit for interviews. It is a pleasure to thank James Engelhardt and Alison Syring of the University of Illinois Press, who edited the manuscript, as well as Alex Sayf Cummings and Joshua Freeman, whose comments made this a stronger book.

As many have before me, I discovered much of what I learned about history by trying to make a little bit of it myself. My time as an organizer for the GWC-UAW and CPW-UAW in Local 2110 taught me not only about how historical change happens but why we study history in the first place. For that insight I am grateful to my leads and comrades: Andy Crow, Alyssa Greene, Lale Alpar, Olga Brudastova, Bradley Gorski, Anthony Romer, Cora Burgantiños, Joy Winkler, Leslie Fine, Michael Belt, Tiffany Yee-Vo, Maida Rosenstein, and Ken Lang. In addition, many colleagues and friends read portions of this work and offered helpful feedback. It is my privilege to name them here: Charles Halvorson, Allison Powers, Mary Freeman, George Aumoithe,

Manual Bautista Gonzalez, Ari King, Amad Ross, Pollyanna Rhee, Ben Serby, Stephen Koeth, Scott MacFarlane, Rebecca Lossin, Mookie Kideckel, Aline Voldoire, Kristina Moore, and Patrick Barrett.

This book benefited enormously from the labor and wisdom of Mae Ngai, Matthew Jones, Eric Foner, Robert Amdur, Anders Stephanson, Herbert Sloan, Richard John, Barbara J. Fields, Nelson Lichtenstein, and Elizabeth Blackmar. I suspect I will never be able to repay Alice Kessler-Harris for everything she has done for me and this project. In addition, for every page that appears in this book I wrote three more, and Casey Nelson Blake read them all; he shepherded this project from the beginning and saved me from many infelicities of thought, fact, and style.

Robert and Sandra Resnikoff, Philip Gary, and Amanda Resnikoff gave me the benefit of their warmth and intelligence; they have these many years sustained both me and this work. And, finally, I could not have written this book were it not for Lou Resnikoff, my unfailing colleague, my teacher, and my comrade.

LABOR'S END

Introduction

It is not from machines that we learn
the purpose of machines.
—Lewis Mumford

The great question will forever remain,
who shall work?
—John Adams

This book is about the meaning of work in the United States after World War II. It did not start out that way. It began, rather, as an attempt to pin down the precise definition of the word "automation," coined by the American automobile industry in the years immediately following the war. I had noticed that some historians of the period granted "automation" a degree of historical agency. Whatever it was, it made things happen. "Although automation's advocates exaggerated its utility and underestimated its costs," writes Thomas Sugrue, "automation sometimes did have dramatic effects."[1] Another historian has written of "automation's role in labor's decline" during that era.[2] I wanted to know what precisely had achieved these results and how.

Yet, surprisingly, while the positive and negative effects of the phenomenon called automation have been the subjects of intense debate since the middle of the twentieth century, the origins of the word have received little attention from historians. This is all the more remarkable considering that at the time when "automation" supposedly achieved its most impressive results, its definition was notoriously controversial. "There is much truth in the quip," wrote John Diebold, who perhaps did more than anyone to popularize the word, "that it is as hard for a group of businessmen to define automation as it is for a group of theologians to define sin."[3] Nevertheless, most historians who write on the subject assume, as I did, that the word "automation" describes a clear-cut technological process—the replacement of human labor with machine action. Regardless of whether they believe it betokens good or evil, scholars have used the word as though it had been summoned into existence by straightforward changes in the means of industrial production.

The origins of automation, however, were not primarily technical. They were ideological. Coined in the late 1940s by an executive at the Ford Motor Company to refer to machines that bored holes in engine blocks, by the early 1950s the word no longer described a specific technology or labor process. It expressed, rather, a conviction: That industrial progress meant the abolition of human labor from industry, and in particular, manual labor. According to this ideological commitment, technological development and the end of human laboring were synonymous. As technology improved, work would naturally diminish. The substance of automation, however, was not the abolition of labor but, instead, its mystification. Hidden behind spectacular new machines and an abiding faith in inevitable technological revolution, human beings continued to labor and produce value.

Rather than describing the state of the mechanical arts, when lawmakers, managers, and union leaders spoke of automation they were talking as much about what they believed work meant as they were the actions of a specific piece of mechanism. The rhetorical power of the ideology called "automation" both revealed and perpetuated a conviction held by Americans from all walks of life that the activity of work was incompatible with freedom. A free person, the proponents of "automation" held, was free from work. Until then this belief had been the conviction of slaveowners, aristocrats, and in the late nineteenth century, a minority of socialist thinkers. In fact, American technological utopians of the turn of the twentieth century had generally believed that a machine-wrought utopia would make work pleasant, rather than abolish it. "We teach that labor is necessary and honorable, that idleness is robbery and disgrace," wrote Henry Olerich in his 1883 speculative classic, *Cityless and Countryless World*. Only with the rise of "automation"—only as political actors, including staunch allies of workers, began to rule out the workplace as a site of political struggle, dismissing speed-up, declassification, and deindustrialization as technical innovation—only then did the notion of technological progress become practically and almost universally synonymous with the elimination of labor.[4]

In this book I refer to this ideological conviction as the automation discourse, or for short, "automation" in scare quotes. With this awkward construction my intention is to clarify consistently for the reader that in the postwar period "automation" was a term of ideology, not a dispassionate description of engineering. The material changes in the labor process that postwar Americans called "automation" were practically indistinguishable from what before they had called mechanization, meant here to mean simply the introduction of machinery or new tools to a labor process. In the postwar period, mechanization was a known phenomenon. It was old, and it was well understood. Sometimes the mechanization of a labor process created more jobs, everyone knew, as when it aided the detailed division of labor; sometimes it allowed managers to hire fewer workers by speeding up an old job so that one person worked harder and could do the work of several people. And sometimes, sure enough, it replaced a task performed by a person with one accomplished by a machine. The past century had shown Americans what mechanization was, and though it could mean labor saving, efficiency, and profit, as often as not to ordinary people coming out of the Great Depression it meant hardship, satanic mills, and alienation. The popular image of mechanization that loomed before the contemporary imagination was not a new world of liberation but Charlie Chaplin in *Modern Times*, eaten alive by the assembly line.[5]

From the beginning, "automation" meant something other than mechanization. "While, in the interests of precision," a congressional subcommittee found during its 1955 hearings on automation and technological change, "there is a natural inclination to narrow the term, it is clearly wrong to dismiss automation, however, as nothing more than an extension of mechanization. We are clearly on the threshold of an industrial age, the significance of which we cannot predict with potentialities which we cannot fully appreciate."[6] A careful investigation of the labor processes that Americans described as being automated in this period, however, shows that they were naming the same diverse changes to the means of production that they earlier had called mechanization. While after the war there was a very public celebration of innovative feedback mechanisms, that alone does not explain the rise of the automation discourse. Self-regulating machinery pre-dated the coining of the word "automation"—including feedback mechanisms—and the history of industrialization had long included many examples of machinery that made labor more productive. From the outset, "automation" meant much more than the development of new feedback mechanisms. Although, like any term of ideology, "automation" had a material referent, its main work was to speak to the grand arc of history and the meaning of human labor; the postwar meaning of the word as a descriptor of a new stage in history far, far outstripped any technical advances made in feedback mechanisms at the time.[7]

Nor do mechanical improvements in labor productivity explain the rise of the automation discourse. While machines could and did make labor more productive through labor saving, increased productivity per worker did not, as the automation discourse held, necessarily mean the elimination of jobs. In fact, well into the 1960s the sectors of the economy that mechanized fastest—those that contemporaries claimed were "automating"—witnessed an increase, not a decrease, in employment. Greater labor productivity lowered prices, generating increased demand, which allowed firms to enlarge their market share, requiring that they hire more, not fewer, workers.[8]

But often enough, what managers called "automation" described practices that increased labor productivity not by means of labor saving but by labor intensification. For example, calling it "automation," managers in the automobile industry sped up workers. Sometimes they used new machines, and sometimes they did not. At certain points in the production process they installed machines that accelerated the speed of production overall, thereby requiring those who continued to work on old machines to labor at a faster pace. What businesses and computer specialists called the "automation" of office work actually *increased* the number of human workers in the labor process as employers used a newfangled machine called the electronic digital computer to break up clerical work into many smaller, more degraded, poorly paid jobs. Union officials and shippers, likewise, described the containerization of dock work as "automation," and by the early 1970s new cranes and docks and the widespread adoption of containers dramatically reduced the number of workers necessary to unload and load a ship. But for the decade when "automation" was supposedly taking place, longshoremen performed the same break bulk handling of individual goods that they had for decades, only now for less money and hauling larger loads—and it was from this pool of excess value, squeezed from human labor, that shippers found the wealth to "modernize" the docks. Workers on the railroads, in coal mines, and in packinghouses—all of whose jobs were undergoing "automation"—complained of speed-up, work intensification, and work degradation.

That "automation" was not an irrepressible and progressive movement toward the elimination of human labor should not surprise us. Between the 1970s and the 1990s historians of technology challenged the notion of "technological determinism," the idea that technology alone produces inevitable social phenomena and that it innovates regardless of its social, political, or economic context. The printing press did not punch out democratic societies along with printed pages, nor did it somehow necessitate the invention of the typewriter (whose origins are distinct). Machines mediate social relations, they do not dictate them. Nor do machines demand their own innovation.[9]

Sitting uneasily with this insight, Americans in the last quarter of the twentieth century spoke often of their new postindustrial society, in which the inevitable thrust of technological development would replace manufacturing jobs with service work and white-collar employment. A worker's ability to manipulate symbols and deploy knowledge was to command more value than his or her ability to perform physical, industrial wage labor. The roots of postindustrialism go back further in time than the 1970s, as others have argued and as this book likewise shows.[10] Nevertheless, although historians of technology have debunked the narrative of ineluctable technological progress that informed much postwar thought on the subject of mechanization, many today still assume that technological trends are their own agents through time and space, and that all technological innovations that can occur, will. According to this line of argument, "automation" is happening, and it falls to historical actors to decide whether to use it—whatever it is—for good or bad.[11]

The practice of most if not all historians of "automation" has been to cut through the vagueness of the word by choosing a specific technological development and treating that apparatus as the real "automation." This book has benefited enormously from those studies, but still they do not explain why Americans after World War II believed that "automation" marked a revolution in the means of production, why its definition was so fraught, or how managers could use it to describe the expansion of a job category rather than its elimination. They do not explain why those who complained most about "automation" on the shop floor were not the minority of skilled workers but rather the masses of the so-called semiskilled, the backbone of the industrial unionization movement in the 1930s and the source of the labor movement's sizable political power in the postwar period. Nor do they explain why so many of these same workers called "automation" a speedup.[12]

The inclination on the part of historians to believe that "automation" was and continues to be a specific technological process, to locate a particular mechanism and treat it as the real "automation," and then to speak of that mechanism as evidence of a coming postindustrial civilization is itself a product of the historical phenomenon that historians intend to explain. I find calling the last quarter of the twentieth century and the first quarter of the twenty-first the "postindustrial era" misleading. Although half a century of deregulation and capital flight has witnessed the reduction of manufacturing employment in the United States, total worldwide industrial employment was higher in the first years of the twenty-first century than it was in the last decade of the twentieth—29 percent in 2010 as opposed to 22 percent in 1994. As Aaron Benanav has shown, increases in labor productivity in the new millennium result not from stupendous labor-saving machines but, ironically, from global industrial "overcapacity," what during the 1930s critics called "overproduction." Labor productivity appears to be rapidly rising only because, with a saturation of industrial producers, manufacturing output has grown so slowly. Too many industrial powers are producing for the same global market, dividing it into ever-smaller shares. That said, although in the United States between 1960 and 2018 the percentage of workers employed in manufacturing fell from

24 percent to 8 percent, in China in 2015, 43 percent of the working population was engaged in industrial production. All of this is to say that the social and practical conditions of profitability, rather than the irresistible current of technological progress, decide whether an employer can or will invest in a machine. When at the turn of the twenty-first century managers shipped factories to the right-to-work South, to Mexico, and to China, they left in pursuit not of "automation" but cheap human labor.[13]

The purpose of business under conditions of capitalism is to make profit. Throughout the history of industrial production, and especially in the midst of postwar "automation," managers showed themselves readily adaptable to using a machine one day and a person the next, and just as often a mix of machines and people. The machine can cheapen the labor; labor can reduce the costs of investment in machines. Throughout the history of industrial capitalism this has been a dynamic, ongoing, circular relationship, not a teleological one. Capital moves. The use of machines in the making of profit is not a straight line driving toward the end of history; it is a whirlwind circling in on itself, unsettling old methods, disrupting the organization of workers, sweeping away anything that does not answer the twists and turns of the market while also bringing in whatever will make money. When it comes to turning a profit, it literally does not pay to be a technological determinist. This is true at present, and it was certainly true in the United States in the middle of the twentieth century.[14]

The belief that "automation" was a technological revolution was practically ubiquitous in the postwar period. "Hardly anybody is against automation," wrote Diebold. "As a matter of fact, nearly everybody is for it, because it is a word that implies 'progress.' Predictions of dire consequences from automation usually end with the warning that it must be controlled rather than stopped."[15] A Ford manager credited with having invented the word called "automation" a "new concept—a new philosophy—of manufacturing." According to James Boggs, a Marxist Humanist and Black liberation theorist who worked on an automobile assembly line in Detroit for twenty years, "Automation is the greatest revolution that has taken place in human society since men stopped hunting and fishing and started to grow their own food," and this required a "New Declaration of Human Rights" in which people were liberated from work. Daniel Bell, a sociologist and public intellectual, wrote in 1956 that automation would do away with the "proletariat," replacing it with a "salariat," and that industrial work "has lost its rationale in the capitalist industrial order." The union leader Walter Reuther told Congress, "We believe that we are really standing on the threshold of a completely revolutionary change in the scientific and technological developments we have experienced. As we in the labor movement visualize this problem, we believe that we are achieving the technology, the tools of production, that will enable us as free people to master our physical environment." Norbert Wiener, a mathematician and guru of the cybernetics movement, insisted that the "second industrial revolution" and "automation" will "undoubtedly lead to the factory without employees." In 1958 the political philosopher Hannah Arendt wrote of "the advent of automation, which in a few decades probably will empty the factories and liberate mankind from its oldest and most natural burden, the burden of laboring and the bondage of necessity." In 1960 President John F. Kennedy said of "automation" that "we cannot stop progress," and it was of national importance that "this public blessing" not become a "private curse." In her *SCUM Manifesto* of 1968, Valerie Solanas, by no means an outlier in this respect, called for society to "institute complete automation," which she believed was entirely possible, in order to liberate women from work.[16]

These individuals did not have a common politics, and yet they were equally committed to the idea that industrial laboring was irreconcilable with freedom. To understand how "automation" could appeal to such a diverse set of actors, we must return to the word's ideological origins; we must consider its place in the longer history of the meaning of work in the United States.

* * *

Throughout the history of the United States, the meaning of work has been a fundamental part of how Americans defined political freedom. With the important exception of the defenders of antebellum slavery, classical American liberalism held that a free person owned productive property and worked for himself. Addressing a largely agrarian country, Noah Webster argued in 1787 that "a general and tolerably equal distribution of landed property is the whole basis of national freedom. . . . While this continues, the people will inevitably possess both power and freedom; when this is lost, power departs, liberty expires, and a commonwealth will inevitably assume some other form." A person who owned property also owned their work. They were independent and decided much of the course of their life. "Work and property," wrote C. Wright Mills of late eighteenth-century political economy, "were closely joined into a single unit." It was this independence that allowed a person to enjoy the privileges and responsibilities of political freedom. When asked in 1865 what freedom meant to him, George Frazier, a Baptist minister who had been enslaved for sixty years, answered: "placing us where we could reap the fruit of our own labor . . . to have land, and turn in and till it by our own labor."[17]

Industrialization at the turn of the twentieth century meant the centralization of productive property. Industrial machines concentrate power. By the early decades of the twentieth century the material processes of reproducing life in the United States all too visibly opposed the political philosophy on which traditional republican notions of freedom were based.[18] Dependent wage laboring could no longer be rationalized, as Abraham Lincoln had done, as the activity of "beginners" in economic life, simply starting out before they owned their own concerns. Free people, Lincoln had said, labored "for themselves, on their farms, in their houses, and in their shops, taking the whole product to themselves, and asking no favors of capital on the one hand, nor hirelings and slaves on the other."[19] Now, for many, wage labor was no longer a stepping stone but a dead end. The logic of profit making led managers to design degraded jobs characterized by harsh regimentation, long hours, dangerous conditions, low pay, exhaustion, and boredom. What I have called the industrial meaning of work, and what others call "bare life" concerns, became prominent: an understanding on the part of workers and managers alike that work in and of itself was essentially unpleasant and that its sole purpose was to keep the individual and his or her dependents alive.[20]

The contradiction between self-rule and industrial wage laboring posed difficult theoretical and practical challenges to the achievement of true democracy in the United States. The Progressive movement of the early twentieth century hoped to reconcile industrial wage laboring and traditional notions of freedom through legal reform, education, and the creation of a welfare state. The labor movement sought to make work and freedom compatible under industrial conditions by securing for workers control over their jobs. Collective bargaining, this reasoning went, would give workers a species of property in their jobs while capitalists would continue to own the means of production. Demands for union recognition and shorter hours animated the growing ranks of the industrial working class in the United States. In demanding shorter hours, however, industrial workers were not anticipating the automation discourse and demanding the mechanical elimination of their jobs. From the Haymarket demonstrations to the 1909 strike of twenty thousand garment workers in New York, the call for shorter hours was part of a larger demand by workers to control the character of their jobs: what they did, when they did it, and for how much.[21]

These concerns gained new urgency in the twenty years between the world wars. The architecture critic Siegfried Giedion would later argue that the period witnessed the "full mechanization" of American society. "Mechanization," wrote Giedion of the 1920s and 1930s, "implanted itself more deeply. It impinged upon the very center of the human psyche, through all the senses."[22] More and more, technically complex networks of power penetrated American society. One can point to indoor plumbing, radio, mass electrification, and the ubiquitous ownership of the automobile. Likewise making an enormous impact on the texture of daily life, mechanization, heavy capitalization, itinerant labor, and distant investor-owners increasingly came to characterize American agriculture.[23] These same years also saw the widespread adoption of practices in manufacturing developed earlier in the century, innovations that have become practically synonymous with workplace alienation—the assembly line (invented in 1913) and the managerial control of workers' bodies known as Taylorism (whose bible, *The Principles of Scientific Management*, Frederick Winslow Taylor published in 1911).[24]

The origins of the postwar coining of "automation" lay in the interwar period. Responding to the record unemployment wrought by the economic collapse of the Great Depression, many liberals came to the conclusion that overproduction had precipitated the disaster. Industrial civilization appeared to have reached its final stage. It produced too much and employed too few. Machines, it appeared, had robbed workers of their jobs.[25] In 1930 John Maynard Keynes dubbed this phenomenon "technological unemployment." Liberals and leftists alike proposed restarting the economy by conserving resources. Congressional representatives proposed national legislation to shorten the workday and even deny patents for "labor-saving devices."[26] The labor movement demanded fewer hours for industrial workers with no reduction in wages, with the aim of distributing wealth more widely by sharing the work. The notion of workers' control gained new persuasiveness in this period with the rise of the industrial union movement and the tactic of the sit-down strike. Militant workers claimed a moral and—after passage of the 1935 National Labor Relations Act—legal ownership of their jobs by means of collective bargaining. Workers' control, unions, and collective bargaining seemed to promise the possibility that although industrial property by its very nature could not be distributed into small-holds, work and freedom could nevertheless be reconciled.

The entrance of the United States into World War II altered the discursive terrain on which Americans debated the meaning of work and its relation to freedom. To meet the war emergency, the U.S. economy shifted into high gear to produce weapons and materiel, in the process reviving the fortunes of industrial capitalism. Overproduction and underconsumption ceased to pose a challenge when the industrial product of the nation was daily consumed in flames. Rather than a temporary mobilization to save the world from fascism, that model became the standard of economic good governance. "The investor, the organizer, the industrial worker, even the farmer, have once again had a glimpse of that hitherto unattainable heaven which the innocent regard as a practical equivalent of the good life: the heaven of full productivity based on unlimited demand and leading to the hope of unlimited profits," Lewis Mumford observed in 1944. "The capitalist dog has returned to his old vomit."[27] Consumption, rather than thoughtful production, became the defining practice of good citizenship.[28] After the conservative reaction to the national strike wave of 1946 and the following McCarthyite purge of the nation's left wing, union leaders bargained away much shop-floor control to win for their members healthcare, unemployment benefits, vacation time, and pensions, all of which a stronger welfare state would have made a citizen's right rather than an employee's privilege. In exchange for a guarantee of physical continuance—the ability to see a doctor, to take a rest, to have enough money when laid off or too old to work—some labor leaders gave up on the principle of worker control of the factory floor. The concession made by the United Auto Workers in the 1949 national Ford contract, article IV, section 4, became a national standard when it allowed management to set "production standards," that is, to dictate how workers did the job, when, and with what machines.[29]

In spite of the general hostility facing the political Left at mid-century, unions and collective bargaining, like Social Security and deficit spending, had nevertheless become for the public essential elements of a humane society. Saddled with unions they could limit but not destroy, trapped by a narrative that banned explicit hostility to the principle of unions and collective bargaining, business interests needed to find another way to escape the bargaining table. The answer came in the form of the widespread technological determinism that obscured the desire for profit and power behind the language of social utopianism. Business interests had celebrated the possibility of technological utopia, a movement sometimes dubbed Fordism, during the interwar period, but the collective effort of waging war on the Axis now allowed them to claim credibly that American corporations, rather than proletarian revolution, could produce a better world.[30] Furthermore, wartime propaganda had billed the conflict as a total war, one in which entire industrial societies fought one another to the death. The detonation of atomic bombs over Hiroshima and Nagasaki fused two different notions of victory: triumph over a human adversary and the conquest of the natural world. "It is an atomic bomb," announced President Harry S. Truman after the Hiroshima bombing. "It is a harnessing of the basic power of the universe. The force from which the sun draws its power has been loosed against those who brought war to the Far East. . . . What has been done," he continued, "is the greatest achievement of organized science in history."[31]

The origins of the term "automation" lay not in a specific technological innovation but, rather, in the semantic needs of postwar Americans. The resurgent faith in the ability of the industrial plant of the United States to overcome hitherto insurmountable political and natural limits seemed to offer a way out of the contradiction between work and freedom endemic to industrial civilization. "Automation" answered the desire to express and discuss the meaning of work in light of the new powers the United States had won for itself, for never before had a nation inherited so much power. The productive and military advantages bequeathed to the country after the war, along with the wealth they brought to millions of Americans, seemed to have consigned the old antagonisms of capitalism to history's proverbial dustbin. With a practically infinite supply of power flowing into American hands, it no longer made sense to speak of its more just distribution. Inequality, wrote John Kenneth Galbraith in *The Affluent Society*, "the old and most agitated of social issues, if not resolved, is at least largely in abeyance, and the disputants have concentrated their attention, instead, on the goal of increased productivity." Leading scholars depicted the era as a new historical epoch—an unprecedented industrial era. "The world is entering a new age—the age of total industrialization," wrote a group of distinguished social scientists that included Clark Kerr, an economist and the first chancellor of the University of California system. But with unprecedented change came uncertainty. "The great transformation continues apace," Kerr and his colleagues wrote in their book, *Industrialism and Industrial Man*, "and no one can really know how it will turn out." From scholars to labor leaders, this double sense of optimism and uncertainty gave the automation discourse much of its discursive power among Americans. That thinkers as careful and empirical as Galbraith and Kerr could believe that the postwar order had overturned the old rules of economics, even history, attested to the stupendousness of both the new powers available to the United States and the excitement they inspired.[32]

The borders of the United States of America could not and did not contain the career of the automation discourse. It led a life in England, Germany, France, Italy, and the Soviet Union.[33] But the origins of "automation" in the middle of the twentieth century were particularly American, as was the distinct role that the discourse played in American society. The weakness of the welfare state and the outsized importance of work in American political life gave "automation" a peculiar significance in the United States. The term lumped many different kinds of material change into a single neat narrative that held that all technological development meant progress and that the inevitable end of progress was the abolition of human labor. The automation discourse perpetuated a degraded understanding of work—usually but not always understood as industrial wage laboring—as the activity of mere survival. "Automation" described a version of events that allowed Americans to reconcile the concentration of the means of production (and the exploitation it often entailed) with the republican notion of being a free citizen. It maintained that true freedom was not simply independence from social oppression but freedom from the demands of biological preservation. The necessity to ensure one's survival was the source of human oppression, this reasoning went, not hierarchy or the actions of oppressors. Injustice originated not from politics but from the functions of one's body. Once the industrial apparatus of the country could automatically produce all that people needed, this logic went, everyone would be released into a life of leisure, for better or for worse. For all people to be free, the discourse held, America first had to conquer nature.

Not everyone believed that freedom required an escape from the embodied condition. A very few influential thinkers, in particular the philosopher Hannah Arendt and the sociologist C. Wright Mills, insisted that work was always a political activity and so, in theory, could be made consistent with political freedom. Mills argued that unless it was understood that the meaning of work resulted from political contest, working-class Americans would be handicapped in their struggle for individual and collective liberation. He worried about the coming of a society of "cheerful robots." Arendt shared much of Mills's disquiet. The desire to escape necessity, she argued, was the equivalent of the desire to escape politics. "Man cannot be free," she wrote, "if he does not know that he is subject to necessity, because freedom is always won in his never wholly successful attempts to liberate himself from necessity." When society failed to see the contingency of its own social life, Arendt reasoned, it ran the risk of perpetrating unspeakable horrors. She urged her readers to embrace what the automation discourse ruled out: the politics of the workplace.[34]

For the most part, the arguments of Mills and Arendt fell on deaf ears. Believing the abolition of industrial labor to be imminent, union leaders, members of the New Left, architects of the war on poverty, feminists, lawmakers, and Black liberation theorists adopted not only the belief that "automation" would soon remove all labor from industry but also the degraded definition of work that this implied.

Drawing on prominent thinkers from across American cultural and political life, what follows is a kind of mosaic that explores how different actors adopted the automation discourse and how its tenets shaped them. The book begins with the material basis of "automation" before moving to the world of ideas, from the tangible to the abstract, from the shop floor to the more airy provinces where national discussion takes place. I have sought at the same time to keep the analysis more or less chronological so that, as much as possible, explanations of cause precede those of effect. Chapter 1 concerns the origin of "automation" in the automobile industry in the late 1940s and early 1950s and the disjuncture between rhetoric and reality in the labor process, while Chapter 2 treats the second point of origin for the automation discourse in the computer industry and, once again, considers the dissonance between what was said of "automation" and the material reality for workers on the job. The middle four chapters of the book relate how the precepts of the automation discourse shaped the ways in which various actors both understood their time and aimed to shape it. With the last chapter, the book ends where it began: in the automobile industry, this time in the midst of revolt. As strikes, absenteeism, and sabotage roiled the U.S. economy in the 1970s, "automation" no longer persuaded. While the automation discourse would persist into the twenty-first century, never again would it command the public imagination as it had before.

In the postwar period, the appeal of "automation" was not absolute, but it was widespread and influential. While managers degraded and sped up the labor process, the forces that could have contested those changes were rhetorically and, to a significant extent, intellectually disarmed by the automation discourse. Most surprising of all was the adoption of the automation discourse by union leaders, those with perhaps the greatest reason to fight against it. Like most of their contemporaries, the leaders of the American labor movement honestly believed that they lived in a historically unprecedented era. They shared the technological optimism of the time and, as much as anyone, they stood in awe of the new powers that had been unleashed. Unsure of what the future would bring and fully committed to the notion of industrial progress, union leaders held a procrustean view of changes to the means of production: It was their job to fight for workers' rights given the changes that management made to the labor process, for union leaders generally understood these changes not as the attempt of capital to wrest control away from unions but as the apolitical development of technological civilization.

Rather than discuss how current powers should be divided so that they could be made consistent with prevailing notions of equity, justice, and autonomy, those who subscribed to the automation discourse made liberation contingent on a surplus of future power. But as observers witnessed in the automobile industry, "automation" obscured the contribution workers made to the labor process. While managers, union leaders, critics, and lawmakers prepared for "automation," workers in the present were sped up, paid less, and laid off. And across the political spectrum, Americans called this degradation of work "progress."

1. "The Machine Tells the Body How to Work"

"Automation" and the Postwar Automobile Industry

In 1950, the same year the Ford Motor Company opened the doors to its new Buffalo stamping plant, many of the factory's 1,250 workers walked out in an unauthorized "wildcat" strike. A union spokesman described it as a "spontaneous reaction on the part of the men in protest of a speedup."[1] The union insisted that the workers at Buffalo Stamping were the most put-upon in the entire company. Managers there demanded more from each worker than at any other Ford plant. "Speed up was the rule on every job," a lawyer for the union said. Anyone who protested was either intimidated into keeping quiet or fired.[2] When Ford opened another new factory the following year, the Cleveland Engine plant, the workers there also complained that management sped them up. Matters became so bad that the union negotiated for specific protections in the local contract, stipulating that the controls to some machines be locked up and the keys kept in the general foreman's office.[3] In a way, there was nothing surprising in all this; since the earliest days of industrial production, workers and managers had fought over the speed of work. Nevertheless, it might have astonished some to learn that the workers at the Buffalo and Cleveland factories were working so hard, especially when, in theory, no one was supposed to be working there at all.

According to Ford, both plants boasted a new technology, a revolution in industrial manufacturing that made human labor obsolete. The company called this technology "automation." Ford itself had invented the term only a few years earlier specifically to describe the kind of production taking place at Cleveland and Buffalo. The boasts were large. "Ours is the only foundry in the world," said one manager at the Cleveland engine plant, "where the molding sand used to make castings is never touched by human hands except maybe out of curiosity." But when two Soviet engineers visited the Cleveland plant with the express purpose of seeing "advanced American automation systems at work in factories," they left disappointed. By then Ford's flagship automated factory was hardly workerless. It employed seven thousand people. More disappointing still, the factory utilized what the visiting engineers said was "for the most part standard manufacturing processes employing methods well known for the last ten or fifteen years." But while there were few new machines to marvel over, the Soviet engineers were very impressed by speed at which the people at Cleveland Engine worked. According to one of them, watching workers was "like looking at a speeding motion picture."[4] The people worked fast. Whatever it was that Ford called automation, it had not eliminated the workers. It had sped them up.

What executives in the automobile industry called "automation" did not describe labor's substitution, but rather its disruption.[5] This disruption did not develop in a single direction. It was a whirlwind, not the straight shot of an arrow. Managers disorganized their workers by decentralizing production and moving factories to the suburbs or to the South, they hired nonunion contract labor to perform work that had been the purview of union members, and they installed new machines to alter and speed up the work process, destroying existing jobs and creating different jobs in their wake. Executives explained this last form of disruption as a natural, inevitable, and beneficial development. They called it "automation." Although auto executives, most famously those at Ford, dreamed of factories where managers could simply think a material object into existence, methods of production were, in the end, defined not by the dreams of technocrats but by profit margins. It was not progress that managers wanted but control, to be free from the demands of workers and government. Stable working conditions were the enemy of managerial control; with a union, workers' expectations all too quickly became privileges, and work incentives expanded to entitlements backed by law. The more workers understood of daily operations, the more they might question their exclusion from the management of their workplace and the better they could resist a speedup of their labor.

The Transfer Machine and Detroit Automation

At a meeting of executives in 1946, Ford's vice president of production, D. S. Harder, stood looking over plans for the installation of a bank of transfer machines. "Let's see some more mechanical handling between these transfer machines," Harder said to his fellow executives and engineers. "Give us some more of that automatic business. . . . Some more of that—that—automation."

It was the first recorded use of the word "automation." A 1948 issue of *American Machinist* had the honor of being the first to print the word publicly, in an article about the opening of Ford's new Automation Department in 1947.[6]

Historians of technology have taken great pains to define automation narrowly with reference to this specific material innovation—the introduction of transfer machines to stamp metal and machine engines in the postwar auto industry, what they have called "Detroit Automation." A transfer machine was an automatic machine tool that executed numerous operations on a piece of material and moved it from one station to another by means of automatic conveyance. Engineers called a series of linked transfer machines a transfer line. Ideally, a human being placed material at the beginning of a transfer line and removed the finished product at its end. The widespread adoption of transfer machinery in the auto industry began in the late 1930s and accelerated with the end of the war. General Motors gained press coverage for its heavy investment in transfer machines at its Buick Division engine plant in 1946. Packard added transfer machines to the line in its engine plant in 1948, and Chrysler used them to make its DeSoto Division's V-8 engine in 1951. Ford installed transfer machines at the River Rouge plant during its postwar retooling in 1947 and then built two new factories—the Buffalo Stamping Plant and the Cleveland Engine Plant—billed as "automated" operations endowed with multiple transfer lines that, theoretically, required the intervention of little or no human labor.[7]

Despite the fanfare with which auto executives hailed the application of the transfer machine to automobile production in the postwar period, however, the mechanism was by no means new; in the 1890s the Waltham Watch Company had used transfer machines to work watch plates and make pinions. New instead was the presence on the shop floor of a militant, national, and largely successful national industrial union.[8] Rather than credit technics with producing the managerial excitement surrounding the transfer machine, we must consider politics. By the early 1950s, "automation," both as a material phenomenon and as a philosophy, had outstripped transfer machinery, and not only among those in the popular press caught up in what one mid-century critic called the "automation hysteria."[9] In 1954, D. S. Harder, the same Ford vice president who coined the word, affirmed: "I, for one, want to think of automation as a new concept—a new philosophy—of manufacturing." Although "automation" entailed "the automatic handling of parts between progressive production processes," said Harder, nevertheless it was "more than merely transferring." According to him, "automation" was "a new manufacturing method," a concept, a philosophy: "Anyone who fails to recognize this fact," he said, "has missed the point."[10]

The Origins of "Automation"

Throughout the 1920 and 1930s, the Big Three of the automobile industry—Ford, General Motors, and Chrysler—had strongly opposed all attempts to bring democracy into their factories. By means of mass organization and sit-down strikes, and with the assistance of sympathetic elected officials, auto workers compelled their employers to recognize their right to organize under the terms of the National Labor Relations Act of 1935. The struggle was bitter, and despite the union's wartime no-strike pledge, worker militancy continued to smolder throughout the first half of the 1940s. With the end of World War II, that repressed militancy exploded; 1946 witnessed the largest strike wave in U.S. history. Week after week, workers across the United States demanded better working conditions and more control over the work process.[11]

The ostensible resolution to this struggle came in the form of the postwar period's grand bargain between capital, labor, and the state. It held that many of the most important protections of citizenship would be realized not in law but through collective bargaining between unions and employers. Full employment was key to this consensus. Only mass employment and mass consumption, liberals believed, would stave off another Great Depression. While managers publicly supported full employment as a matter of general government policy, they contested any claims that their workers made for control over their own specific jobs. At the same time, auto manufacturers awash in war wealth made enormous fixed capital investments in their factories. They expanded production, and as they did, they decentralized the industry away from Detroit, the capital of auto manufacturing and a center of union strength. Not only were manufacturers hoping to take advantage of the consumption bonanza following the war, they also longed to undermine the UAW, one of the most powerful unions in American history.

It was at this time that managers in the automobile industry began arguing that the human body had reached its industrial limits. Advancement, they said, could continue only if human labor were removed from the production process. As one socialist commentator put it at the time, "Close to $3 billion has been allocated by GM, over $1½ billion by Ford, and $300 million by Chrysler for a modernization program so stupendous that the new word, 'automation,' had to be coined to describe it."[12] At heart, "automation" was a term of ideology, not a dispassionate description of the substitution of machine action for human labor. Like any term of ideology, automation's metaphysics seemed to explain a physical reality. There were indeed new machines on the shop floor, and many people called these machines "automation." But "automation" was not a specific technology; instead, it was an argument about the meaning of labor and its relation to technological change. It was, above all, a discursive tool that allowed managers to pry workers away from a moral claim to their jobs: If work could be performed without a human being, the story went, then it was technology that determined whether a particular job was necessary. The automation discourse held that private industry was not obligated to provide for the welfare of its workers, not when technological change, rather than politics, made workers obsolete. According to this discourse, these acts of dispossession were not labor degradation; they were industrial progress.

A perusal of postwar union resolutions, minutes of bargaining sessions, and countless grievances, however, reveal the same thing: Workers sought security, while management designed upheaval. In making changes to the means of production, management's purpose was not to destroy jobs but to maintain a regime of fiat production in the pursuit of profit. A factory of robots was only an evocative and ultimately metaphorical articulation of the dream of a labor force with no power to challenge management. From the beginning, executives understood that a completely automatic factory would be too static a construction to answer changes in the market. Harvard Business School professor James Bright explained in 1958, "The more automatic and integrated the production system, the more management's hands are tied by the performance range of this supermachine."[13] Instead, managers deployed machines and labor in an ever-changing mix, using one to make the other cheaper. To keep workers from gaining too much control over their working conditions, managers installed machines; to keep the cost of fixed capital investments down, managers used human labor. Even as it dedicated itself to "automation," the auto industry made no commitment to the workerless factory.

Rather than use machines to abolish human labor, under the aegis of "automation" postwar managers effected a tremendous speedup of workers. Executives aimed that speedup at semiskilled workers, those who made up the backbone of industrial unionism. For production workers, "automation" did not mean relief from physical labor—the obsolescence of the industrial value of the human body. Instead, ironically, it signified an intensification of physical labor.

The Twilight of the Semiskilled Worker

Traditionally in the auto industry, new production processes handed down by management were incomplete until workers redesigned them. "We tried the engineer's way of using the guns for two days," a worker at Chrysler's Mack Avenue plant recalled of a new labor process introduced in the late 1940s, "and the best we could get was fifty jobs an hour." That only amounted to one-third of their original output. "Each of us decided to do the job his own way. We started figuring it out for each other. . . . After we found the best way to work, the superintendent and the engineer came back down. The superintendent could only ask questions—he didn't know anything. The engineer didn't say anything. They decided to let us work as we wanted."[14]

Historically, managers despised this situation. "Automation," Harder said, was "a new method of manufacture . . . a way of controlling the various processes. Automation is a philosophy of design, it is a manufacturing method, and it is control within a machine."[15] Design, control, machine: These words summed up the allure of the automation discourse for managers. Advanced machines seemed to promise the power to design a product in the boardroom and maintain complete control of its production on the shop floor by means of mere mechanism. These were old managerial desires. Frederick Winslow Taylor had given them clear expression in his push for "scientific" management in the early twentieth century. But whereas Taylor had hoped to achieve managerial control of production by disciplining workers, postwar technological optimism held out the promise of managerial control through eliminating workers altogether.

Harder's emphasis on design—the top-down planning of production—was a reaction to countless embarrassing scenes like the one at the Mack Avenue plant in which relatively uneducated, semiskilled workers corrected the plans of engineers. "Automation" was a vision of management's freedom from its workers, one in which a solitary man, educated and white-collar, could manifest the ideal car part directly from his mind. "In place of the old, complicated maze of machinery," said Ford vice president R. H. Sullivan, "we visualized long, clean production lines along which intricate parts would flow smoothly and evenly—just as fast as modern machines could handle them. . . . The new lines would be almost entirely self-maintaining, with various control devices to assure preventive maintenance. . . . That," he said, "was our dream of things to come."[16] By act of mere thought alone, said G. G. Murie, Ford's supervisor of design and engineering in the Engine and Foundry Division, the heart of Detroit Automation, "the automation engineer" would "coordinate all phases" of design. "Automation," he hoped, would change design from a social task to an individual one, with the company placing "all responsibility for automation with one person."[17] Furthermore, with "automation" managers could depict their desire for control as a general social good. "Greater productivity is almost *always* the result of two factors: better methods and better machines. Often these have been installed only over the objections of the labor unions," said Kenneth D. Cassidy, Ford's vice president of industrial relations.[18] Labor, remarkable only in its periodic interruption of production, was incidental to a process in which capital reproduced capital, or so Cassidy argued.

The auto industry's framing of its own desires as a social boon gained credibility from the commonplace belief that the nation had entered a new era of power and technological achievement. Sober opinion held that an awesome and utterly different future portended. In 1950 Robert Oppenheimer described the postwar period as a time of "new insight and new mastery." The otherwise staid *Saturday Review* boasted of a "new power for a new age" and "revolutions of power." Union leaders, businessmen, workers, lawmakers—all suspected that an epoch of extraordinary and unbridled power floated on the horizon.[19] With so much confidence abroad that technological utopia was imminent, when Ford executives suggested that human labor, especially semiskilled labor, would cease to hold any value in the near future, they persuaded. "Automation," said the sociologist and liberal stalwart Daniel Bell, would "create a new *salariat* instead of a *proletariat*, as automatic processes reduce the number of industrial workers required in production."[20] Harry Braverman, a labor organizer and intellectual, agreed that the hardest hit by "automation" would be "the giant layer of semi-skilled workers—the biggest portion of the country's working class—the class of workers created by the Industrial Revolution and the rise of mass-production methods."[21] According to Ford managers, the elimination of an entire class of workers did not mean disaster. "Automation," they held, would replace blue-collar work with a "demand for skilled maintenance and repair technicians" and "vast new opportunities to the worker who is willing to work and learn."[22] But it was not only journalists and cultural critics who found this claim reasonable. Surprisingly, so did the leaders of the UAW.

Along with other unions in the Congress of Industrial Organizations (CIO), in the 1930s the UAW had transformed the labor movement by extending union organizing beyond craft workers to include the great armies of semi-skilled laborers in mass manufacturing. Less interested in the sanctity of craft, industrial unions sought to win for the semiskilled—machine operators and line workers—power over their jobs. Historically, worker control had been the privilege of skilled craftsmen, most of whom were native-born, white, and male. These were the workers whom the old labor movement, epitomized by the American Federation of Labor (AFL), had organized. When during the Industrial Revolution scientific managers expropriated knowledge of the work process from under the craftsman's cap, they had done so by creating detailed industrial jobs. In the process, they opened up wage work to a cheaper but also more diverse cohort of workers. Industrial unionism sought to organize these new workers, the semiskilled, those who only held industrial jobs because managers had broken up the old crafts.[23]

Like Ford executives, union leaders in the postwar period understood "automation" as the process by which semiskilled work, the bedrock of their industrial organizing model, would cease to exist. Following what seemed the inherent logic of technological progress, they believed that "automation" would reintegrate the detailed division of labor into a single complex megamachine. In this hazy future, some union officials spied a potential wasteland, a new order in which the union had lost its bargaining power and its members were consigned to quotidian precariousness. In the future, they concluded, everyone would be either a white-collared, salaried professional or a member of a low-paid "unskilled" underclass. But, like Ford's management, union leaders also saw utopian possibilities. They agreed that "automation" in the 1950s was, in the words of the UAW's national director for the Ford Motor Company, Ken Bannon, "a far cry from the crude transfer machines and the in-line machine process" that marked its origins.[24] At the national UAW convention in 1957, officials invoked the founder of the cybernetics movement, Norbert Wiener, and proclaimed that "automation" was inaugurating a second Industrial Revolution. "For the first time in history," they announced,

> we have the means at hand to free mankind from the ancient struggle for material survival, and to replace scarcity and poverty with economic abundance and the good life for all. The scientist and the engineer are providing us with the physical means by which our material problems can be solved. We in the UAW welcome the opportunities they offer us to usher in a golden age of plenty for all mankind.[25]

Not proletarian revolution, said union leaders, but the white-collar scientist and engineer would provide the means to overcome the old antagonisms of capitalism. From splitting the atom to reaching the Moon, there seemed little that the technological prowess of the United States could not achieve. In this spirit, rather than fault the owners of capital for poverty and inequality, the UAW's leaders blamed the demands of embodied existence, "the ancient struggle for material survival." These demands, the union officially said, not the unfair distribution of society's wealth, were the ultimate cause of the exploitation of workers. In a time of economic boom, this rhetoric made sense. When society had so much, surely it was reasonable to distribute that wealth more equally. But in this rhetoric lay an enormous concession, one made across the political spectrum: that nature, not politics, was to blame for hierarchy and injustice; that the demands of the body, not the decisions of the powerful, had necessitated the unforgiving exploitation of men and women. The automation discourse justified this line of reasoning so that it made sense, not only to managers but also to union leaders . If society could exploit machines with the same tenacity it had working people, perhaps even workers could benefit from industrial capitalism, with blue-collar workers all graduating into the ranks of white-collar management. This was a vision of capitalism perfected, and though some union leaders might have remained skeptical as to who ultimately would benefit from the new age of power, few doubted that it had arrived.

Across the postwar CIO, union leaders did not know what to make of the unprecedented era supposedly dawning before their eyes. At a meeting of senior administrators from ten of the largest unions in the United States, the participants agreed that no one understood what precise material changes "automation" signified. "Not enough is known about what happens specifically in a plant or office when automation takes place," said a representative of the Communications Workers of America. She warned the group against "the labor movement becoming identified as 'weepers' on this subject." Any union resistance to technological progress, she found, led to negative press coverage. "We are identified as those heralding calamity." The solution to the problem was obvious: "Use our influence to get AFL-CIO spokesmen to point not only to the problems and difficulties of automation but to acknowledge the tremendous benefits it provides."[26] "Automation," whatever it was materially, had also become the moment's watchword for the arrival of technological utopia. Union officials did not want to appear as obstacles on the road to progress. Unsure of what the future would bring, they too believed that "automation" held a great, vague promise.

The consequences of this technological fatalism were evident even in the language of the UAW's collectively bargained contracts. The union's basic acceptance of inevitable, apolitical, technological change made it difficult for production workers to argue that they should have a direct say in any changes to the means of production. As early as 1949, the UAW's national Ford contract stipulated that workers could not bargain over production standards except in cases of health or safety. In exchange for a measure of security—sufficient wages, unemployment benefits, a pension—the workers would have no control over production decisions, but nor were they to be overworked. For anyone interested in immediate shop-floor democracy, the production standards clause spelled a crushing defeat. The agreement would hold for practically the entire automotive industry throughout the postwar period and beyond.[27]

In theory, the potential elimination of the semiskilled from industry posed a grave threat to postwar liberalism's commitment to full employment. Keynesianism held that the masses of semiskilled wage earners played a crucial role in the fortunes of industrial capitalism. Unless average Americans possessed enough either in wages or credit to consume the products of American industry, the United States would once again find itself locked in a downward spiral of overproduction and underconsumption. Job holding served as the nation's primary mechanism for distributing wealth. According to the automation discourse, however, the abolition of semiskilled human labor in industry was the inevitable outcome of technological development.

The discourse's adherents resolved this contradiction by arguing that while progress might do away with the need for the laboring body, it would also make greater demands on the human mind. The highest authorities validated this rhetorical move. After nine days of hearings, a Senate subcommittee concluded that "automation" would displace some workers but that the real challenge it posed was to the nation's brainpower. Although they conceded that "automation" appeared ready to eliminate those employed in industrial line production, the senators found that "the most disturbing thing which came to the subcommittee's attention during the hearings was the near unanimous conclusion of the witnesses that the Nation is faced with a threatened shortage of scientists, technicians, and skilled labor."[28] When another Senate subcommittee revisited the question of automation eight years later, lawmakers and their witnesses remained convinced that technological progress meant a move away from the laboring body and toward the professional, skilled exertions of the mind. In his opening remarks at the 1963 subcommittee hearings, chairman Joseph S. Clark uttered what was practically a truism of the automation discourse when he said that because of "automation," the United States faced the paradox of millions of unemployed workers, on one hand, "and severe shortages of manpower needed to run our highly complex technology," on the other. "As technology replaces human labor and the skilled needs of society are elevated," he continued, "a whole new set of political, social, and educational challenges are posed." Authorities agreed. "We may be facing a period in the next 20 years where the semiskilled factory operation would be very substantially eliminated by these new technological developments," said the chair of Harvard University's Economics Department, John T. Dunlop. Willard Wirtz, President Kennedy's Secretary of Labor, spoke of "the very rapid pace of the automation and technological change which is resulting in a shift in employment to relatively more skilled occupations."[29]

To the UAW, then, "automation" seemed to pose an existential threat: the end of the working class itself. But rather than fight progress by contesting the nature of these historical changes, the UAW hoped to place itself at the head of the revolution and to guarantee for its members a share of the wealth the new industrial order would bring. The Guaranteed Annual Income, steady pay regardless of layoff (and UAW president Walter Reuther's contractual white whale for most of the postwar period), was union leadership's anticipation of the inevitable. Even if "automation" destroyed semiskilled jobs, Reuther reasoned, a guaranteed income provided by the employer would make the remaining UAW members, the degraded unskilled workers, as good as salaried workers possessing benefits and security befitting the middle class. "Salaried people do not get cut as a result of automation," Gene Prato, the chairman of the union's Ford Committee, asserted as late as 1967 during contract negotiations with the Ford Motor Company. In that same round of negotiations, a UAW representative argued that the company needed to offer "training and retraining programs" to allow "blue collar" workers to become "white collar."[30] Caught between its belief in progress and its mandate to protect union members, unable or unwilling to fight with the automation discourse or mechanization itself, UAW officials chose to see "automation" as a way for workers to enter the middle class. In anticipation of the possible expansion of skilled jobs, in 1951 the UAW created a "Skilled Trades" department. As one member of the new department put it: "With the shadow of automation hanging over us the skilled worker will play an ever increasing part in union affairs."[31] Although "automation" meant that the human body would lose its industrial value, the faith in its power to turn semiskilled workers into highly skilled professionals allowed Reuther to hold out deeply democratic hopes. "Every person," he said, "has to have a place in society and meaningful work, creative work. Work of a social usefulness is essential to achieve a measure of dignity." But this work was not industrial labor, nor was it workers' control of basic industry. It was, instead, a celebration of the dissolution of the industrial working class. The leadership's answer to progress was not for the workers to make the shop floor a democracy but for them to stop being workers altogether. These leaders had no desire to change history, only to be on the right side of it.[32]

But while union leaders prepared for the end of semiskilled labor, managers in the automobile industry were discovering that revolution, technological or otherwise, was risky business. In response to critics who interpreted "automation" as a betrayal of the postwar industrial peace, in the early 1960s Ford's management began to walk itself back from some of its boldest claims. The dream of workerless factories suggested that technological progress and rising profits were not exactly compatible with full employment, the cornerstone of postwar economic policy. As early as the mid-1950s, auto executives found themselves on the defensive against allegations that "automation" was a weapon that automakers were using to break the UAW. During congressional hearings, D. J. Davis, vice president of manufacturing at Ford, struggled to answer a question about whether the company's turn to "automation" had been a response to "labor difficulty in the collective bargaining process" and a way to "eliminate certain workers and certain job processes." He dodged the question by describing technological change as an organic, inevitable process.

"You can't bury your head in the sand to progress," he replied. "If a machine-tool manufacturer comes out with something better than he did last year and it saves us money, your competition is going to buy it if you don't."[33]

When unemployment rates rose in the early 1960s, President John F. Kennedy expressed the same unease that "automation" stirred in much of the liberal establishment: "I regard it as the major domestic challenge, really, of the '60's, to maintain full employment at a time when automation, of course, is replacing men."[34] If the automakers wanted to align their postwar reinvestment program with the Keynesian moral code, they needed to dispel fears that "automation" was an unprecedented innovation that would upset the grand economic bargain. To that end, and in direct contradiction to all its previous claims to the contrary, the Ford Motor Company argued that "automation" was nothing new, only the latest "manifestation of the search for ways of doing things better, doing them more efficiently, doing them more effectively, that long has characterized" American business. "Automation," the company held, "describes an evolutionary process that started centuries ago."[35]

In private correspondence with members of Congress, Ford's Vice President of Labor relations sought to distance the company as much as possible from the revolutionary implications of "automation". Though "automation," he wrote, "originally had a very precise, technical meaning"—by which he meant the transfer machine—the word was now, lamentably, "used to describe virtually any improvement in manufacturing process or technique." As regarded the transfer machine, he said, in metal stamping Ford had recently been "forced to reduce the level of automation in order to obtain greater flexibility in responding to changes in consumer demand. . . . It is erroneous," he asserted, "to think of Ford as an 'automated' company in any sense other than that it seeks with all the determination, ingenuity, and constancy it can muster to improve its efficiency." This was, to say the least, a far cry from Harder's "new philosophy of manufacture."[36]

In an attempt to depict the company that bore his name as economically responsible, company president Henry Ford II defined "automation" as merely technological innovation more generally and its critics as luddites opposed to progress. Ford called "automation" a "first-rate scareword." Although one of his own vice presidents had quite recently invented the word, he referred to it as "that old devil automation." It was an "old wives' tale" and "as old as the hills." To fear it was to fret over "phantoms." But even as Ford dismissed "automation" as an empty signifier, he also claimed it was synonymous with historical progress. "Why," he asked, did "otherwise enlightened people persist in the notion that productivity or automation is something we must fear, use with caution, and regard with suspicion?" To listen to Henry Ford II, one would have thought that "automation" was literally meaningless. At the same time, one would have concluded that it was a hallowed concept from time immemorial synonymous with innovation and productivity.[37] In any case, whatever "automation" was, Ford assured his audience, the company his grandfather founded had not invented it. Private industry could be trusted with the fate of the American economy.

Mechanized Disruption and Speedup

For managers and union officials "automation" described a revolution in the means of production. For workers the word meant something quite different. Rather than signifying progress, to those on the assembly line "automation" was another word for a material process as old as industrial production itself: mechanized speedup.

Among workers, speedup was well understood and universally detested. It cast in stark relief the discrepancy between the hourly wage and the value of labor. In the normal wage relationship between company and hired hand, a manager bought the labor of a worker for a period of time, which is to say, a manager did not really know what he bought. Every day he lived the possibility of making a bad deal. In order to profit from the labor he purchased, a manager needed to receive more value in work than he paid out in wages. Speeding up the pace of production was the most blatant way to assure the manager that he indeed had the better end of the bargain. Running the line faster allowed management to *see* the nature of its relationship to workers, a relation manifested in the form of hundreds of worried bodies twisting, sweating, and exerting themselves at their stations.[38]

But just as speedup clarified for management the disproportion between the high value of the work done and the relatively small wage paid out, it also made that asymmetry obvious to workers. It should then come as no surprise then that with the adoption during the interwar period of the assembly line and the time study, speedup became one of the central grievances of workers in automobile factories. When auto workers unionized during the Great Depression, they rallied around an end to speedup. "It was the speedup that organized Flint," Henry Kraus remembered in 1947, "as it was the one element in the life of all the workers that found a common basis of resentment. Wives who feared intervention of the union vented their execration on the speedup which left their husbands trembling and exhausted after their work and narrowed the life of the family to the mere acts of physical continuance."[39]

Management sped up workers in order to compensate for slack in planning or logistics. A late shipment of materials, a breakdown at one point on the line, or labor unrest in another department could threaten an entire day's quota. In response, a foreman turned up the pace of work, forcing hands on the line to rush for an hour, three hours, or the whole day. If demand for a particular product was unexpectedly robust, the heightened speed could become the new normal. More frequently, workers experienced speedup in bursts. Because skilled machinists had more power to determine the pace of their work, speedup was the special bane of the semiskilled, hitting the likes of line workers, machine operators, assembly workers, and hired hands sweating in the foundry. Typical throughout the auto industry, speedup was especially bad at Ford. "For years and years and years," UAW president Walter Reuther remembered in 1949, "the Ford Motor Company, instead of developing efficient management procedure, just drove the guys. You didn't have to be efficient—just kick the guys along when they were behind." Donald E. Peterson, who would serve as CEO of the Ford Motor Company in the 1980s, agreed. When he had first come to work at Ford in 1949, he remembered, "[he] was introduced into an environment that was largely run by fear."[40]

Between 1946 and 1949, the war finished and with it the union's no-strike pledge, management and workers at Ford battled for control over the speed of production. Workers wanted the company to commit to a set line speed for the life of a contract. Management insisted on its right to manipulate line speed at will. In 1949, workers struck. As part of the settlement that followed, Ford agreed to set speeds at the beginning of each workday and hold to them until the whistle blew. Workers did not have a say over the speed of production (with an exception for the right to bargain over "health and safety" standards), and management could change the speed from day to day, but not from hour to hour. This agreement constituted one of the most important elements in the production standards clause of the new contract.

It was in the middle of the postwar speedup dispute, in 1947, that Ford founded its Automation Department. The conflict, however, was years in the making. The auto industry, like other mass manufacturing industries, had introduced new machinery to speed up production before, churning out more product with fewer people. In 1930 the economist John Maynard Keynes coined the term "technological unemployment" to describe the phenomenon.[41] The machines behind technological unemployment, however, were often not labor *saving*, but labor *intensifying*; they required each worker to produce more in less time. When AC Sparkplug invested in new punch presses in 1934, the machines allowed three hundred workers to accomplish the same work that five hundred had performed the year before, much of it the result, according to one electrical worker, of "pure sweat." So said a sparkplug gapper in the same factory. In 1927 she gapped forty-five hundred sparkplugs per day by pressing a powered foot pedal nine thousand times over the course of a ten-hour shift. In 1934, by means of a new machine, she gapped ten thousand sparkplugs per day by pressing a new power pedal twenty thousand times during her now eight-hour shift. In return for her increased output, the result of twice as much effort in two hours' less time, she earned one dollar and thirty cents less than she had before. Quite often, it was not the machines that replaced workers; rather, human beings replaced other human beings, their labor sped up and intensified by means of a machine.[42]

The postwar period in the automobile industry was an era of speedup. The record echoes with a chorus of outraged and exhausted workers from all three of the major automakers. According to labor organizer Nat Ganley, postwar speedup was perhaps worse than what workers experienced in the Depression. The fight in the 1930s had been "for wage increases, for the union shop, for paid vacations and an end to SPEED-UP." Yet in 1954, workers found that "the vicious speed-up system" with which management once ruled the shop had returned with a vengeance. Despite "the most modern push button machines, the most wonderful technical improvements," workers were still "compelled to turn out more production on the same machines, and the same job, than they were a dozen years ago." They now worked longer hours, and "example after example may be pointed to where workers now run three machines on the same job." Every minute of the worker's day, Ganley said, was "being made to count by more being pushed upon him than in the days before the union." Because of this, he noted, "more quickie strikes take place around the speed-up issue than any other single issue."[43]

"Today the workers are doing in eight hours the actual physical work they used to do in twelve," said James Boggs, engine jitney driver at Chrysler's Jefferson Avenue assembly plant.[44] In 1961 the president of Local 862 in Louisville wrote to the head of the UAW's Ford Department to tell him that management had assigned assembly workers an "impossible" number of tasks at the body jigs. "Management," he said, "intends to force slave conditions in Louisville in these bucks and then use this as a spring board in the rest of the Assembly Plants."[45] In the same year, a proposed UAW resolution claimed that "there is an apparent concerted effort now in progress on the part of Managements to increase production, without regard to the human aspects of the speedup of production." In the words of one GM worker: "The speed-up is the burning issue among production workers." Workers called this postwar speedup "automation." Or, more simply, the "new Automation speedup."[46]

Although speedup was the bane of the line worker, the Reuther administration had priorities other than fighting for workers' control of production. It hoped instead to win company-provided welfare for its membership, "fringe benefits" such as healthcare, supplemental unemployment insurance, vacation time, and a guaranteed yearly income. In exchange for the security of the members, union leadership agreed to maintain industrial peace. The problem of speedup upset that plan. An official fight against line speed and for workers' control ran the risk of becoming a discussion of who ran the factory, of nothing less than the rights of private property in the United States. As a result, according to Ganley, workers saw "no struggle against speed-up coming from any section" of the union's leadership. "Militant UAW leaders know that to open your mouth on speed-up charges in the UAW," he said, "is to have all hell let loose on you."[47]

Automakers achieved speedup by means of disruption. Managers invested in machines that disorganized workers, obscured the logic of the overall labor process, and physically prevented workers from coming together. On the factory floor, workers experienced "automation" not as efficiency but as chaos. In 1961 Walter E. Schilling, representing the GM workers of UAW Local 25, St. Louis, reported that "the constant changing of automation and technical improvements made by Management" generated "a never ending stream of production standards grievances." Plant managers introduced new machines and assigned fewer workers to their operation even when they knew, as the workers did, that in order to meet production standards the machines would ultimately require more workers. "As a result of this type of manoeuvre [sic]," an exhausted Schilling explained, managers achieved "efficiency savings for short periods of time," but workers suffered "hardships and overloaded operations, loss of earnings when bumped down to lower rated jobs and loss of earnings when laid off through reduction in force." When the union brought grievances against these changes, it was forced to dispute each disruption separately. In the meantime, management used the new organization of production to squeeze more work out of the people who remained on the line.[48]

Management often introduced "automated" processes during a model changeover, after many of the workers were already laid off. When the workers returned, they found a new and bewildering scene. The former layout gone, it was difficult to understand how everything was connected, to establish clear cause and effect in the work process. Managers moved jobs from one factory to another, and often the old machines that remained in the factory were moved to different places. Workers might wander the floor trying to find the new locations of their old places. Those assigned to the new machines experienced the greatest disorientation. As one union official summarized it, "With all of that junk around it how are we going to get next to our old machines or those new machines?"[49]

The medal of managerial disruption had two sides, "automation" on one, decentralization on the other. Much of the UAW's leadership recognized this. "One of the dangers of sweeping technological change," the UAW's 1957 resolution on "automation" warned, was the "management decision to move whole plants from one community to another."[50] Rank-and-file workers also understood this connection, calling the following year for a special "automation and decentralization conference."[51] Electrical worker Angela Terrano explained Chrysler's decision to ship production away from two plants in 1957 as a response to the shop-floor resistance of workers who didn't "take their speedup and automation-machines so lightly." Of the company she said, "They want to break up what's left of the union." Collective resistance to a mechanized speedup, Terrano believed, had encouraged auto manufacturers to move their factories out of Detroit. "All the women at work are saying Detroit will become a ghost town soon, with all these companies moving out."[52]

In the "automated" factory, automakers invested in strategically placed machines that were faster than previous equipment but still required human operators. The constant change of equipment disoriented workers. An experienced worker returning to a retooled factory felt as if he was starting his first day on the job. One worker in a Chrysler auto-body shop claimed that the new arrangements in his plant made the place "a crazy house." "I've been there over 15 years," he said, "but when I went in, two weeks ago Friday, I was lost. It looked like a new plant—all full of electronics machines. One foreman said that, in my department alone, one thousand workers who worked on the 1956 model won't be called back to work on the 1957 model."[53] A new assignment could involve a completely different kind of machine—or no machine at all. While old skills lay fallow, the conditions of work, too, might change. A worker might earn ten cents less an hour or work a different shift. With familiarity went security.[54]

It was fitting that workers confronting the "automated" factory should have felt as though their history had been erased. Years of seniority provided little protection from a pay cut, if for some it warded off a pink slip. Semiskilled workers might find themselves reduced to common manual labor, little better in the hierarchy of manufacturing than janitorial or foundry work. Workers returning to a plant that was "automated" in their absence would go to work on another machine or a similar machine in a different location on the line. Even these workers might feel that their history had disappeared from the record, punching in on an utterly different shop floor, away from old co-workers, laboring in a terrain they could not yet decipher. "The loneliness that is brought about by these monster machines is terrific," a Chrysler worker wrote. "Every worker feels it. When you work one of these machines you have no one to talk to. Before there used to be eight or ten guys doing the same job." Another preferred working on a machine he called the "merry-go-round," which he considered, in terms of the physical motions necessary to operate it, the worst job in the plant. "Even though it's the worst job, you're working next to someone. It makes it different. You forget the strain and pressure you're under when you're talking. Sometimes I forget the time and the day goes by."[55] The new equipment left workers atomized, deprived of company and conversation on the job, and, to some extent, the opportunity to organize collectively.

This uprooting was precisely what company officials at Ford hoped to achieve with "automation," not only in terms of a worker's subjective experience of his or her job but in the very language of a local's collectively bargained contract. Ford workers in the UAW were covered by a national contract, but job classifications, wages, and seniority were negotiated locally, plant to plant. New machines generated a contest between the union and the company over the classification of jobs: Was a new job an entirely novel introduction to the line, or was it merely an old job performed on a new machine? The presence of new apparatus made it difficult for union leaders to maintain established pay rates and uphold labor standards. At the newly built "automated" Cleveland plant, for example, a union survey found that workers earned eleven cents less an hour on average for work similar to that performed at the Dearborn plant. "Where a job was on the borderline between two classifications at the Cleveland plant," the union found, "the Company had classified the worker in the lower paying classification." It was clear to union representatives that "automation and down-grading as a result of job dilution had gone hand-in-hand at the Cleveland plant." Using the claim that "automation" had fundamentally changed the nature of the work, the company introduced a program of new job classifications according to which workers earned less and did more. Overwhelmed by a new landscape of jobs and contractual language, the UAW was forced to "formulate an entirely new wage and classification structure, and bargain for it."[56]

Before the UAW was recognized as the official collective bargaining agent at the "automated" Buffalo stamping plant, management condensed seven recognized skilled trades—die maker, machine repairer, millwright, welder, hydraulic worker, pipe fitter, and tinsmith—into one job under the classification of "Automation Equipment Maker and Maintenance." After the workers elected to join the UAW, union officials fought to break up the classification. The same thing happened at the Cleveland engine plant, but the membership there resisted attempts by the union's leadership to reintroduce the previous distinctions because all skilled workers who fell under the simplified classification received the highest rate, that of a die maker. The union argued, however, that consolidation was only the first step toward "the deterioration of skilled trades standards." Lumping all of the trades into one classification would ultimately degrade the value of the job, union leaders argued, leaving "men who are jacks-of-all-trades and masters of none." But the leadership's plea to the workers "fell on deaf ears." With the consolidation of trade classifications, management could assign an "Automation" worker any kind of trade work, allowing the company to hire fewer workers to do more.[57] With the automation discourse Ford expunged the history not only of entire job classifications but also of the struggle that produced them and was set down in the workers' collectively bargained contract.

By means of mechanized speedup, management laid off thousands of workers and forced those who remained to work mandatory overtime. It was a stark, maddening contrast between unstinting labor and idle penury. In October 1956 Ford claimed that its Detroit plants were functioning at full production with overtime for all. In November one Ford worker complained that everyone in his department as well as two other departments was to be laid off. At the same time, Chrysler scheduled Saturday hours and demanded that workers put in six-day weeks until Christmas. In the words of a Detroit *News and Letters* editorial: "Full production has never meant full employment, and since automation it certainly doesn't." Or as one worker put it: "All Automation has meant to us is unemployment and overwork. *Both at the same time.*"[58]

According to some, the introduction of new productive machinery could have had no result other than incredible speedup. In the pages of *The American Socialist*, H. Butler wrote, "Automation forces the industry to produce at a greater percent of capacity in order to 'break even.'"[59] Ford vice president D. S. Harder acknowledged as much. "We now have machines capable of turning out parts at a much more rapid rate than they are actually doing," he said. "Automation, in at least some of its aspects, fills this void. Devices can be made to enable a machine to attain its designed production rate." At the same time, however, Harder recognized that a factory completely bereft of human workers "depends upon so many other considerations that its existence is far in the future—if it ever can be achieved."[60] In other words, no matter what, human beings would remain in the "automated" factory. This was practically the definition of a speedup. For the new machines to turn a profit, they needed to work at top speed. But the advantage of that speed was only valuable if the rest of the factory could match the new pace. If "automation" was to break even, pre-existing machines, and their operators, had to be run as fast as possible. And in the Ford Motor Company, at least, managers found a way to make the machines not merely break even, but pay out. In 1954 a Ford executive wrote in the pages of *Advanced Management* magazine that the company's postwar reinvestment program had reduced manufacturing costs by "330 million dollars annually compared to the level at which they were running in the second half of 1948." Speaking of his fellow managers, he said, "Our 1953 performance was the best in our history of cost control." Socialist Butler responded, "Only the Ford workers can fully realize where this 330 million saving came from. Ford speedup is exceeded nowhere else in the industry."[61]

That would explain why workers at Chrysler's Lynch Road plant who were not working on what was called automated equipment found themselves nevertheless laboring at an automated pace: "Automation has affected most production operations in the Chrysler Lynch Road Plant," a union member said in 1961. "It is highly conceivable that the cycle time of most other operations is more rapid to meet the parallel of those that are mechanically operated in an automated setup. This establishes an inhuman rapidity which the operator is suppose [*sic*] to endure."[62] Ted F. Silvey, a researcher for the CIO, also found that "automation" sped up old operations. "When changes occur at great speed even with familiar things," he wrote, "the rapid change makes the old things actually new." The same old factory running at twice the speed was, as experienced by a worker, like a different factory altogether.[63]

The more marginalized a worker, the more he or she felt the effects of mechanized speedup, and workers continued to complain of speedup well into the late 1960s. In 1969 organizers for the League of Revolutionary Black Workers reported that for "the black worker the pressure of production never ceases." These workers, they claimed, "are now producing at least twice as much as auto workers twenty years ago." According to the league, "because of the super exploitation of black labor, profits in autos have soared. A process called 'niggermation' is more pervasive than automation. Often new black workers are forced to do the work of two white men." Organizers for the league found that one young Black worker was producing more than 120 units per hour working a job at which previously two white men had each completed 70 per hour. Both white workers had invoked their seniority to transfer to another task, saying that their current assignment was "too strenuous." Still, members of the league acknowledged, white workers continued to suffer from speedup. "Speed up, safety hazards and unhealthy working conditions," they wrote, "have become regular fare for all auto workers."[64]

Few understood better the connection between "automation" and speedup than Simon Owens. The son of sharecroppers and the grandson of slaves, Owens left his home in Lowndes County, Alabama, for Detroit, where, during World War II, he found a job in Chrysler's Briggs Mack Avenue plant. He worked there for the next three decades, witnessing time and again as a Black man how employers deployed the color line to turn workers against one another. Organizing within the UAW as well as working with numerous political organizations, Owens spent years seeking a group that advocated for both workers' rights and the overthrow of American racism. He found it only in the late 1940s with the anti-Stalinist Johnson-Forest Tendency, a Marxist-Humanist splinter group led by Raya Dunayevskaya and the West Indian philosophe C. L. R. James. In their newspaper, *News and Letters*, the Johnson-Forest Tendency reinterpreted Marxism in light of American history, seeking to explain how racism, class exploitation, and industrialization combined to forestall a proletarian revolution. Owens became a regular contributor to the organ.[65]

In 1960, based on his experience as both a full-time auto worker and a journalist, Owens published a short book: *Workers Battle Automation*. Unlike most authors treating the subject, Owens recognized that the technical vagueness of "automation" was essential to its meaning. The many warring definitions of "automation," he argued, testified to a reality of social relations, not mechanical essences. "Automation is not an abstraction," he wrote. "It is a reality. Toward this fact of life, two opposed class attitudes stand out." The first, that of management, understood "automation" as a labor process in which "the machine can almost run by itself, and the men are expendable." But from the workers' point of view, Owens wrote, "the machine is a man-killer. Half the men it throws out of work, and those it keeps at work it sweats so mercilessly that it would seem, that, far from running by electricity, it runs on the nervous system of the men themselves."[66] While proponents of "automation" spoke of its future possibilities, Owens insisted on defining it as it existed in the present. "The point, however," he wrote, "is: we are not talking about what Automation could do if we lived under a different system, but what Automation is right here and now." And "now," Owens argued, "automation has not reduced the drudgery of labor. Whatever Automation means to management, labor bureaucrat, or engineer," he continued, "to the production worker it means a return to sweatshop conditions, increased speedup and gearing the man to the machine, instead of the machine to the man. The union contract assures management increased productivity by robbing the workers of control over the conditions of labor."[67]

Management achieved speedup by a combination of new machinery and the notorious time study, a practice popularized by Frederick Winslow Taylor and his method of scientific management. When conducting a time study, a manager or hired consultant stood over a worker while he or she completed a task. The time measured became the shop standard. Owens noted that "automation" had meant an increase in the frequency of time studies. "We used to see the time-study man once a year," he said. "Now you see him forty times a day. He's standing there all the time. I've actually caught these guys standing behind a worker with a stop watch in his hand and his hand behind his back, clocking the guy." Whereas earlier, workers had been allowed to rest if they met the hour's quota before the hour was up, now managers insisted more strongly on maintaining "a flowing line," meaning that they wanted jobs done "to the minute of the hour so that the line keeps moving with no stops." A superintendent told Owens, "We would have to stop the machine if you didn't work this way." Owens called this "murder," writing, "You're just standing there, grinding your life away. . . . They want those machines to be in charge of the course of the man's destiny every moment he is in that shop."[68]

For management, the increased frequency of time studies and the relentless "flowing line" were essential if the company wanted its postwar investments in heavy capital to show a return. Owens saw why at first hand; machines kept breaking down. The flowing line was, in fact, a fiction, but not an entirely useless one. In factories crowded with new, untested equipment, failures were inevitable. When, therefore, the machines did function, they needed to work quickly and consistently to recoup the value lost while mechanics had scrambled through the inert, labyrinthine mechanism searching for the latest problem. For production workers on the line, that meant speedup. More important, workers proved necessary to keep the new machines in operation. "Those machines have to be watched constantly because if nobody watches, everything goes wrong," an autoworker told Owens.[69] Contrary to what the UAW leadership might have wanted to believe, the workers' responsibility to watch and fix the machines did not make them as good as white-collar employees. Owens himself went through retraining to work on what he called "an Automation machine." The experience left an impression. "I have never worked under such brutal conditions before," he said. "He [Reuther] certainly can't mean re-training to become the kind of technicians that do nothing but push buttons and get good pay doing it."[70] Tending the new machines had not transformed the workers into respectable engineers.

Owens, like many in the postwar period, believed that the technology available to industry was unprecedented in scope and power. The new equipment impressed him. "It is a whole series of automatic machines linked together," he wrote, "to produce either a finished or semi-finished product which has gone through an assembly process as its various parts come together in the automation complex." Some of these machines were programmable, "controlled by a recorded tape"—Detroit Automation. But Owens saw many other kinds of machines that he and other workers also understood as "automation."[71]

Consider, for example, the car frame welder that Chrysler bought to speed up production. It placed frames on a bed while, Owens noted, "workers practically touching each other are welding on both sides of it." A worker had twelve seconds to finish his part of the job. Then a buzzer would sound, warning workers to step back. "The frame leaps out of its bed above your head and beds down a few feet beyond you," he wrote. Simultaneously, the next frame would be lowered into place. Owens complained that the company had attempted to reduce the time for this task from twelve seconds to seven. "Every time they try it," he wrote, "something dangerous happens." The frames had the tendency to leap out too quickly, spraying the workers with unwelded pieces that broke loose. If something went wrong, a worker could punch an emergency button to stop the line. But workers hesitated to push it, Owens wrote: "When someone uses this it is like shifting a car in reverse when it's traveling at a high rate of speed . . . there is a bang and a crash as if two freight cars have met head on. The superintendent comes running and wants to know who stopped it." When a representative from the company that designed the frame welder came onto the shop floor to inspect it after repeated failures, he noticed that the speed gauge was set too high. He dialed it back to a rate of one job every twelve seconds. The foreman returned it to where it had been set earlier that day, one job every nine seconds. The representative from the machine company turned it back to twelve and told the foreman it could not operate faster without leading to mechanical breakdown.[72]

Owens also used the word "automation" to describe a particularly ghoulish piece of equipment. Chrysler's management installed it during the 1959 to 1960 model changeover. It was a cutting machine, evidently so fast that one of its human operators—for it still required not one, but two people to run it—could only use it if he or she were strapped into leather cuffs that ran along the operator's arms, under the armpits, and over the shoulders. The cuffs were connected to a steel cable. The operators placed a piece of metal into the machine. By means of electric eyes the mechanism sensed the material's presence and activated automatically. The steel cable went taut and pulled the workers' hands away as a blade came slicing down. "The machine works so fast," one maintenance man said, "it isn't humanly possible for the worker to get his hands back out of the way before it cuts." The machine supposedly had a breaking point of one hundredth of a second. As one might imagine, it caused quite a stir when management ordered its installation on the shop floor. The workers refused to belt themselves into it. Finally, a superintendent forced a foreman to cuff himself to the machine and, by way of demonstration, show the workers that the device was perfectly safe. After running a few pieces through, Owens wrote, "the foreman begged them to turn him loose because he was forced to go to the bathroom."[73]

Although that particular cutting machine was especially horrific to many of the workers, other machines that they considered "automation" evoked similar feelings of danger, exhaustion, and claustrophobia. One Chrysler worker employed in Detroit, most likely in the heavy truck plant at 9 Mile and Sherwood, said: "You can't turn, you can't do anything. They got you sewed in with these automation machines. You got to work as regular as the wind blows, hour by hour—and you got to get it to work. I'm no good at the end of the day." A worker at the Chrysler Trim-Shop in Detroit had a similar experience with "automation": "They've got us pinned down so bad, we can't move around, can't talk to anybody, can't do a thing."[74]

With untried machines and a faster pace came physical danger. "Minor injuries are a daily occurrence," Owens wrote. "To the production worker in auto," he elaborated, "Automation means physical strain, mental fatigue, heart attacks—death by Automation." With mechanized speedup, safety precautions went by the board. The "speed from automation," Owens said, was disastrous. Remembering the first day of the installation of a bank of new machines in his department, he recalled crushed hands, lost fingers, and workers strained to the limit passing blood in the factory lavatory.[75] "These," Owens maintained, "are everyday occurrences in automated factories today." The speedup left workers exhausted. Many reported that they were so tired at the end of the day that they no longer had regular sexual relations with their spouses.[76] "A man's body has to be trained to work like a machine," he said. "The machine tells the body how to work."[77]

Another worker experiencing the mechanized speedup he and others called "automation" put it more succinctly. Describing how it felt to work a long day in an auto plant under these conditions, he said: "You are not human."[78] But that, of course, was the dream of "automation": a factory without human beings.

And as the automation discourse moved from the automobile factories into industries across the economy, so would the speedup and degradation of human labor.

2. The Electronic Brain's Tired Hands

Automation, the Digital Computer,
and the Degradation of Clerical Work

"As for the word 'automation,'" said John Diebold in 1955, "I quite frankly find it very difficult to define." Some might have found this admission surprising, for Diebold, a recent graduate of Harvard Business School, also claimed that he had invented the word. More than the newspaper and trade journal articles coming from the automobile industry in Detroit, it was Diebold's 1952 book *Automation: The Advent of the Automatic Factory* that elevated "automation" to its status in the postwar period as the watchword of technological progress. The *New York Times* called Diebold the "high priest of automation," its "evangelist" and "prophet." Hannah Arendt consulted his work and cited him as an authority on the subject, and when the United States Congress held hearings on the subject of "automation" it called him as its first witness to testify to the word's meaning. But by then events had outpaced him; the word had become the property of the public, and though Diebold remained certain that "automation" referred to something epochal and historically unprecedented, he could not be sure what that was.[1]

As the evangelist of "automation," Diebold made his name and his fortune popularizing the idea. He built a trans-Atlantic empire around it, the Diebold Group, a consulting firm that advised the likes of Boeing, DuPont, IBM, the government of Venezuela, and even the Communications Workers of America.[2] As the expert on "automation" he befriended characters as diverse as Henry Kissinger, Walter Cronkite, and Princess Beatrix of the House of Orange-Nassau, heir apparent to the Dutch throne. Flipping through the pages of his twelve guest books, one saw many familiar names. There were Richard Nixon and Gloria Steinem. Daniel Bell, Marshall McLuhan, Isaac Asimov, Ted Kennedy, and Henry Luce all put their names in Diebold's book, as did a secretary of labor and a secretary of state, along with CEOs from across the American industrial firmament—IBM, NCR, Alcoa, Sperry Rand, Mobil, RCA, Westinghouse, and AT&T. Diebold held "Monday Luncheons" that Alan Greenspan so enjoyed that on one occasion he brought Ayn Rand with him. "I keep relearning afresh," Diebold confided to his diary at the pinnacle of his success, "that throughout my life the people I have gotten along with most easily were the men at the very top."[3]

It was through "automation" that Diebold gained entrance to the very top, for the origins of the automation discourse intersected with one of the most consequential events in the history of technology in the twentieth century: the creation of a mass market for the electronic digital computer. In the immediate aftermath of World War II few if any predicted that the digital computer would one day become a ubiquitous feature of daily life. The idea of the broad diffusion of computers would have struck the ear as about as sensible as an x-ray machine in every home. Early computers were large and very expensive, but more to the point, it was unclear why anyone other than a government agency or university would desire the ability to perform astronomical computations with lightning speed. This posed a problem for those in the business of selling computers. Only businesses could afford to buy or rent one, and in the early postwar period it remained far from obvious how the new machines could help a company make money. If there was to be a mass market in digital computers, boosters would need to conjure it into existence; they would need to find a way to make it valuable to American businesses. Their answer was the contrivance of a newly minted commodity called "information."

By 1973 Daniel Bell would argue that the coming "post-industrial" society was to be "organized around knowledge" rather than "the coordination of machines and men for the production of goods"—and not just any knowledge, "*theoretical* knowledge—the primacy of theory over empiricism." The move from empiricism to theory as the source of value was, Bell maintained, in part a result of such "intellectual technology" as the electronic digital computer, and Bell had considered several other possible names beside "post-industrial" for the future society it heralded: the "professional society," the "knowledge society," and the "information society."[4] Like other critics in the last quarter of the twentieth century, Bell believed he was witnessing what later scholars called an "information revolution" in which the digital computer was replacing the need for embodied human labor. Information and the digital computer's ability to manipulate it were a new and decisive source of value, the proponents of the information revolution held, while the motions of the human body, no longer fetching a return, had been superseded as an agent driving social change.[5]

These claims had their origins in the early postwar period and grew directly from the automation discourse, the same discourse that played a crucial role in the creation of a mass market for computers. The narrative that "information" would replace physical production as the ultimate source of economic value first appeared in Diebold's 1952 book *Automation*. There, he argued that the value of the digital computer lay in its ability to do away with human labor, specifically by handling "information." "Automation" and the early diffusion of the computer went hand in hand, and in selling "automation" to corporate America, Diebold became an influential salesmen of digital computing technology. Management guru Peter Drucker claimed that it was Diebold who announced "the arrival of not only a new technology but also an altogether new way to look at work and at the economy." Diebold, he said, had been among the first to realize that "the ability to handle information efficiently is as important as, a hundred years ago, the ability to produce cheap mechanical power, that is, electricity, proved to be."[6]

The Second Coining of "Automation"

Whereas in 1952 Diebold's definition of "automation" had been rather straightforward—"a new word denoting both automatic operation and the process of making things automatic"—barely a year later he was no longer certain what exactly it meant. Shortly after the publication of *Automation* he discovered that he was unable to publish a magazine with the same title, although he had registered "automation" as a trademark. His lawyers told him that the term was already too widely in use. "Automation," they said, had become a "descriptive word in the field." The word had taken on a seemingly objective character that purported to describe a material reality, although the precise nature of that reality remained vague. Regardless, whatever "automation" meant it was no longer for Diebold to decide; the word had ceased to belong to him.[7]

In fact, it had not quite belonged to him in the first place. Only as the manuscript for *Automation* was going to press did Diebold learn that his invention was actually a reinvention. "It has recently been brought to the author's attention," he acknowledged in his preface, "that Mr. D. S. Harder, Vice President in charge of manufacturing of the Ford Motor Company, has for some time used the word *automation* to describe the automatic handling of materials and parts in and out of machines."[8] Diebold had known nothing of Ford's Automation Department. The coincidence of two individuals who knew nothing of each other, both managers, inventing the same term at more or less the same moment speaks to the difficulties Diebold discovered in defining his own word. More than the Ford Motor Company's mechanized speedup or Diebold's aspirations to drum up business, a broader semantic need in postwar society summoned the idea of "automation" into existence. The postwar concentration of powers political and technical inspired a sense, a feeling, an intuition that humanity had crossed the threshold of a new stage in history. That impression needed a name, one that described not a specific technological innovation but something deeper—a reassessment of the value of human labor in industrial society.[9]

In retrospect, one can perceive in the years preceding the word's invention the discursive void that "automation" would fill. Take, for example, a 1946 article in *Fortune*, "The Automatic Factory," that spoke of the potential for "automatism" in American manufacturing, of "threat and promise," of something that was bound to happen but had not happened yet. Thanks to the technological wonders produced during World War II and the wealth that had fallen to the United States in its aftermath, it now appeared, the article said, that "all the parts are here" to build an automatic factory. *Fortune*, in preparation, published a speculative series of illustrations demonstrating what that factory might look like. "The automatic factory does not exist," it said, "and, indeed, when it comes will not look much like this. But all its parts exist in bewildering variety." All this heralded "a new industrial order." Included was a photograph of workers in a factory captioned "The old production line," which was, actually, a picture of a current production line.[10]

The word "automation" both affirmed and described the technological enthusiasm of the moment, the common belief that what historians have called the "affluent society" and a "consumer's republic" was not simply a postwar boom but rather a new stage in history. It provided a seemingly technical explanation for the dramatic social changes taking place in the United States. By means of technology, economic policy, and world hegemony, the nation appeared to have solved the problems of capitalism: both its instability and the way it encouraged the owners of capital to exploit workers. With new wealth and new technical powers, critics reasoned, the United States could engineer its way out of the historical antagonisms endemic to industrial capitalism. Mass home ownership, mass consumption as a social duty, broad access to higher education, the widespread presence of unions, and widely shared material security all seemed to point toward the graduation of the working class—industrial, hourly wage workers engaged in physical labor—to middle-class, white-collar, professional jobs with yearly salaries that did not require physical exertion. "It is to this white-collar world," wrote the sociologist C. Wright Mills in 1951, "that one must look for much that is characteristic of twentieth-century existence."[11]

Diebold's *Automation* was a response to this heady atmosphere of capitalism revived and labor entrenched. The book's immediate origins lay in a report that Diebold and a group of colleagues wrote while attending Harvard Business School in the 1950–1951 school year. "Making the Automatic Factory a Reality" was their final assignment in Professor Georges Doriot's year-long manufacturing course, and it served as the basis for Diebold's later work.[12] A brigadier general in the Quartermaster Corps and Director of the Military Planning Division in charge of the Army's program of research and development during World War II, Doriot witnessed at first hand the remarkable technological developments made possible by the allocation of capital to targeted scientific investigation. Immediately after the war, he founded the first venture capital firm in the United States. "The research for war," he lectured his class, "does not have the primary restriction of money. For this reason, projects can be attempted by the government which private industry could hardly justify. . . . Though these releases have not been publicized widely," he continued, "it will be your responsibility to find out what has been done. If you do not, then your competitor will and you will be lost by the amount of the advantage he thereby gains."[13] He invited guest lecturers including K. T. Keller, president of Chrysler, Jay W. Forrester, a key figure in the development of the digital computer, and General Leslie Groves, military director of the Manhattan Project, to speak to the next generation of American managers.[14]

In his lectures Doriot taught his students what he considered to be two basic truths: first, that graduates of Harvard Business School should be ready to oppose the "little CIO girl" and her allies "with [their] own energy which is directed more intelligently" and second, that "the ideal factory has no men."[15]

Taking seriously Doriot's call to make use of the latest technological insights, the authors of "Making the Automatic Factory a Reality" sought out experts in the field of automatic machinery, including such pioneers in digital computing as Julian Bigelow and Howard Aiken. They also met with three founding members of the cybernetics movement: John von Neumann, Norbert Wiener, and Claude Shannon. Concerned with feedback, or the way self-regulating systems control themselves, cybernetics became its own field of study in the late 1940s.[16] In Wiener's words, cybernetics was the "study of control and communication in the animal and the machine," an analogy whose usefulness occurred to him during the war when he tried to construct a self-aiming anti-aircraft gun.[17] Claude Shannon made his contribution to the field through his work in wartime cryptography. John von Neumann, one of the twentieth century's great mathematicians, had been a major contributor to the development of the first electronic digital computer, ENIAC, and had helped design the explosive lenses used in Fat Man, the atomic bomb that destroyed Nagasaki. Diebold and a colleague began by driving to Princeton to consult with von Neumann:

> One of the questions I asked of him was whether it would not be possible to use computers to control the various kinds of process plants, petroleum refinement and chemical processing. He made several calculations on a blackboard in his room as a demonstration on how he felt it would indeed be possible for computers to control these plants. I then asked what will you do about this, and he said, nothing at all. He said that I am now convinced that it will be possible, and I have no further interest whatever in spending any further time on the problem.[18]

Despite having sought the advice the founders of cybernetics, in the final draft of their report Diebold and his colleagues distanced themselves from the movement. Cybernetics, they argued, hoped to explain how a person or a machine might react to its environment autonomously. They, however, wanted machines that could actually *handle* materials as effectively as a person could. They called for "the automation of fabricating and materials handling functions which are now performed manually." They used the new word almost in passing. They did not define what they meant by "automation" or note that the word was in any way extraordinary, although it seemed to mean, quite simply, making something automatic: "The approach most popular among those seeking automation in industry is that of reducing control mechanisms to their basic elements."[19]

After graduating from Harvard, Diebold created his own company with the intention of advising manufacturers as to how they might remove human workers from their factories. To promote the business, he rewrote the Harvard report and published it as *Automation*. From the margins of the earlier paper, "automation" shot to the center of the analysis. Now it was "a distinct phase in industrial progress" that offered "an escape from designing in terms of the limitations of human operators." Cribbing from Wiener, Diebold now spoke of a "second industrial revolution."[20] Since the late 1930s corporate America had seized on the language of socialist utopians, offering to consumers visions of a technologically sublime future provided not by revolution but by private enterprise.[21] In his book Diebold made use of the same rhetoric but condensed it into a single word, one that married sober technical discussions to broad claims about the coming of a brave new world. From then on, he consistently spoke of "automation" as a revolution that would "take us *beyond* the civilization of an industrial society, a revolution in which human beings will be largely freed from the bondage of machines." Machines, he would write, were "*agents for social change*" that were to usher in the "age of automation . . . a golden Periclean age in which a society based on the work of the machine—not of human chattel—rises to the full heights of which the human spirit is capable."[22]

Diebold premised the "automation" revolution on the notion that the human body had reached its industrial and historical limits and, so, no longer produced value. To elaborate on this point, he chose as the symbol of human weakness what until then had represented the ingenuity and resourcefulness of the species: the hand. Whereas archeologists and anthropologists extolled the thumb as the author of civilization, Diebold saw it as the obstacle to progress. "The greatest pitfall to avoid is the assumption that the design aim is reproduction of the hand movements of the operator or laborer," he wrote. The italics were Diebold's: "*The strong tendency in this direction may be due to the assumption that human hands guided by human brains represent optimum efficiency and should therefore be copied as closely as possible. Such an assumption, in most cases, is unwarranted.*" A human being, he wrote, possessed eyes, hands, fingers—all undermined by "limited dexterity." It was time to move beyond these organs. "All too many of our present machines have been built around these limitations," he concluded.[23]

Diebold's contempt for the hand went beyond its supposed inefficiency; hands also threatened managerial control. What made "automation" different from the mere use of "automatic controls," he argued, was the way it ruled out the possibility that a hired hand might interrupt the work flow. He asked his reader to consider a steel factory that had recently installed new, supposedly automatic equipment. "Two years ago I had the opportunity to visit one of our largest steel plants," he wrote.

> At a long line of open hearth furnaces, the guide proudly explained the use of a new device for determining the optimum time for tapping the furnaces. As we watched, the workmen dutifully referred to this device and noted the readings on log sheets. Yet no furnace was tapped until an old foreman squinted through a piece of colored glass at a sample of molten metal that had been poured on the brick floor and nodded his approval.[24]

Here was the problem. Despite investments in the latest mechanisms to rationalize production, the company still relied on a foreman who evidently had the power to decide when and if to tap a furnace. Regardless of the ready availability of "de-skilling" equipment, the organization of workers in the mill meant that a potentially unreliable human foreman still controlled the work. The application of the new technology had not guaranteed greater managerial control over the factory. This problem was not mechanical but political. As long as there were workers on the shop floor there would also be politics.

But if executives achieved a "truly automatic" factory, argued Diebold, they would have accomplished something wholly unprecedented: a factory without politics.

When Diebold went into business in the early 1950s, he assumed that he would advise factories and offices in the ways of eliminating human workers by means of machinery, and for the most part the public focused its attention on the prospect of a workerless factory. But while enough manufacturers and many more besides spoke of the imminent "automation" of industrial production, it seemed that few manufacturers actually cared to invest capital in making their factories automatic. An internal memorandum for Diebold's company noted as much. Whereas the company's reputation rested on "factory automation," it remarked, in truth it "performed a very small amount of professional work in this area."[25]

Industrial manufacturers did not desire Diebold's services. His lack of success was best captured by the speech he gave to the National Machine Tool Builders' Association in 1963 titled "The Revolution That Fails to Take Place." The "business of supplying machine tools should be in the midst of a revolution," he told the assembled representatives of some of the oldest tooling firms in the country. They should have been developing the means to produce automatic machine tools, he said, but for some reason they were not. Their mistake, he informed them, was that they assumed the presence of the human body. Building machine tools with the motions of a craftsmen in mind, he said, was "too limited."[26] But his listeners, arguably in closer touch than Diebold with the demands of industrial manufacturers, did not see a profit to be made in throwing their all into the development of automatic machine tools. As the automobile industry had discovered, making a factory entirely automatic was by no means necessarily consistent with making a profit. And by the mid-1960s, enough failures to win factory contracts convinced Diebold that the "manless factory is a technical possibility, but there are good reasons for thinking it will never be built." Looking at Plymouth's use of transfer machines in the production of engines, he noted that "the number of workers could probably be cut in half if the line were made as automatic as present technology permits. However, the cost of the engine would go up, because on some of the stations it is cheaper to use conventional assembly methods than to automate."[27]

Factory managers clearly did not believe that doing away with the detailed division of labor would fatten the bottom line, although often enough they deployed the language of "automation" to describe the technical innovations they did in fact make. Rather than actually producing automatic factories, the ultimate value of the automation discourse lay in how it joined a language of no-

nonsense engineering with utopian breathlessness. If Diebold wanted to make "automation" profitable, he therefore needed to find a place where uncertainty was high and where the postwar technological innovations could plausibly offer the most. Ultimately, the best ground for Diebold and those like him was not the shop floor. In the end, the apparatus that he and a growing number of consultants promoted in the name of "automation" would not be the machine tool but rather a new and untried device: the electronic digital computer.

"Automation," Information, the Digital Computer, and Clerical Work

Diebold's decision to apply "automation" to the digital computer grew from the final report that he and his fellow students had written for Doriot's manufacturing course. In preparing the report, they had consulted with Claude Shannon, a major figure in early computing history who provided much of the theoretical language of what would be known as information theory. In an influential 1948 article Shannon defined "information" as the statistical likelihood that a certain signal would be transmitted. For example, if someone were transmitting a word to another person, letter by letter, let's say, the word "Quiet," he or she would begin by transmitting the letter Q. According to Shannon, because the person receiving the transmission had no idea what word was being sent, one could consider this Q to have a high quotient of information. But the following U that the transmitter sent would possess hardly any information at all, because in English a Q is almost always followed by a U. The certainty of its transmission was practically 100 percent. If one wanted to compress the transmission of the data being sent, one might well be able to omit the U entirely. The higher the certainty of a signal's transmission, the lower its value as information in this particular sense. This statistical likelihood of transmission, Shannon realized, could be quantified, and he used a special term to denote a unit of information: the "bit," short for "binary digit," which had been used originally in relation to the either/or of a telephone switch. On one point, however, Shannon could not have been more explicit. "Information" in this engineering sense, he insisted, was not a synonym for the more colloquial understanding of the word "information" as valuable knowledge. In fact, a bit of information possessed no semantic value whatever. It was only the measure of a statistical probability.[28]

In "Making the Automatic Factory a Reality" Diebold and his colleagues considered the possibility of an automatic office, but this concern was secondary to the workerless factory. Here the influence of the cybernetics movement was clearest. The authors of the report asked of office work, "What is the function of the man?" and answered: "He gathers information." That is, he enters data into some kind of processing system. "He puts this information in useful form." He manipulates it. "He constantly changes his files, adds and deletes, manually lifting bits of paper and rearranges them. He refers to his bits of paper in the file and arranges the information in useable form at a date after it has entered the material in the file."[29] It is not clear whether the authors misunderstood Shannon's definition of "information" or intentionally expanded it, but in describing the human function of the clerical worker they made an elision between the colloquial meaning of "information" and its engineering sense. In this analysis, human labor and moving bits of information were the same thing. The information to which they referred was useful knowledge, some valuable fact recorded on a bit of paper. The human clerical worker assessed and manipulated this valuable fact and rendered it into an even more valuable form, something that could return a profit. With this conflation the group made what would become a common claim in the middle of the twentieth century—that human labor, especially in the office, could be replaced by disembodied information handled not by the human hand but by a digital computer.[30]

If the conflation of the concept of valuable knowledge and Shannon's "information" had been a mistake on the part of the Harvard group, it was one that Diebold perpetuated throughout his career. "Our clerical procedures," he argued in *Automation*, "have been designed largely in terms of human limitations." In this case, those limitations came in the form of clerks and middle managers. "At the present time," he continued, "much lower and middle management time is devoted to processing information and drawing from raw data the significant facts necessary for making top management decisions." The computer, he wrote, would process that "information" and create "significant facts," that is, useful knowledge, with which a lone executive could make decisions. Rather than rely on an office of low-level managers and clerks to synthesize raw data into actionable knowledge, Diebold maintained, an executive could make use of a computer. Clerks, in this case, were understood to be women.[31]

Automation was the first example of a management theorist arguing that information was a discrete commodity that was valuable to businessmen. The justification of information's value was, according to Diebold, its ability to replace human labor—that the digital computer could "handle" information as human clerical workers had—and by 1955 information had made its way into the center of Diebold's understanding of "automation": "The technology of automation is incredibly complex," he told lawmakers. "Fundamentally, it deals with the transmission and use of information for the purposes of machine control, and for the purposes of optimizing production." Information was both the means to effect automatic production and sometimes was the product itself. According to Diebold, "automation" reunited in one supermachine the labor process that industrialization had broken up into the detailed division of labor. Now, he maintained, no human being would interfere with the labor process from raw material to finished product. "This may be a physical product," he said, "or (in a business process) it may be information."[32]

The Postwar Office and the Digital Computer

Diebold's move from factory to office was a response to the recent expansion and feminization of office work. The number of clerical workers in the country rose dramatically with the postwar boom in American business. Between 1947 and 1956 the number of white-collar workers employed in the United States ballooned by more than 50 percent; in that group, clerical workers made up the largest single occupation.[33] This development took the nation by surprise. "The white-collar people slipped quietly into modern society," went the first sentence of C. Wright Mills's seminal 1951 book *White Collar*. They were, to go by Mills, a confusing people, without history or clear common interest. Wage earners in factories, the famed industrial working class, could, if they wished, understand themselves as the vanguard of the revolution. White-collar workers, on the other hand, were something else—not a class, neither clearly bourgeois nor explicitly proletarian, and for the most part not unionized.[34] Some believed that the growth in the number of professionals, managers, salesmen, retailers, and clerks indicated that the United States was on the verge of becoming an essentially middle-class society. But as Mills wrote, "In the lower reaches of the white-collar world, office operatives grind along, loading and emptying the filing system; there are private secretaries and typists, entry clerks, billing clerks, corresponding clerks—a thousand kinds of clerks." A significant cohort in this army, those at the bottom rung of respectability, were the people who used machines—clerks who ran comptometers, sat at typewriters, and worked keypunches. They were women. Nationwide, more women were employed in clerical work than in any other kind of job, over one-fourth of all the women in the workforce.[35]

Office managers worried that the proliferation of clerical jobs would eat into profits. Summarizing the lessons learned at the American Management Association's Office Management Conference in October 1957, one manager reported, "The same principles of scientific planning that have brought us from the cottage system and dependence on master artisans in the factory to our highly mechanized lines are applicable to clerical functions as well." Like the Taylorists before them, office managers wanted to find ways of "getting the work out faster, at lower unit costs." This move to render clerical labor as much like factory labor meant managers consciously adopted the practices of speedup, mechanization, and regimentation. In part this involved "eliminating human hands and handwriting." And, as one might have expected, as clerical work became ever more like factory work and the white collar took on a shade of blue, managers began to fear a proletarian rebellion in the office suite, or so wrote the authors of *White-Collar Restiveness: A Growing Challenge*.[36]

Into this boom in clerical employment stepped those, like Diebold, who hoped to sell a new generation of business machines.[37] Computer manufacturers and their allies claimed that they could sell to offices the power to do away with the growing ranks of clerical workers cutting into profits and threatening to proletarianize the workplace. They assured employers that digital computers would bring "automation" to offices. Computers, they argued, rather than human hands, would channel business information, the equivalent of a company's thoughts. If the boosters were to be believed, the new machines would allow a company to escape practically all physical limits. "And information," Diebold wrote, "is the great central, all-important element in our personal lives and in the life of our society and our world. Once we have enough information and use it well enough, who is to say that even the speed of light could not be surpassed! I certainly would take no bet on it!" All this was "made possible by computers," said Diebold, "by automation."[38]

Beginning in the mid-1950s, "information technology" became a common term in publications aimed at persuading executives that computers were good for business.[39] In his 1956 book *Office Work and Automation*, Howard S. Levin, formerly of the Manhattan Project, argued against Claude Shannon and held that one could, indeed, make a distinction between information and data: Data was the raw material of knowledge; information was knowledge rendered into a useful form. "Distribution of information completes a data-processing operation," he wrote. "Thus, information serves the purpose of getting things done." Useful knowledge was knowledge that had a relative value—a use value.[40] The office was like a factory, he maintained, in that it produced "the information needed to guide and operate the business." That information had to be distilled from a great deal of paperwork. But mere "information" on its own was not enough to convince employers to purchase the new machine. Although Levin promoted the digital computer as a machine of remarkable potential in addition to its supposed ability to replace human beings, he found that managers were not particularly interested in buying vague promises of power or "the creation of a more useful office." Instead, they valued the computer according to the same criteria they had applied to earlier generations of office machines—its ability to reduce their workforce. "Saving money through reduction of clerical payrolls," Levin said of office managers, "is proving a more powerful motivation."[41]

By the early 1960s, consultants, technicians, and computer manufacturers called this vision of "automation" Management Information Systems, or MIS. According to one proponent, MIS was a "totally automated, fully responsive, truly all-encompassing information system embodying the collection, storage and processing of data and the reporting of significant information on an as-needed basis." The purpose of MIS was to reduce the number of people between the source of a business's information and upper-level management.[42] According to one business executive, a researcher reported, managers installed "integrated data-processing" in order to, in the executive's words, "chop heads off payroll." Managers, acting on the advice of consultants, sought to apply the digital computer to repetitive tasks, as this researcher put it, "to cut clerical costs and thus hasten the break-even point." Such tasks, when performed by hand, "are the province of unskilled high school girls who on graduation turn to the banks and utility and insurance companies for employment."[43] These were the untrustworthy hands, counted in the millions, that managers hoped to mechanize away.

Computers, according to boosters such as Levin and Diebold, allowed a manager to gain access to hitherto unimaginable deposits of useful knowledge. A mass of undifferentiated, worthless data became "information," which was discrete, transferable, and valuable—valuable because it was useful and because its creation required no labor costs. An internal report for Diebold's company captured this sense of the profitable distillation of a normally diffused resource: This "new concept of data organization" made use of "the *value* of a data element." Speaking of the value of new technology, Diebold maintained that "the root is not the computer. . . . The root is information theory and its ability to build a wide variety of brand new families of machines to handle information." This was because, as another company report claimed, "Every person who handles the data is a potential source of introduction of bias in shaping the 'facts.'"[44]

Computer companies embraced the automation discourse's celebration of the freeing of "information" from the body of the worker. Take, for example, Jim Henson's promotional film for IBM, *The Paperwork Explosion*. A montage of talking heads all spoke the same lines: "Today there is more paperwork than ever before," they said. The answer to this problem, they held, was the computer. "With IBM dictation equipment I can get four times as much thinking recorded as I can by writing it down, and twice as much as I can by dictating to a highly skilled secretary." Finally, the film riffed on the company's slogan,

FIGURE 1. The workers supposedly eliminated by the digital computer. *The Information Machine* (1958), courtesy of the Eames Office, LLC.

"Think": "IBM machines can do the work, so that people have time to think. . . . Machines should do the work, that's what they're best at; people should do the thinking, that's what they're best at"—and finally—"Machines should work, people should think."[45]

Since the 1950s IBM had sold the digital computer as a device that would remove human labor from clerical work. Take, for example, Charles and Ray Eames's promotional film *The Information Machine,* made for the IBM pavilion at the 1958 World's Fair in Brussels. The film touted the computer as a "control" mechanism, one that could maintain "complicated systems," among which it included clerical work, represented by a group of women engaged in filing.

"Data processing removes the drudgery," the film's narrator went on to say, "but it imposes new and broad responsibilities." The viewer was then shown a man in a tie thinking deeply while a long mechanical arm fed punched cards into a computer.

Despite the film's claims, however, the job of that mechanical arm was never the work of machines. Preparing and entering data into a computer remained a human's job, the job of thousands upon thousands of poorly paid female

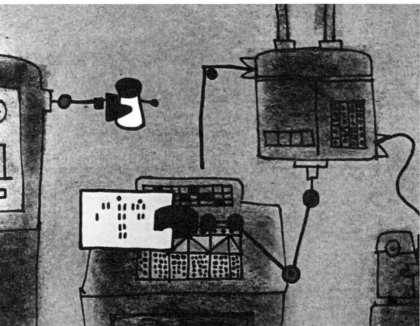

FIGURES 2 AND 3. A fantasy of the manager's thoughts made into material reality without the intervention of human labor. *The Information Machine* (1958), courtesy of the Eames Office, LLC.

workers. In order to show how computers did the work, IBM chose to erase the essential human action required to make a computer in any way useful. The appeal of the computer was that it promised a manager a world where pure thought encountered no physical limitations. The thinker was understood to be a white professional man. The worker was depicted as an inhuman machine. But this machine was, like other science fictions, a metaphor for poorly paid people.[46]

For regardless of the celebration of the new commodity called "information" and the spectacular displays of the electronic digital computer, the postwar mechanization of the office followed the same logic it had since the turn of the twentieth century: As employers added new machines to the labor process, they feminized their workforce. That way, rather than eliminate workers, they simply made them cheaper to employ. At the end of the nineteenth century, for example, the typewriter had been a new machine, and employers had with comparative ease sex-typed typing as feminine work. In coding the keyboard as a feminine apparatus, managers made the job of clerk one that was fit primarily for female workers, which is to say, cheap workers. In 1880, approximately half of all stenographers and typists were women; by 1930, practically all were. As other machines entered the office, managers sex-typed them as feminine also, including the keypunch machines that would be used to translate data into a language a computer could understand, usually in the form of holes punched into paper cards.[47]

Beginning in earnest in the late 1950s and accelerating throughout the 1960s, managers availed themselves of these same time-honored methods of cheapening the cost of labor, only now by means of the digital computer. Although they brought in many different kinds of machines during this period, at the center stood the large mainframe computer. The mainframe enabled offices to perform "batch processing" of data, usually entered into the computer in the form of punchcards or punched tape, a process known as electronic data processing, or EDP. Mainframe computers could calculate quickly, perform certain office procedures rapidly, and store and retrieve files. Nonetheless, the human hand remained irreplaceable at one particular bottleneck: data entry. And as computing power increased, so did the number of clerks necessary to enter data.[48]

It was precisely here that the automation discourse obscured rather than eliminated the value of human labor. While the notion that commodified "information" could replace labor in the office was the brainchild of managers, union leaders also believed that "automation" was on the verge of removing all clerical labor from the office. On its face, this was surprising. No one knew better than union leadership that the number of clerical workers in the United

States was rising, not falling. As the secretary-treasurer of the AFL-CIO's Industrial Union Department observed, "The number of white collar workers rises constantly."[49] Nevertheless, many union officials worried that soon there would be no more white-collar jobs. "I don't know how many office workers or how many retail workers will be displaced by automation," Walter Reuther said at a conference on the future of white-collar work. The legions of clerical workers grew daily, but they were also "in the middle of the revolutionary changes that are going to sweep the American economy."[50] The nation stood on that threshold, he said. According to these labor leaders, white-collar work was one of the fastest-growing segments of the labor force and, incongruously, they also agreed that very soon there would be no more white-collar jobs.

The gendering of work in the automation discourse helps explain this apparent contradiction. The director of the Organization for Office Employees International Union demonstrated as much: "Statistics prove many things, he said, "but they do not ease the burden of paying rent, buying the groceries, or explaining to the displaced employee's child why she cannot have a new dress because daddy's job has been eliminated by an electric brain." The worker in danger of losing his office job was assumed to be a man. The entity supposedly replacing him was a machine, an electric brain. For labor leaders thinking about workers in the office, the presence of women's bodies was subsumed into the new office equipment. The human labor necessary to make the fantastic new machines work—the typists, the file clerks, and the keypunch operators—seemed incidental to the laboring power of the machine. The workers were there, clearly, but simultaneously not there, invisible appendages of the new mechanisms. And as long as the majority of such workers were invisible, one might well argue, as did the same director, then (male) office workers would "see machines do in a second work that takes them days and weeks to accomplish. They will see machines replace the jobs that they . . . have come to feel are their permanent niches in the office world."[51] The menial clerical jobs that women performed were not real jobs, union leaders could say to themselves, and even if they were, soon, because of "automation," the supposed tendency of all technological development to eliminate human labor, those little women's jobs would soon cease to exist.

It would take union leaders decades to recognize that the tasks women performed in offices constituted real jobs worthy of representation in collective bargaining. Twenty years later, a female organizer for District 65 in New York who went on to help form several clerical workers' unions would say, "This is one of the things not only with our union but with all unions. Sometimes they've looked on the office workers as being sort of invisible, although we do have many office workers in our textile and garment industry. But sometimes the people in a shop or a warehouse just haven't paid attention and the women haven't sought out a union."[52] The belief in the inevitability of technological advance toward laborless machines contributed to labor leadership's inability to see these female clerical workers as real workers, or to see them at all. It most certainly played a part in holding back the unionization of the office in the middle of the twentieth century. Not until the late 1970s would female clerks in such organizations as 9to5 and Women Office Workers, inspired by the women's movement of the 1960s, began to demand full recognition of the value of their labor and their right to unionize. In the eyes of most union leaders in the 1950s and 1960s, the dramatic increase in the number of women working in the office was an incidental phenomenon in the larger story of machines taking over the office.

But, if anything, office computers seemed to create more of a need for human labor than before. "The traditional promise of electronic data processing is the possibility of actually eliminating—or at least reducing to a minimum—the processing of paperwork," one office manager said in 1958, announcing a given among managers hoping to save on labor costs. But in rendering the data into a form in which it could be fed into the computer, he complained, "the magnitude of paperwork now is breaking all records." Referring to the introduction of a large computer into the office, this manager noted that "the computer was installed cleverly and smoothly, and is now producing excellently. However, there are just as many clerks and just as many key-punch operators as before. . . . In most cases, paperwork is actually increasing in the input area."[53] This is not to say that mechanization did not increase productivity. Rather, in order to increase productivity with a machine, offices also needed to hire more workers. As a 1966 study by the Bureau of Labor Statistics put it: "It was possible to handle an increasing workload without increasing employment as much as would have been necessary if EDP had not been introduced."[54] With a new source of machine power, employers needed to increase, not decrease, the amount of human labor power necessary to make the machine power useful. This was not the same as machines bodily replacing human beings; it was not what John Diebold and the computer industry promised when they proposed "automation" to offices, although it was entirely consistent with the long history of industrial mechanization.

Despite claims by proponents that "automation" created more skilled work, by the middle of the 1960s three-fifths of the workers directly involved in the use of the central office computer in the insurance industry, one of the most paperwork-heavy of businesses, were low-level clerical workers, more than 90 percent of them female. Direct clerical computer work comprised several tasks. Besides performing data entry itself—keypunching—clerical workers

FIGURE 4. Keypunch operators at work in the insurance industry in the 1960s. From Freeman, *Impact of Office Mechanization in the Insurance Industry*, 43.

"coded," converting records from English into languages the machines could understand. They were also librarians who physically took out or put away reels of punched-paper or magnetic tape.[55] Sometimes these jobs were broken up, and sometimes employers asked clerical workers to do a mix of them, including more traditional tasks such as answering telephones, typing, operating mechanical tabulating machines or bookkeeping equipment, running errands, and doing office chores.[56]

Even as the common method of data entry began to shift from use of punchcards to keyboard typing in the mid-1970s, the problem had not changed. Human labor remained essential and was, often, grueling. "Many jobs can't be done by machines," wrote Jean Tepperman, an activist in the women's movement who conducted a series of interviews with clerical workers in the 1970s and also worked closely with 9to5, the National Association of Working Women. "And even when they can," she continued, "people are needed to operate the machines. . . . Hardly a computer in the country 'knows' anything unless a person—usually a low-paid woman worker—tells it the information on a keyboard." Responding to a bank officer who hoped to minimize the importance of human data entry by saying, "The girl just keys in the information directly," Tepperman answered, "The 'girl' is still an essential part of their multi-million dollar computer system—even if one of the cheapest parts!"[57]

FIGURE 5. A clerical worker feeding punched cards into a digital computer. From Freeman, *Impact of Office Mechanization in the Insurance Industry*, 21.

When Mary Roberge went to work for Monarch Insurance in Springfield, Massachusetts, in 1959, she was equally shocked by how poorly management treated clerical workers, as well as by how onerous their work with an IBM computer was. She was employed as a "math clerk," but, she said, "my job title was a misleading euphemism, as I did no math—simply stamped, punched, and endlessly filed and refiled IBM cards, standing in front of row upon row of drawers." Roberge worked in an environment typical for computer clerical work in banking and insurance: "a large open area, part of a sea of desks, occupied by women and men in a ratio of about 20 to 1." The male bosses, Roberge remembered, sat in glass-paneled offices that surrounded the clerical workers and looked out onto the working floor where they transformed written reports into a machine-readable form. "Except at new business time," Roberge remembered, "when we['d] spend some time key-punching, then hours standing at the file drawers, we sat at our desks all day doing the work the supervisor parcelled [sic] out to us. It consisted of memos with instructions on which IBM cards to pull and which of our half dozen rubber stamps to use on them—'Cancelled,' 'Lapsed,' 'Extended to _____,' change of state or agency." The workers were not allowed to get up from their desks except to pull a file or use the bathroom. "There were no coffee breaks," Roberge remembered, and talking was discouraged. One day, during a slack hour, Roberge put her head down on her arms, resting on her desk. "The young supervisor came flying over and told me in a voice of gentle alarm that if I didn't feel well, I should go to the nurse's office, but I could not 'rest' that way at my desk." Roberge earned $47.50 a week, "and that was extremely low pay," she said, "even in 1959."[58]

While Roberge was sometimes bored on the job, many clerical workers in offices with computers were snowed under with work. In 1960 Mrs. Duncan, a keypunch operator, found that the introduction of a computer allowed management to speedup employees. All the operators were "nervous wrecks," she said. "If you happen to speak to an operator while she is working, she will jump a mile. You can't help being tense. The machine makes you that way." She went on: "Even though the supervisor does not keep an official count on our work, she certainly knows how much each of us is turning out—by the number of boxes of cards we do." Said another keypunch operator, "Everything is speed in the work now," the pace of work "terrific." While speaking with a researcher, a vice president at an insurance company pointed toward a room where keypunch operators furiously typed and said, "All they lack is a chain."[59]

A clerical worker employed at Travellers Insurance Company in the early 1970s reported similar conditions working not on a keypunch machine but on one that entered data on magnetic tape. "Everything is time-rated," she said. "They give you x number of minutes to do a piece of paper, a sheet of work. . . . Each sheet has a number that comes on automatically when you push the button. It automatically goes on the tape . . . so you can't really cheat."[60] In this way the machines simultaneously sped up work and surveilled workers. A clerical worker employed at a Bank of America "data processing center" reported that they were required to "mark down every time your machine is not running so if you go to talk to somebody you write down from 17:10 to

17:20, talking, or you have to mark down when you have to go to the bathroom, anything over 5 minutes. Of course it takes you 5 minutes to get through the man trap to get out to the bathroom so you have to mark it down."[61]

Computers often broke down. "Computers! You can have them!" said Shirley Haapanen, who at Liberty Mutual Insurance was still doing batch processing in the late 1970s. There were two computers in her section. "It seemed like there was a [line a] mile long waiting to use that computer. And it was always on the blink. It just wasn't working half of every day, and it was so frustrating."[62] Even when machines worked, management often did not know how best to incorporate them into the labor process, creating significant problems that workers had to iron out. One clerical worker remembered when her employer introduced a digital computer to mechanize her job. "You see," she said, "we went on this new system in Sept. of '72, and they did a real half-assed job on it."

> One of the men from the home office came and told us how great this new system was going to be. We'd be totally computerized in a few years. . . . Well, they did it wrong in the beginning, and ever since then we've been trying to prove it. We keep adjusting figures, and doing all kinds of things to make it prove, but it never proves. The last time we did an inventory, my particular group was $56,000 off, and we couldn't find it. It's not us. We added everything correctly, and we did everything as best we knew how. It just is nuts.[63]

Although this worker believed that the computer might have been useful "for doing written business," she was unimpressed with its ability to handle claims. "They'll still need people," she said. "There's going to be a lot of key-punch jobs . . . and it's going to be really boring work for anyone who has to work there."[64]

Working directly with computers was often physically exhausting. "They like it if you dress nice," said one clerical worker in the insurance industry, "but in most of the departments you can't afford to dress nice because you end up tearing your hose. You have to move this or that, you get dust on your clothes. . . . It's a very dirty job." Every hour she needed to pick up jobs that had been run on the computer. "And when you pick those things up, you get it [dirt] on your clothes. And then you have to file them. You pull this big truck along, shove it against a wall and this is no position to be wearing a dress or skirt." The folders were large, and the inserters in which they were entered into the computer were made of metal. "They catch on your clothes and pull," she recalled. "You cut your fingers."[65]

A worker entering data on magnetic tape at Travellers Insurance Company said of the machines she used, "I can't hear anything when people talk to me.

I have to turn off the machine." She found it surprising that it should be so physically demanding to operate the apparatus, "especially for a machine that was designed to be typed on all day long." It was like "driving a big truck with standard, without automatic steering. It's very hard and it's very noisy."[66]

A clerical worker at Bank of America was also impressed by the physical effort needed to operate a computer. She worked in a centralized facility that employed approximately four thousand people in three shifts, including a weekend shift, operating an IBM machine that microfilmed and sorted checks. Frank Benson, director of Commonwealth Edison's Treasury Department in Chicago, praised such check-reading machines because "long after the remittance staff has gone home for the day, the main accounting computers update the permanent records." But in her section, this clerical worker was on the swing shift from five in the evening to two in the morning, doing the night work that Mr. Benson implied the computer accomplished entirely on its own. She worked on piece rate, meaning that her earnings were directly related to the number of checks she processed. "You're working faster because the item count is going to be part of the statistics in your review," she said. "At the beginning of the night there's very limited work because the branches haven't all got in yet, so people are almost fighting to get work because they want their item count up there." Most of the employees in this section were men, although the number of women had doubled since she had started the job a year earlier. Although the computer sometimes broke down or rejected checks that it could not read, still the machine's pace was "a constant thing." Workers taught themselves how to fix most of the machine failures so they would not have to call in "the I.B.M. man." The machines were so loud that the bank provided ear plugs; the machines kicked up so much dust that management gave the workers masks. The bank no longer allowed men to wear ties when operating the computers because "ties went through the machine, with the guy attached to it." In order to use the machine, she said, "you have to stand."

> The machine is tall so when you're feeding it in you're moving to empty the pockets at the same time that you're feeding it and turning around filling up the tray and putting the tray when it's full on the other side so you can put an empty one in there. So you're standing on your feet constantly but you are moving. . . . When I first started I did [get tired] but now I got used to it. You just keep going, you just wear the right shoes. Some of the girls come in with heels like that in the first few days and they can't take it. They're sitting down constantly.[67]

In addition to reducing labor costs by means of job degradation, companies brought in computers and computer consultants to undermine existing union contracts. Unionized clerical workers at the Blue Shield office in San Francisco in Local 3 of the Office and Professional Employees International Union found that, in the words of a clerical worker named Toni, "bargaining unit jobs are slowly disappearing and the people that make them disappear is [*sic*] this computer organization." Blue Shield had hired a consulting company, Electronic Data Systems (EDS), ostensibly to advise on how to mechanize clerical work with digital computers. The head and founder of EDS was, in the words of Ramon, a claims examiner at Blue Shield of California, "this guy named H. Ross Poreau," that is, Ross Perot, future third-party candidate in the 1992 presidential election. "And E.D.S. started going in companies that had computer problems, saying—We can run your whole system a lot cheaper." It was true. Ross Perot founded EDS in 1962 after working for five years at IBM. He began making money through EDS in 1966 by advising Blue Cross Blue Shield of Texas regarding how best to use its computers to process claims made under the new Medicare and Medicaid programs. At the time when he secured that job for his company he was, in fact, also employed by Blue Cross Blue Shield of Texas. He won the contract without its having gone out to bid and without the authorization of the Social Security Administration, "raising," in the words of the *New York Times*, "the issue of conflict of interest." The stroke that made Perot's fortune came in 1968 when he won a million-dollar-a-month contract for EDS with Blue Shield of California. According to Ramon and Toni, Blue Shield called in EDS in order to undermine the clerical workers' collectively bargained contract on the pretext of installing and running digital computers.[68]

Toni noted, "E.D.S. is actually doing management and that is against our contract. Instead of your supervisor telling you about something, there's an E.[D].S. guy saying, 'That will be your desk over there, you're not to talk to this person. Your production's been such and such. We're moving you over here.' Pure and simple management responsibilities. And we don't even work for these fucking guys." After EDS came in, Blue Shield cut at least two hundred union jobs in the California system, and by the end of its first year of consulting fifty workers were bumped to a lower job classification. "Most [of] them lost about 60¢ to 80¢ an hour in pay," Toni noted. "It's more efficient production, speed-up as they call it."[69] This was not an isolated event. As late as 1980 the National Association of Office Workers reported that "too often, highly paid consultants brought in to ease the transition to automation play a dual role as anti-union or union-busting advisors . . . company officials flatly challenge job titles, telling employees 'You're not a file clerk anymore, you're just a machine operator.'"[70]

"Automation" by means of the digital computer—like "automation" in the automobile industry—degraded, intensified, and expanded the human labor necessary to make the office work. By the late 1970s a growing contingent of managers would come to agree that "automation" had not reduced the office's reliance on human clerical workers. "The incongruity between the enormous growth in the automated office systems and the virtually non-existent rise in office production clearly points out that creating equipment alone cannot solve today's management problems," wrote a consultant for Booz, Allen, Hamilton. The machines had not chopped heads off payroll.[71] At the dawn of the next century, the United States Bureau of Labor Statistics confirmed this impression. Clerical workers had made up 5.2 percent of the total workforce in 1910 and reached 19.3 percent in 1980 before taking a small dip, ending the millennium at 17.4 percent. Although certain clerical occupations would shrink—in particular stenography, typing, and secretarial work—nonspecialized forms of clerical work as a percentage of the total workforce grew in the twenty-first century. Data entry in the office was still performed, for the most part, by hand.[72]

In many ways, the postwar mechanization of the office followed the same model of industrial mechanization that dated back to the nineteenth century. Managers used machines to degrade an expanding occupation by means of the detailed division of labor. The automation discourse allowed managers and union leaders to describe this expansion of an occupation as evidence of its imminent abolition. The combination of sexism and technological utopianism hid the labor of workers. The digital computer made its way from postwar novelty to mass-market commodity by means of "automation," through the understanding that machines should work and people should think. But as long as workers were hidden behind the machine, they would be expected to work like machines. And as the automation discourse became a topic of national discussion, those laboring bodies became practically invisible. Not labor but leisure would be the public's concern.

3. The Liberation of the Leisure Class

Debating Freedom and Work in the 1950s and Early 1960s

On February 24, 1949, a rocket took off from the White Sands Missile Range in New Mexico and flew higher than any machine before it ever had. As it climbed to its apogee of 244 miles above the Earth's surface, a camera housed in the rocket's nose snapped a photograph of the planet falling away below. Taken from this previously unattainable height, the photo showed something new: the convex horizon of the Earth against the uniform darkness of outer space. The photograph accompanied an article by Robert Oppenheimer in *Scientific American* in which the father of the atomic bomb claimed that the year 1950 was witnessing a revolution in "the material conditions of man's life." According to Oppenheimer, humanity now boasted an unprecedented wealth of resources, powers heralding a new historical epoch. The present, he said, was a time of "new insight and new mastery."[1]

In the main, Americans spoke of the effort to escape the planet as a quest in search of freedom. Reflecting on the 1957 Soviet launch of *Sputnik*, the first human-built satellite to orbit the Earth, one American newspaper celebrated the launch as a "step toward escape from man's imprisonment." No less sober a figure than the Ford Motor Company's head of engineering and research, expanding on the theme of the flying car, announced before an audience of fellow engineers, "We nourish the hope that all men may break free from their earth-bound existence." When the navy launched a rocket on the Fourth of July, 1957, the *Washington Post* reported that it flew in search of "new freedoms and powers for mankind." After Alan Shepard became the first American in space, riding to low Earth orbit in 1961 in a capsule named *Freedom 7*, President Kennedy asked Congress for billions in fiscal appropriations to send a man to the moon, "with the full speed of freedom, in the exciting adventure"

FIGURE 6. A snapshot of Earth taken from the nose of a rocket launched from the White Sands Missile Range, February 24, 1949. Courtesy of the White Sands Missile Range Museum.

of space. "This is not merely a race," Kennedy told the nation. "Space is open to us now; and our eagerness to share its meaning is not governed by the efforts of others."[2]

Outer space beckoned as a new and final frontier, a place for free people. Some found this puzzling. "Nobody in the history of mankind has ever conceived of the earth as a prison for men's bodies or shown such eagerness to go literally from here to the moon," wrote the philosopher Hannah Arendt. To her, the launch of *Sputnik* was more momentous than the splitting of the atom. Humanity today, she wrote, seemed "possessed by a rebellion against human existence as it has been given," a gift it hoped to exchange for something the species had made for itself. It was this same impetus to escape necessity, she argued, that led postwar Americans to celebrate "automation," a phenomenon that, like most at the time, she considered the "last stage" of industrialization and "the culminating point of modern development." The desire to leave the influences of the Earth, "the very quintessence of the human condition," wrote Arendt, was founded on the same conviction that made "automation" attractive to postwar Americans: the belief that the United States had become a technological society capable of overcoming the limits of the natural world. The source of life, the Earth, also represented life's limitations—the labor of living and the seemingly immutable necessities of maintaining a human body.[3]

For those who would subscribe to the automaton discourse in the postwar period, "leisure" and political freedom became synonyms. They believed that industrial progress would inevitably produce both. Referring to repetitive factory tasks, a review of Diebold's *Automation* announced that "automation" held the promise of "freeing the worker" from "this kind of slavery." The review called this freedom from work "leisure."[4] The postwar understanding of leisure implicitly rested on a denigration of the value of work and folded neatly into the discursive divorce of politics from the workplace. In *White Collar*, C. Wright Mills saw the ideological opposition of work and freedom as a recent development. When considering postwar wage workers, specifically the lower rungs of the white-collar professions, Mills wrote, "Whatever satisfaction they gain from life occurs outside the boundaries of work; work and life are sharply split."[5] Ironically, the celebration of the coming leisure society took shape at precisely the moment when the shorter-hours movement in the United States stalled.[6] Historically, the movement had not been a work-abolition movement but, rather, one aspect of a larger demand for workers' control of industry. Its goal had not been to degrade the value of work. In fact, it was just the opposite. Workers wanted less work time to fetch higher wages; they wanted a say about their working conditions. An aspect of that control meant winning time away from work, but that did not mean the end of work. Workers wanted to increase their control over their jobs, not surrender them altogether.[7]

American thinkers sympathetic to the plight of exploited workers had traditionally understood work and freedom as compatible. In *Looking Backward*, Edward Bellamy had imagined an egalitarian society where all had a place in an industrial army, worked until middle age, and then retired at forty-five.[8] Thorstein Veblen, in his 1899 book *The Theory of the Leisure Class*, argued that far from a social ideal, leisure was the product of a "predatory culture," a weapon of class oppression with which the powerful displayed their superiority in order to cow their inferiors. An exploitative upper class did not need to work because it had gained its free time at the expense of those forced into the lower orders. For Veblen, as for many in the American shorter-hours movement, a truly equal society would guarantee its individuals time to do what they would like by sharing the burden of work more fairly. Nothing about work itself contradicted the full development of an authentic individual. "Labour," wrote Veblen, "acquires a character of irksomeness by virtue of the indignity imputed to it."[9]

But as postwar Americans from across the political spectrum increasingly depicted the reduction of the working day as the apolitical product of technological progress, a new take on leisure became commonplace. In 1952 the U.S. Department of Commerce found it newsworthy that two years earlier Americans had spent more than eleven billion dollars on "recreation." This was possible, it reported, only because of the broad institution of high wages and the shortening of the workday, all of which the department depicted as the result of technological advance, or as one newspaper put it, "the five day week itself is largely due to the ability of American industry to meet all the country's requirements with its employees working shorter hours."[10]

These claims would persist throughout the postwar period and come from all corners. A body known as the Outdoor Recreation Resources Review Commission reported to the president and Congress that by the year 2000 Americans should expect to enjoy a thirty-hour work week, four weeks of paid vacation each year, and an increase of over four hundred hours more "free time" than workers possessed in 1962. This increase in nonwork time would occur more or less organically, the commission believed, a natural byproduct of "automation" combined with the basic control of collective bargaining insuring that union members received a share of industrially produced free time. "The real question," said the director of the AFL-CIO's Community Services Activities section, was not whether Americans would work shorter hours but "What are we going to do with our free time?"[11] Americans should expect a four-day workweek in the foreseeable future, Vice President Richard Nixon said on the campaign trail in 1956. "These are not dreams or idle boasts," he said. "They are simple projections of the gains we have made in the last four years." He spoke of the "unbelievably prosperous" future that America could anticipate, a new way of life to come because "back-breaking toil and mind-wearing tension will be left to machines and electronic devices." There was no longer any use, he said, for talk of "the bitterness of class struggle."[12]

The combination of technological optimism and organized labor's move away from the demand for workers' control lent credibility to the claim that a technical solution to the problem of labor exploitation was not only conceivable but necessary. At the same time, the possibility that industry would once again fail to provide gainful employment to millions of Americans, as it had during the Great Depression, inflamed a general anxiety that industrial development was incompatible with a Keynesian dedication to full employment. One headline succinctly expressed this concern: "Automation: Man vs. Machine, Golden Age of Leisure or Nightmare of Lost Jobs?"[13]

A moment of economic uncertainty catalyzed this combination of anxiety and hope into the automation discourse. Since the late 1940s, the word "automation" had led a subterranean life, appearing mostly in trade journals if it appeared in print at all. That changed in the winter of 1953–1954. Occurring at the same time as the post–Korean War recession and a spike in unemployment from 2.9% to 5.5%, the word began to appear regularly in the mass-circulation press.[14] Over the course of the intervening year and a half between the publication of Diebold's *Automation* and the recession, his name was all but scrubbed from the coining of the word. By the mid-1950s reputable newspapers referred to "automation" as a wholly impersonal, technical phenomenon, often making no mention of either Diebold's book or the Ford Automation Department. "Automation Is Upon Us" was the headline of a 1953 article in the *Los Angeles Times*: "Automation is a new word." It "is not exactly synonymous with Paradise," the article claimed, "but it does connote Progress, which in American idiom is a comparable state. . . . [M]achines do not eliminate jobs but create more, and so will automation." The paper reported that "automation" would eliminate blue-collar jobs and replace them with white-collar positions: those of engineers, personnel managers, lawyers, and financiers. "Automation Stirs Revolution" read the headline of a similar article in the *New York Times* in early 1954.[15]

The flowering of the automation discourse in the midst of a recession pushed Congress to act. In early 1955 the Senate held hearings on automation and technological change, "automation" having almost overnight become practically a synonym for technological development. The interest that had prompted the hearings, according to the chairman of the hearings, Illinois senator Paul H. Douglas, "has since grown by the week and month as the newspapers, Sunday supplements, and magazines report ever new and startling developments in automation. The frequency with which not only the trade magazines but the mass-circulation popular magazines have devoted articles to this subject is a striking indication of the public concern as to its economic and social implications."[16] Although the word had become divorced from both the automobile industry and *Automation*, Diebold nevertheless parlayed his book into a business, John Diebold and Associates, Inc. He could not claim ownership of "automation," which now appeared to be an objective description of a revolutionary era in industrial civilization, but he could claim expertise. Having started his own consulting company advising factories and offices as to how they might install new machinery to decrease the number of workers in their concerns, it was natural that Congress called him as its first witness.

The definition of "automation" was a consistent concern of the hearings. Both senators and witnesses assumed that the word represented an objective and material phenomenon. "I think it is a curious paradox that the more we talk about automation, the less confidently we can assume a common understanding of the term," Diebold told the senators. "The word has come to mean so many things, to so many people, that (for the moment at least) it seems in danger of losing a great deal of usefulness." He continued by asserting that "automation" was not a specific technology. "It is a basic change in production philosophy." A person could distinguish "automation" from, say, mechanization, because "automation" reintegrated the detailed division of labor by which managers had over the previous century and a half broken up old crafts into numerous small, mechanized jobs. The basis of the new era of industrial production, he said, was not specific machinery. For Diebold, "automation" came to signify the conviction that human labor should and inevitably would be removed from industrial production. Of course, that conviction had been the true substance of "automation" since the word's coining—a desire, joined with a belief in the insufficiency of the human body.[17]

The senators called a bevy of manufacturers, union leaders, academics, and prominent scientists to testify. Walter Reuther spoke, as did Vannevar Bush, who had led the U.S. government's scientific research projects during World War II. The narrative of unstoppable technological change was an attractive one. Speaking on behalf of the leadership of the UAW, Reuther proclaimed: "We believe that we are really standing on the threshold of a completely revolutionary change in the scientific and technological developments that we have experienced."[18] Organized labor needed at all costs to depict itself as standing on the right side of progress. In conceding the meaning of technological "progress" to big business, Reuther was not alone. He and other labor leaders hoped to leverage acquiescence to the managerial control of the labor process to produce some kind of welfare state and ensure a more or less equitable distribution of wealth, whether it was won in Congress or at the bargaining table. In preparation for bargaining with mechanizing telephone companies, the Communications Workers of America's president, Joseph Beirne, captured the spirit of that strategy:

> A century and a half ago, men, women and children threw wooden shoes into the new looms that were newly-powered by steam. The working people of that day tried to stop the new mechanical machines. They did so because industry and government were callous and unconcerned with the needs of the people. We do not expect to repeat history, nor do we want to. We welcome the new machines, rather than try to stop or destroy them. But we believe that the divine guidance given to our scientists and engineers should be sought by our social engineers so that we do not find ourselves with greatly increased productivity but without equivalent purchasing power for the American people.[19]

With that crucial concession made, both Beirne and Reuther found it easy to share the increasingly popular notion that freedom meant freedom from physical labor. Evidently it was the needs of the human body, not politics or moral failing, that were to blame for the unequal distribution of resources that had dogged the human species since the earliest days of recorded history: "As we in the labor movement visualize this problem," said Reuther, "we believe that we are achieving the technology, the tools of production, that will enable us as free people to master our physical environment . . . Automation is the second phase of the industrial revolution." Karl Marx, Reuther added, "was wrong because historically he analyzed the world in terms of a struggle between people and nations and groups to divide up economic scarcity . . . he did not and perhaps could not have visualized the unlimited possibilities of cooperating in the creation and sharing of abundance."[20] "Automation," what Reuther understood as the imminent abolition of the industrial working class, allowed society for the first time in history to escape class conflict, so long as the benefits of this new stage of civilization were justly distributed.

> For centuries and centuries and centuries people have been struggling to find a way to satisfy their basic economic and material needs, to get enough food in their empty bellies, to get enough warm clothing on their naked backs, and to provide decent shelter. For centuries they have struggled with the economics of scarcity. . . . And so here we are, standing on the threshold of a development of science and technology that will enable us to solve the problems that have plagued the human family for these many thousands of years. . . . We welcome any development that will lighten the burden of human labor.[21]

Despite his encomiums, Reuther did not intend his endorsement of "automation" to serve as an act of surrender. "What we do insist upon, however," he told the Senate panel, "is that we find a way to gear this developing technology, this greater economic abundance, to the needs of all the people."[22]

With witnesses like Reuther, it was no wonder that the subcommittee embraced Diebold's definition of "automation" as a revolutionary development in the means of industrial production. After the hearings finished, the panel members would conclude in their findings that "the economic significance of the automation movement is not to be judged or limited by the precision of its definition." Despite the desire to "narrow the term," the subcommittee argued, it was important to avoid technical specificity. "We are clearly on the threshold of an industrial age," it wrote, "the significance of which we cannot predict and with potentialities which we cannot fully appreciate."[23] Awed by technological innovation and predictions of an unpredictable future, the subcommittee decided that "automation" was also *the* word for a new era of technological progress, one without human labor. Others agreed, and, ironically, it was precisely the word's technical vagueness that became its chief advantage. "At first it was just a word," reported *Business Week* that same month, "a handy tag for a single engineering concept. But there was excitement in the air—a sense that something new and revolutionary was being born in the laboratories and the factories. The word became a focus for the excitement. Now it's agitating businessmen, unions, politicians. And it means something different to each."[24]

Despite the sweeping nature of the changes to come, the subcommittee found that "no specific broad-gauge economic legislation appears to be called for." It recommended that the government hold to the spirit of the 1946 Employment Act, which called for the maintenance of full employment but gave the government no decisive powers to do so. Instead, the subcommittee suggested improving the collection of employment statistics, educating young people for a future that it admitted could not be foretold, asking employers to ease voluntarily the burden of unemployment on workers, especially older workers, and insisting that unions "continue to recognize that an improved level of living for all cannot be achieved by a blind defense of the status quo."[25] In sum, the subcommittee recommended: Wait, watch, and do nothing while the owners of capital did what they would to the means of production.

Leisure and Freedom

The prospect of an age of unprecedented wealth and power posed unique difficulties to those who had never fully made their peace with democracy. If a people idled by unemployment had threatened to unravel both economy and body politic during the Great Depression, twenty years later the mass distribution of leisure likewise presented itself as a grave social problem. "The salient fact about leisure is that it is growing much faster than is our capacity to use it wisely," said James C. Charlesworth, the president of the American Academy of Political Science. He explained what he meant: "Leisure time without education on how to use it will create disturbances for a great many people." Listeners were meant to understand that the trouble with leisure lay not with freedom. Rather, Americans themselves were the problem. "What you have to distinguish between is the difference in leisure time for the professional and unprofessional person," Charlesworth informed his audience. Educated people would want to use their leisure well and expand their interest in "art, literature and music." That was good. Unfortunately, most people, at least in Charlesworth's estimation, were not well educated.[26] These fears were not limited to academicians alone. The director of the clinic of the Neuro-Psychiatric Institute of UCLA worried, "We will have a lot who will simply be lost—those who will pass a lot of time sitting and watching TV indiscriminately."[27] At a 1963 AFL-CIO conference on the coming leisure society, participants expressed apprehension at George Gallup's findings that more workers watched television than read books in their free time. As one might have expected, a few union members at the conference resented the assumption that workers needed to be saved from their own lack of sophistication. "You can't cram this stuff down people's throats," said one. A union official reported that he would be voted out of office if he "went home and told [his] union how to use their free time."[28] Nevertheless, the vast majority of Americans were, it seemed, not gentlemen, and this was a problem. At least, it was a problem for the coming "automated" society.

Walter Reuther's depiction of biological necessity as an obstacle to human liberation was typical of the automation discourse's conception of freedom. "Leisure" was the word most commonly used to describe that liberated state. Leisure as the ideal of human liberation had an ancient pedigree. It was, historically, the aristocratic definition of freedom, one that vouchsafed autonomy for only a minority of people. Without question, leisure's most celebrated theorist was Aristotle, and the rising popularity of Aristotelian thinking among postwar American intellectuals showed just how persuasive the automation discourse had become. Aristotle's definition of freedom presumed that social domination was the inevitable consequence of the human biological condition, not the result of decisions made by human beings. There were natural rulers and natural slaves, he argued. No amount of political negotiation could change that fact. Not crime but the human condition had produced the great slave societies of old. This was because work was an activity befitting only slaves, or so Aristotle and his postwar adherents thought. Therefore, a just society did not share work equitably, for to do so would only mean sharing the condition of enslavement. If Aristotle was right and nature, not politics, made work unfit for people, it therefore followed that for all to be liberated, society would first need to conquer nature. With "automation," however, it seemed that finally and for the first time in human history society possessed the power to do just that.

Few at the time recognized the unintended implications of the aristocratic understanding of freedom. The aristocratic ideal confused cause and effect, laying the blame for social oppression not on the actions of oppressors but, rather, on the constitution of the natural world. In accepting an essentially degraded understanding of work, those who subscribed to the automation discourse's definition of freedom as leisure consigned those still at work to equally degraded conditions. Under those terms, even Americans dedicated to democracy and equality found themselves defending the theoretical necessity for human slavery. Rather than consider how current powers might be distributed so that social necessity could be met in the present without crushing the human spirit, adherents of the automation discourse apologized for those soul-crushing conditions while they planned for a future glut of power that would make questions of necessity irrelevant. Some of the most vibrant of progressive thinkers lifted their gaze from the shop floor to the technicolor horizon. The results in the present would be disastrous for those still at work. It remains to the historian to explain this theoretical abandonment of the workplace.

The aristocratic ideal could only persuade liberal and left-wing Americans because they believed that a new era in the history of humanity had dawned. To that end, defining humanity in light of technologically produced abundance became a cottage industry in the postwar period.[29] With the natural world understood as subdued, postwar intellectuals were left with the task of defining the new entity that had escaped its bodily limitations. "Leisure," John Diebold told *Playboy* magazine's roundtable on the issue of the uses and abuses of the new leisure, "is going to test man's conception of himself." The conquest of nature would force people to ask themselves "what our nature is." Society had until then placed a premium on work, Diebold asserted. But now that "work is becoming the fringe and leisure moving to the center," he said "only his leisure pursuits, will distinguish him from the machine."[30]

One attempt at defining true humanity came in the form of the historian David Potter's 1954 *People of Plenty*, a book that sought to investigate the effects of "economic abundance" on the "American character." In the process, Potter trespassed on hallowed historiographical ground—Frederick Jackson Turner's frontier thesis—and there floated a revision. He suggested that it was not the ever-retreating frontier that historically had decided the American character but, rather, abundance. "Many of the traits which were attributed to the frontier influence, it is argued, could equally well be accounted for by the impact of abundance, and thus abundance, rather than the frontier," Potter wrote, "is proposed as the historical precipitant which produces what have been regarded as frontier aspects of American culture." The foundation of American character did not reside in the rugged individualism and the yearning for independence that, Turner claimed, had conquered a continent. Instead, the crucial "American" attribute was access to wealth, life beyond the minimum—a thick cushion of material surplus. Potter reversed Turner's equation: Independence and democracy were not the preconditions of wealth; wealth created the conditions of independence and democracy.[31]

With leisure as their ideal, mid-century Americans became accidental Aristotelians. In the *Nicomachean Ethics*, Aristotle had defined the good life as the pursuit of worthy ends. The function of a human being was the use of reason, and therefore anyone who did not possess this quality was incapable of being a complete person. Bodily demands were common to human and beast alike, and therefore to answer the needs of the body constituted a subhuman task. A full human being required freedom from necessity, above all freedom from the demands of the body, in order to enjoy full human status as a reasoning and politically free person. This did not consign all of humanity to servitude, however. In his *Politics*, Aristotle argued that humanity was already biologically divided into superior and inferior versions of itself, between those meant to work—to ensure the biological perpetuity of the species—and those destined for freedom. Freedom and work therefore required no reconciliation. Women and "natural slaves" were not intellectually capable of ruling themselves. It would have been a contradiction in terms for women and natural slaves to have any power over their lives, for freedom was self-rule, and for Aristotle the absence of reason was the absence of self-control.[32]

Not since the antebellum defense of southern slavery had Aristotle's philosophy enjoyed such a vogue in America.[33] The 1952 translation from German into English of Josef Pieper's 1947 *Leisure: The Basis of Culture* attested to the new interest in Aristotle in a society that increasingly viewed work and freedom as mutually exclusive. A neo-Thomist, Pieper argued that "work" meant any activity that was a means to an end. Because true human life consisted in the life of the soul, he argued, leisure was the only truly human activity. Pieper's Aristotelian definition of "human being" was one that a generation dedicated to reaching the Moon could easily understand: "to be human is: to know things beyond the 'roof' of the stars, to go beyond the trusted enclosures of the normal, customary day-to-day reality of the whole of existing things, to go beyond the 'environment' to the 'world' in which that environment is enclosed." But like the rocket ships that would send human beings beyond the limits of the Earth, Pieper's philosophy did not have room for everyone. The purpose of leisure was to keep "the functionary *human*," he wrote, "so that he can stay a *gentleman*," and whether because of circumstance or temperament, not everyone could hope to be a gentleman.[34]

Several postwar American intellectuals, like David Riesman in *The Lonely Crowd*, wanted "to increase the automatization of work," not "for the sake of work" but for "pleasure and consumption." Riesman called this species of freedom "play."[35] Others worried that Americans were not ready to become aristocrats, that their machine-made leisure would be synonymous with idleness. Pieper was Daniel Bell's source in his discussion of the classical definition of leisure in his 1956 book *Work and Its Discontents*. Bell believed that "automation" would soon abolish industrial wage labor. (By 1965 he would change his mind, calling "automation" a "bogey.") And what the masses did in their free time, Bell argued, was not true leisure, not activity worthy of a human being. "Play, it should be pointed out," Bell wrote, "is not leisure—at least not in the classical image as it has come down from Plato to T. S. Eliot." Ideally, Bell insisted, leisure was "a full-time cultivation of the gentle arts." It was a specific kind of activity: the calling of "a gentleman."[36]

Even on the Left there was ambiguity about the place of work in a socialist utopia. Did freedom mean workers' control or a society where individuals were free from necessity? Marx's writings made arguments in both directions, with the early Marx seeming to argue that people would work in a communist society and the late Marx making claims to the contrary.[37] The technological optimism and abundance of the postwar period, including the big promises of the automation discourse, brought out in bright colors the Aristotelian tendencies in Marxism. Nowhere was this clearer than in the work of Herbert Marcuse, a Marxist-Humanist and a center of intellectual gravity for the New Left. In his 1955 classic *Eros and Civilization*, Marcuse offered a reinterpretation of Marx through the lens of Sigmund Freud that might account for a country seemingly sated with material goods, bereft of an active political Left, and miserably repressed. Work, Marcuse wrote, had been imposed on humanity not only by cruel taskmasters but also by "brute necessity." A person, he elaborated, could not consider him- or herself liberated under conditions of "scarcity." Industrial civilization had eliminated scarcity, although capitalist oppression continued to impose artificial scarcity on workers. "Freud's consistent denial of the possibility of an essential liberation of the former [the pleasure principle] implies the assumption that scarcity is as permanent as domination," Marcuse wrote, "an assumption that seems to beg the question." Melding Marx and Freud, Marcuse insisted that "the historical possibility of a gradual decontrolling of the instinctual development must be taken seriously, perhaps even the historical *necessity*—if civilization is to progress to a higher stage of freedom."[38]

Three years later Marcuse elaborated on this point, and in the name of freeing the proletariat reproduced practically all of the leisure ideal's assertions. Just as important, Marcuse claimed that these insights did *not* belong to Marx: "As long as man's struggle with nature requires human toil for procuring the necessities of life, all that can be attained in this sphere is a truly rational societal organization of labor. . . . For Marx, it is to be solved by a revolution which brings the productive process under the collective control of the 'immediate producers.' But this is not freedom. Freedom is living without toil, without anxiety: the play of human faculties." To achieve this required "the highest possible degree of mechanization." And just as Pieper and Bell insisted, for Marcuse the "play of human faculties" was something more than self-directed free time, what Riesman had called "play." Freedom required instead "the development of those human faculties which make for the free (in Marx's words—the 'all-round') individual, especially the development of 'consciousness.'"[39]

In a letter to Raya Dunayevskaya, Trotsky's secretary during his Mexican exile and fellow Marxist-Humanist, Marcuse claimed that "genuine automation" would "explode" capitalism. Referring to one of the workers who told Dunayevskaya that this "genuine automation" sounded more like a life of pointlessness than liberation, Marcuse said, "You should really tell her about all that humanization of labor, its connection with life, etc.—that this is possible only through complete automation, because such humanization is correctly relegated by Marx to the realm of freedom beyond the realm of necessity, i.e., beyond the entire realm of socially necessary labor in the material production." Therefore, in order to set workers free, "total de-humanization of the latter is the prerequisite." Only when human beings were freed from the production of bare life, he continued, could they consider themselves free. Marcuse's definition of freedom promoted what he claimed were Marx's "deep-rooted anarchistic and libertarian elements," freedom as the kind of unbounded time in which a person was absolved of meeting any social obligation whatsoever.[40]

The automation discourse revealed the dangers of blaming political oppression on the biology of the human organism. Although few remarked on it at the time, in retrospect one discovers in the automation discourse a remarkable defense of the institution of slavery, a defense that was in fact the logical conclusion of the reduction of freedom to leisure. Since antiquity, political theorists hostile to democracy had worried that the leveling tendencies of democratic societies prevented them from achieving true greatness as civilizations. The automation discourse allowed those who considered themselves allies of democratic governance to nurse the same suspicions. "Up to the present day," wrote Sebastian de Grazia, a liberal professor of political science and the author of the popular 1962 book *Of Time, Work, and Leisure*, "though we have given birth to many genial tinkerers, we have produced no great theoretical scientist. The foreigners have taken the seven-league steps." The heroes of the revolutionary generation, such as Thomas Jefferson, had been the last gentlemen to enjoy leisure of the ancient Greek variety. And so, with its rejection of aristocracy, the United States had lost its ability to produce geniuses. "The brilliant theoretical capacity of the Founders disappeared along with the leisure they had."[41] Senator Joseph Clark, a Democrat who wanted to expand Social

Security and repeal the Taft-Hartley Act, agreed in 1963 that "most of the other great civilizations were founded on slave labor."[42] "Our economic system has come of age," said the president of the American Academy of Political Science. "If we are not fatuously to conclude that we should work for machines instead of making machines work for us, we must consider all of the little and big iron men as our slaves and ourselves to be entitled to a demigodlike personal development."[43] Robert Theobald, a left-wing economist and popular critic of postwar capitalism, wrote: "It is not hyperbole to suggest that we could be the modern Greeks, with mechanical slaves to take the place of human toil."[44] The progressive critic W. H. "Ping" Ferry uttered what at the time appeared to many a mere statement of fact when he told an audience that "technology is carrying us rapidly into a twentieth-century version of the half-free, half-slave society of fourth century Athens" and that technical advance seemed to have accomplished the impossible by making slavery theoretically compatible with true democracy. "Today's slaves, the machines," Ferry wrote, "are creating a new class that democratic theory never wound into its calculus."[45]

The implications of this conviction did not seem to trouble many Americans, though it conceded a crucial point that militant labor organizers of the 1930s never would have allowed: that work was oppressive not because of its political organization, but by its very nature. "Slavery has very little to do with a political system," wrote Alice Mary Hilton, a prominent promoter of "automation," coiner of the word "cyberculture," and a member of the Ad Hoc Committee on the Triple Revolution, a left-liberal coalition that called for the divorce of income from job-holding. "Slavery is economically conditioned. The world never before had the opportunity for the kind of equality as I understand it, or for all human beings to live truly human lives. The mere end of brutal demands, of biological survival, has made it necessary for some disagreeable, dangerous and undignified work not worthy of human beings to be done." This was, amazingly, not the argument of an archconservative but, rather, a thinker on the Left. "For the first time," Hilton continued, "now, we are on the threshold of a world where real abundance is possible and real leisure feasible. All the work that is necessary for biological survival can be done by machines under the direction of electronic computing machines."[46]

The Marxist Humanist and Black liberation theorist James Boggs, a descendent of slaves, might have seemed unlikely to agree with Hilton. But when arguing in the mode of the automation discourse even he could subscribe to a tacit defense of the necessity of slavery: "All societies at one time or another have had slaves," he wrote in 1964. "What I *am* concerned about is that we, today, at *this* stage of industrial development, are still so concerned with imposing and maintaining the slavery of jobs *when this is no longer necessary* and is indeed cruel and absurd."[47] In this analysis, Greek and antebellum slavery ceased to be a crime committed by notoriously unjust societies and became, instead, an inevitable product of human biology. Until then, only the most inveterate social conservatives had dared to argue that the institution of slavery was summoned into existence by the natural order.

Defenders of Work

Not all intellectuals in the early postwar period subscribed to the automation discourse's definitions of work and freedom. A small but diverse group of critics in the 1950s argued that freedom and work could and ought to be reconciled. Often enough these thinkers, like many of their contemporaries, believed that "automation" in fact described a technical revolution that was in the process of making the laboring body obsolete. They did not agree, however, that this development meant universal liberation. But calling the values of the automation discourse into question in the 1950s and early 1960s meant arguing against the temper of the times. Critics who expressed doubt in the technological faith of the postwar period risked the danger of appearing hopelessly out of touch. Those who did so often harbored radical doubts about the character of modernity itself; they worried that infusing their current society with immense power would only further empower its shortcomings.

It therefore made sense that traditionalist conservatives counted among the earliest critics of the automation discourse. Unlike the pro-business managerial wing of the American Right that coined the word "automation," these conservatives had no love for industrial progress. "Industrialism was a harder knock to conservatism than the books of the French egalitarians," explained Russell Kirk in *The Conservative Mind*. The most astute of these conservative thinkers shared the criticisms of industrial capitalism that came from the Left, chief among them that the Industrial Revolution had dispossessed people of the older social structures on which they had relied. Generally, however, these thinkers mentioned the significance of the material changes wrought by industrialization only in passing. They focused instead on culture, arguing that failures of character and faith—rather than economic exploitation and changes in the means of production—had brought about a society that held nothing sacred. *Ideas Have Consequences* was the title Richard Weaver gave his popular 1948 defense of traditionalist conservatism, for like others of that stripe he believed that the ills of society stemmed from the supposedly wrongheaded ideas that individuals held. Social conservatives such as Weaver lamented that both society and the state had been demystified, shorn of the sacred trappings that legitimated inequality; they held out as superior a polity in which hierarchy was justified by vague if not supernatural forces: morality, religion, tradition, honor, God. That these hierarchies were steeply unequal and static did not trouble this strain of postwar conservatism. Or as Kirk put it: "We must purge ourselves of the notion that pure equality is consonant with liberty and humility."[48]

Traditionalist conservatives felt no need to reconcile work—in particular, bodily labor—and freedom, not when a defense of hierarchy lay at the center of their politics. As a result, they also had little need for the automation discourse. There were natural aristocrats and there were natural servants, they argued, and it remained the duty of natural servants to support the greatness of their betters. "They who work with their minds should rank above those who work with their hands; but men engaged in a genuinely ethical working are higher still," wrote Kirk. "Any real civilization must relieve certain individuals of the necessity for working with their hands so that they may participate in that leisure which is an indispensable preparation for leadership." Kirk himself called this "the Aristotelian view of human nature, which defines the truly natural state as the cultivation of what is highest in man," and, as this view implied, the highest men. "We need to examine our definition of work— which depends upon our definition of nature. What we mean by 'liberty,' in turn, depends upon our meaning of work," wrote Kirk. Whereas subscribers to the automation discourse saw industrial progress as creating a nation of aristocrats, traditionalist conservatives viewed the same material changes as the proletarianization of the elite. Allen Tate of the Southern Agrarian movement praised Pieper's *Leisure* and its celebration of Aristotelian thought as "a comprehensive indictment of a decaying civilization," a work that to his eyes correctly described how "the modern reduction of all human action, including philosophy, to servile labor is daily creating a proletarian society from top to bottom, from executive to machine tender." Work had a special meaning; it applied to those who naturally should serve society with the effort of their bodies. Aristocrats had their own role, and perhaps one could call it work of the mind, but it certainly was not the activity of sustaining bare life or continuous physical exertion.[49]

Weaver in particular was quite frank in stating that his defense of work was necessary to maintain a hierarchical and unequal society. The reduction of the meaning of work to nothing more than pay, he said, "increasingly poses the problem of what source will procure sufficient discipline to hold men to production." If work meant only the meeting of bare necessity and nothing else, he asked, if it could not be reconciled with the good life, would not the individual "constantly seek to avoid it?" This, of course, was precisely what the automation discourse held out as progress. "Science encourages [man] to believe that he is exempt from labor," Weaver wrote. "And what possible lesson can man draw from this but that work is a curse, which he will avoid as far as possible until science arrives with the means for its total abolishment . . . and we are assured daily by advertisements that the goal is not too far off. How obvious here," he mourned, "is the extinction of the idea of mission."[50]

While traditionalist conservatives saw no need to reconcile work and freedom, those dedicated to the premise of human equality on the American Left had more reason to adopt the values of the automation discourse. Only a minority dissented. They did so because they embraced the belief that the fundamental organization of social life was the result not of an inevitable natural or technological order but of a contest over power. The sociologist C. Wright Mills stood out among this group. Placing politics at the center of his analysis, Mills tracked how the meaning of seemingly timeless social categories such as "work" responded to historical forces.

To that end, Mills sought to explain the new character of the postwar American middle class. The new professionals of the office, he showed, had much in common with industrial workers. Unlike the middle classes of old, who often owned their businesses and enjoyed a certain degree of independence, the new white-collar people worked for wages in large businesses; they owned little or no productive property; they had bosses and worked set hours. The concentration of productive property through industrialization into an enormous and complex apparatus had pushed farmers off the land and the petty bourgeois out of their small shops. Now practically everyone was a wage earner. These deep structural changes, argued Mills, had also thrown the meaning of work into question.[51]

Mills was one of the few thinkers of this time who argued that the meaning of work was conditional—that people could decide what it should mean. "Work," he wrote, "may be a mere source of livelihood, or the most significant part of one's inner life; it may be experienced as expiation, or as exuberant expression of self; as bounden duty, or as the development of man's universal nature. Neither love nor hatred of work is inherent in man, or inherent in any given line of work. *For work*," Mills argued, "*has no intrinsic meaning*." Culture, technics, and above all politics played a part in deciding how people defined what activity counted as work. So few had looked at work this way before that for the most part Mills found himself forging ahead alone: "No adequate history of the meanings of work has been written," he noted.[52]

The key term for Mills was "alienation." Without any meaningful control in the workplace, the social conditions surrounding the daily grind had lent a negative meaning to the activity of work itself, "a fatalistic feeling," he wrote, "that work *per se* is unpleasant." The disagreeableness of working under hierarchical conditions had made work seem like the cause of the worker's alienation, and Mills doubted that the American working class would be able to assert itself to demand that work and freedom be reconciled. Instead of blaming bosses for the oppressive conditions of wage work, workers blamed "work" itself. They did not appear poised to redefine it in a way that could be made consistent with traditional republican notions of freedom. Worse, Mills suspected that most people did not actually desire freedom. Managers, it seemed, desired that the mass of people in the United States should be "cheerful robots"—hard-working and obedient on the job—and Mills feared that one day managers might actually get what they wanted. As far as he could see, the so-called Protestant work ethic no longer drove most Americans to work, if it ever had. "For the white collar masses," said Mills, "work seems to serve neither God nor whatever they may experience as divine in themselves." Instead, workers were driven by another vision of the good life: not eternal rest in Heaven, and not the Jeffersonian political independence of working their own property. Rather, wrote Mills, "now work itself is judged in terms of leisure values. The sphere of leisure provides the standards by which work is judged; it lends to work such meanings as work has." The "gospel of work," said Mills, had been replaced by the "leisure ethic."[53]

Besides Mills, however, there were few writers whose experience in the industrial workplace led them to challenge the automation discourse. Harvey Swados, a writer and metal finisher at the Ford Motor Company's assembly plant in Mahwah, New Jersey, could call on almost no allies when he reported in the *Nation* that industrial workers most certainly still existed in the United States and that by no means had they all metamorphosed into happy middle-class professionals leading lives of leisure. To him, it appeared as though liberalism had decided simply to erase the presence of the worker from its picture of American society. "There is one thing that the worker doesn't do like the middle-class," Swados observed: "he works like a worker. The steel-mill puddler does not yet sort memos, the coal miner does not yet sit in conferences, the cotton millhand does not yet sip martinis from his lunchbox." In proclaiming the working class a thing of the past, he argued, critics all too often also ignored the quotidian struggles of working people—long hours, grueling conditions, and crushing debt. "As for its toll on the physical organism and the psyche," Swados wrote, "that is a question perhaps worthy of further investigation by those who currently pronounce themselves bored with Utopia Unlimited in the Fat Fifties."[54]

Others on the Left also shared Mills's refusal to accept the automation discourse's denigration of work. For Harry Braverman, editor of the socialist publication *Monthly Review*, "automation" meant the proper apportioning of work to people, not its total abolition or de-politicization. For years an industrial worker and no stranger to the shop floor, Braverman refused to abandon work as a site of political struggle, although until the early 1960s he too believed "automation" to be the technological phenomenon so many of its boosters claimed it was. In 1955 he said it was "unmatched in history," a "genuine innovation, not merely 'a little more of the same.' It is already on its way and will be broadened in scope at a rapid pace. It will have smashing consequences upon [the] economy." He predicted that all industry in the United States would soon be "fully automated," by which he meant "one man will do at least the work that five do now." By 1963, almost ten years later and the technological revolution still unconsummated, he extended his forecast.[55]

Unlike most adherents of the automation discourse, however, Braverman, with his dedication to the politics of the work process, would not equate freedom with leisure. "Leisure which does not alter the conditions of work," he argued, "does not succeed in reconstituting a new and integrated human being, but sharpens the present division between the meaningful and mean-ingless hours of the worker's life; the same hold[s] true of hours that are merely reduced without being altered in content." This was not a call to increase alien-ation from the work process but to reduce it. To that end, Braverman called for the "total work" society that Josef Pieper feared, the "total professionalization of the working population, coupled with the sharing of the production and housekeeping chores of society on an equitable basis." Braverman saw a way to reconcile his technological enthusiasm with his dedication to the political character of socially necessary activity. The application of the "vast techno-logical progress open to humanity," what Braverman called "automation," should be used to redistribute the burden of meeting chores and also reduce their onus. Many hands, in other words, made light work. If all shared the work equally, society would arrange the conditions of work so that it became consistent with human dignity. The source of the oppression at work was not work itself, he argued. It was inequality.[56]

Perhaps the most nuanced postwar defense of work as an activity consis-tent with freedom came from the philosopher Hannah Arendt. It made sense that a thinker whose politics were as unclassifiable as Arendt's would dissent from the general consensus surrounding the automation discourse. Like Mills, Arendt feared the possibility of a society of cheerful robots. Totalitarianism had, in her view, benefited from the de-politicization of communal life. Fascist governments outlawed dissent, negotiation, and collective reasoning. The evacuation of politics from work celebrated by the automation discourse, therefore, appeared to her as a threat, regardless of whatever benefits its pro-moters perceived on the horizon. Beginning from the same starting point as many of her contemporaries, Aristotle's *Politics*, Arendt drew a very different conclusion about the definition of freedom.

Like most of her contemporaries, Arendt believed that the postwar period was a truly unprecedented historical epoch—"the advent of a new and yet unknown age"—on account of the impressive concentration of powers converging in the United States. And, like her contemporaries, she proposed to reconsider the human condition in light of the recent revolution in technological prowess, a new world that, she said, "was born with the first atomic explosions." She published that reconsideration, fittingly, under the title *The Human Condition*. To an extent unmatched by any other creature, claimed Arendt, human beings now built artificial worlds for themselves. People created artifice, were "world-builders," but they could not escape the fact that life came from beyond, not arising out of their own fabricated world but rather from the Earth itself. With the new powers of production at its disposal, however, it seemed to her that humanity was on the verge of finally replacing first nature with second nature, the Earth with artifice, "cutting the last tie through which even man belongs among the children of nature." She did not doubt that people had the power to effect such an exchange; she wrote her book specifically to call into question their desire to do so. The word she used to describe the powers that made this new era of human escape possible was "automation."[57]

Arendt did not define the term, nor was she particularly interested in the technological specificities it might represent. Instead, she took it to signify a fast-approaching and self-evident material reality: the end of human intervention in the industrial labor process, a phenomenon that, she said, "in a few decades probably will empty the factories and liberate mankind from its oldest and most natural burden, the burden of laboring and the bondage of necessity." (Her primary and perhaps only source on "automation" was Diebold's 1952 book on the subject.) Considering that possibility as an imminent reality, Arendt performed a close reading of Aristotle in order to divide human life into her three now-legendary, categories: labor, work, and action. "Labor" was the activity that fulfilled the necessities of bare life, of biological being; "work" meant the activity of constructing the artifice of society beyond mere biological sustenance; and "action" signified deliberate political activity, the world of public speech and the most contingent and mutable of all human creations. The articulation of these categories allowed her to level her main argument: that with the rise of industrial capitalism work had collapsed into labor. In other words, people treated political activity as though it were prescribed by nature. They failed to see just how much of the world that they inhabited was subject to historical change and, therefore, renegotiation. Increasingly, she argued, people understood all socially useful activity as the fulfillment of "labor," of mere survival and nothing more. And simple survival appeared to be wholly unconditional. One is alive, or one is dead.[58]

Although she came to a far different conclusion than did others who took their cue from Aristotle, Arendt nevertheless shared many views with other postwar Aristotelians. "Freedom from labor," she wrote, was the traditional privilege of aristocrats. The threat to society from reduction of all human activity to labor, she continued, was that "there is no class left, no aristocracy of either a political or spiritual nature, from which restoration of the other capacities of man could start anew." In the middle of the twentieth century, she claimed, even kings and queens justified their activities as nothing more than "a job necessary for the life of society." She argued that the danger of this radical denigration in meaning was nothing less than the almost complete eviction of politics from social life. When a society viewed all its functions and all its activities as natural, immutable, and nonnegotiable, it ran the risk of perpetrating unspeakable horrors. With no politics, no contingency, no culture, it became that much more difficult to challenge the existing social order. This was the problem with "automation," she argued: It encouraged individuals to treat the political world as though it were the natural world. In this situation, people would cease to believe that they could consciously alter their own society in keeping with their values. That fatalism amounted to nothing less than a surrender of all civic and moral responsibility.[59]

As the world rocketed into the future, Arendt kept her eye on the recent past. A Jewish refugee from Nazi Germany, she remembered all too well how the Nazis had conceived of the Final Solution as a biological mandate, an apolitical necessity to purify both reich and race. She considered these high stakes not in *The Human Condition* but in *Eichmann in Jerusalem*. From the 1961 trial of Adolf Eichmann in Israel she concluded that another genocide, this time worse than the Holocaust, seemed all too likely. "The frightening coincidence of the modern population explosion with the discovery of technical devices that, through automation, will make large sections of the population 'superfluous' even in terms of labor, and that, through nuclear energy, make it possible to deal with this twofold threat by the use of instruments beside which Hitler's gassing installations look like an evil child's fumbling toys, should be enough to make us tremble." The possibility of "superfluous" people, people rendered useless to capital because of their mechanical substitution, sounded too similar to the plight of stateless people. Believing that "automation" was a fast-approaching technological certainty, Arendt hoped that civilization could reintroduce politics back into work so that humane values, rather than technocratic bureaucracy, would inform how the state treated the people under its control.[60]

The reduction of political life to the terms of mere survival was ubiquitous in the postwar period. In a public address in January 1958, a few months after the launch of *Sputnik*, Walter Reuther considered the possibility of nuclear war over the city of Detroit and told his audience: "We live in a world in which the common denominator that binds the human family together has been reduced to its simplest fundamental term, human survival."[61] In the proposed collective bargaining program for 1958, the executive board of the UAW pointed to the "launching of the Sputniks" as a threat to all life in America. They called for full employment—"our need today, in fact our hope for survival." Despite the hoped-for freedom of space flight, the actual realization of the power to break away from the Earth seemed only to reduce the range of human experience. The board cited *Sputnik* and the threat it posed as the reason why in 1958 they would not bargain for a shorter workweek. "We believe," they said, "that UAW members and their families will share our belief that in this hour of freedom's crisis the real need is to get the unemployed all back to work and to get those on short workweeks back on a full workweek, and that greater leisure, for the time being, can wait."[62]

With the eviction of the idea of politics from the workplace, the opposing vision of an incorporeal life beyond the clouds gained adherents. The desire to leave the Earth appealed to those who wanted to imagine humanity as a species that could live beyond its body, that could thrive anywhere in the cosmos. With that boundlessness also came a radical denigration of embodied life. This disembodied ideal, this misanthropic sublime, was the same ethic that informed the automation discourse. It gave daily reality the sheen of something one expected to read in the science fiction pulps—a genre Arendt called a "highly non-respectable literature" that unfortunately had not yet received the attention it deserved as "a vehicle of mass sentiments and mass desires."[63]

With increasing frequency, Americans thought of space as an Eden where humanity wielded immense, godlike powers. Arthur C. Clarke's popular 1953 novel *Childhood's End* was typical, telling a story of humanity growing beyond its crude, Earth-bound condition to achieve interstellar inorganic liberty. The novel concludes with the species evolving into a single disembodied hive mind, launching itself into the cosmos by devouring and ultimately destroying the planet Earth and all life on it—a positive development, or so the reader is led to believe.[64] At times science fiction bled into forms of speculation meant to be taken more literally. Certainly the space race lent gravity to what at another time might have been dismissed as idle fancy. In 1960 Manfred Clynes coined the word "cyborg," short for cybernetic organism, in an article he wrote with Nathan S. Kline in *Astronautics* titled "Cyborgs and Space." Rather than send human beings to space in a ship that reproduced an Earth-like environment, the authors proposed, it would make more sense to re-engineer the human body itself so that it could survive beyond the influences of the planet. The human mind would conquer the bodily limitations that held the species back from its destiny among the stars. The goal was to reinvent the natural world and the seeming automaticity of the biological functions of a human body in order to allow a man to "live in space *qua natura*." "This self-regulation," they wrote, "needs to function without the benefit of consciousness. . . . If man in space, in addition to flying his vehicle, must continuously be checking on things and making adjustments merely in order to keep himself alive, he becomes a slave to the machine." The purpose of re-engineering human biology was so that the "robot-like problems" of maintaining bodily survival "are taken care of automatically and unconsciously, leaving man free to explore, to create, to think, and to feel."[65]

In *Cyborg: Evolution of the Superman*, a popularization of Clynes's neologism, D. S. Halacy Jr. could have been speaking for the automation discourse when he wrote that "the cyborg concept helps man overcome the limitations of his earthly birth" to take him "a step nearer to understanding the relationship between inner and outer space (or mind and universe)" and "fly away from earth to become a new and, he hopes, better being."[66] Rarely did critics say why exactly outer space was the realm of freedom while the Earth and the human body posed unfortunate encumbrances. Halacy's division of inner from outer space, "mind" from "universe," and the chance for humanity to become itself among the stars found a less breathless expression in the 1963 Senate hearings on automation, when Secretary of Labor W. Willard Wirtz spoke of automation's making a "progression" through key industries, closing off potential frontiers. There was no field of activity left to absorb human energies. "That," said Wirtz, "is the reason automation is the problem now that it was not before." His interlocutor, Senator Joseph S. Clark, responded, most likely in jest: "Maybe there is outer space." Wirtz answered, "The point is I am sure not made lightly. The point remains that the concentration of the effect of automation on unskilled jobs is posing some very real problems for us. I don't think we exaggerate a bit," he continued, "in suggesting that it is the opening of the doors of space that probably presents part of the answer to those who get so gloomy about the future of unemployment."[67]

Some of the most thoughtful artists working within the world of postwar science fiction, however, produced early criticism of the automation discourse. Often in these stories outer space was the place people went to discover how ill prepared they were to use the powers they had inherited. Kurt Vonnegut's 1952 novel *Player Piano* comes to mind, as do Ray Bradbury's short stories from the late 1940s and early 1950s—"There Will Come Soft Rains," "The World the Children Made," and "The City." Perhaps the most significant work to criticize the presumptions of the automation discourse was the 1956 movie *Forbidden Planet*, a brilliant adaptation of Shakespeare's *The Tempest*. In it, explorers to a far-distant world encounter a device that transforms pure thought into material reality. They activate it, only to discover that it inadvertently also realizes the Id, the atavistic and violent tendencies of the human unconscious. In the end, in an inversion of Clarke's vision of apocalyptic transcendence, the machine blows itself up, along with the planet on which it resided—pure mind, the viewer sees, leads to total destruction. Returning home, the explorers conclude that humanity's biological boundaries exist for its own good. The horizon of the body limits an individual's power with all the wisdom of a hundred million years of evolution.[68]

In reducing the idea of work to mere labor, Arendt had argued, moderns had ceased to act as though they made the world they lived in. On one hand, people could not imagine opening the daily travails of maintaining life to political renegotiation. On the other, men and women denied that they were biological beings at all.[69] While machines took the place of nature, human biology loomed as a tyrant opposed to the realization of universal liberation. In response, Arendt defended the importance of necessity in her definition of freedom. She imagined freedom as a state that an embodied entity could enjoy. "Man cannot be free," she wrote, "if he does not know that he is subject to necessity, because his freedom is always won in his never wholly successful attempts to liberate himself from necessity." For a human being, the experience of the body *was* life. Aristotle's twentieth-century disciples wanted to imagine that the bodily pains supporting an aristocrat's life could be offloaded onto the bodies of others or their artificial substitutes, the machines. But life, Arendt argued, was inalienable: "The human condition is such that pain and effort are not just symptoms which can be removed without changing life itself; they are rather the modes in which life itself, together with the necessity to which it is bound, makes itself felt. For mortals, the 'easy life of the gods' would be a lifeless life." The necessity to eat, sleep, and reproduce was not a prison sentence. Given the right political conditions, feeding yourself could be the dignified activity of a free person. Perhaps that was why initially Arendt intended to name her book not *The Human Condition*, but *Amor Mundi* (For the Love of the World). Necessities, she argued, could be sources of profound meaning. But their meaning was political. In order to reclaim the dignity of necessity and make it consistent with freedom, mid-century Americans would have to recognize that these necessary activities were subject to political negotiation, something the automation discourse ruled out.[70]

Although *The Human Condition* became an instant classic, along with Mills's *White Collar*, few in elite intellectual circles paid any attention to its reconciliation of freedom and work. After all, even Arendt believed John Diebold when he claimed that machines were, at that moment, abolishing all industrial labor. That had become practically the definition of progress. Nevertheless, Arendt was right to ask why people thought fleeing the Earth and biological necessity meant freedom, especially when the first people to make their escape reported that the most beautiful sight from space was, in fact, the planet they left behind. Looking down at Earth through the periscope of his spacecraft, Alan Shepard spontaneously exclaimed, "What a beautiful view!" A few days after completing his historic mission, reporters asked Yuri Gagarin, the first human being in space, what the Earth looked like from high up. "Blue," he said, "like a blue globe, a wonderful picture." But when they asked, "And what is the sky like up there, in space?" Gagarin could only answer: "Dark, comrades, very dark."[71]

4. Anticipating Oblivion

The Automation Discourse,
Federal Policy, and Collective Bargaining

While a few concerned themselves with the differences between leisure and freedom, by the mid-1950s the word "automation" had all the appearances of an apolitical technical term; it meant the inevitable abolition of the industrial working class. But as the automation discourse became postwar commonplace, lawmakers, union leaders, and workers grew worried, for "automation" posed a direct theoretical challenge to the foundations of postwar liberalism. Economic good governance held that John Maynard Keynes and the school he inspired had discovered the solution to capitalism's volatility. If government could ensure full employment and a reasonable distribution of collective wealth, economists reasoned, never again would the country face anything like the Great Depression. "In my book," Joseph Beirne, president of the Communications Workers of America, told the 1955 CIO Conference on Automation, "increasing productivity and static or decreasing purchasing power spells depression."[1]

In the postwar period, this was the utterance of a platitude. Staving off depression required insuring the mass purchasing power of the people. Other than a state-provided guaranteed income to every adult citizen—a measure few in the leadership of the labor movement, big business, or the halls of government seriously considered—full employment was the answer. Now, however, the decidedly un-Keynesian desire to reduce employment had acquired a special name. "Automation" implied that the very practices that might unravel the postwar consensus were, in fact, the definition of technological progress. Lawmakers and concerned citizens faced a paradox. On one hand, full employment was the main safeguard against another depression; on the other, full employment was, evidently, an impediment to industrial development.[2]

During the 1955 congressional hearings on automation and technological change, the Senate subcommittee considered the possibility that the word "automation" described nothing other than mechanization, a known quantity dating back to the dawn of industrialization. "So long as one understands that machines and processes can be automatic, more automatic, and still more automatic one can accept automation as an old concept and merely an extension of familiar forms of mechanization," wrote the subcommittee in its findings. But because "automation" indicated not simply more mechanization but, rather, a new and historically unprecedented era, the word justified increasing unemployment as evidence of, ironically, economic health. "It is clearly wrong to dismiss automation, however, as nothing more than an extension of mechanization," the subcommittee found. "We are clearly on the threshold of an industrial age, the significance of which we cannot predict and with potentialities which we cannot fully appreciate."[3]

Another element of the automation discourse allowed critics to embrace the prospect of the elimination of industrial jobs without compromising their theoretical dedication to full employment. "Automation," many believed, would replace industrial wage work—often understood as semiskilled manual labor—with the skilled professional work of the mind. It seemed a reasonable deduction: With the supposed increase in the intricacy of America's industrial apparatus, more brainy white-collar workers would be needed to manage that complexity. John Kenneth Galbraith, economist, presidential advisor, and liberal-left public intellectual, articulated this element of the automation discourse in his 1958 classic *The Affluent Society*. Galbraith spoke of the rise of a "New Class" of Americans that would soon replace the industrial working class as a result of "automation." This New Class would hold jobs that were more interesting, better remunerated, and characterized by their "exemption from manual toil," or what Galbraith called "work." Freedom would mean the escape not from job-holding itself but from bodily industrial labor. In order to perform these higher functions, he argued, the New Class needed to meet loftier "intellectual, literary, cultural, and artistic demands." Its members would need the kind of education befitting a middle-class professional. Galbraith equated human liberation with the development of this New Class, affirming that, other than avoiding nuclear war with the Soviet Union, it should be "*the* major social goal of the society." A strong welfare state, he concluded, was therefore necessary to ensure that the ranks of the soon-to-appear unemployed would receive the education they needed to fit into this new thinking society.[4]

Galbraith's understanding of "automation" as the replacement of physical toil with intellection was so broadly shared that it was practically a truism.[5] "Most of the current planning to ease the impact of automation is based on the belief that new jobs will develop to replace the old," reported the *Congressional Quarterly* of federal government planning. "Justification for these efforts is that, as technology advances, the need for unskilled workers will decline but the need for highly educated and skilled workers will increase."[6] "As technology replaces human labor and the skilled needs of society are elevated, a whole new set of political, social, and educational challenges are posed," said Senator Joseph S. Clark, chairman of the Congressional Subcommittee on Employment and Manpower. Secretary of Labor W. Willard Wirtz agreed. "The very rapid pace of the automation and technological change," he said in 1963, was resulting "in a shift in employment to relatively more skilled occupations."[7]

The premise that "automation" replaced the labor of the body with that of the mind seemed to resolve the contradiction between the claims of technological progress and the demand for full employment. The 1958 recession, the worst to hit the United States since World War II, tested that reconciliation. As unemployment rose to 7.5 percent, the automation discourse threatened that the current crisis might become a mere taste of things to come. With the economic stumble, "automation" became a useful word for politicians. During Adlai Stevenson's failed 1956 president bid, an advisor to the campaign suggested that if unemployment were to worsen, candidate Stevenson "might call for the establishment of a semi-permanent Presidential Commission on Adjustment to Automation" to study the problem. To exploit the measure to the greatest political advantage, Democrats would tacitly, or maybe not-so-tacitly, ask: "Can Republican single interest, big business government be trusted to take the nation through the coming phase of technological revolution?"[8]

Recession, coming a year and a half too late to help Adlai Stevenson, proved useful material for John F. Kennedy. In his acceptance speech for the 1960 Democratic presidential nomination, Kennedy introduced his "New Frontier," a heady mix of technological utopianism ("beyond that frontier are uncharted areas of science and space," he said) and a commitment to provide everyone a share in the postwar affluence by addressing "unanswered questions of poverty and surplus," or what would come to be called The Other America.[9] During the primary, both Kennedy and his rival for the Democratic nomination, Hubert Humphrey, had visited impoverished mining towns in the hills of West Virginia. The plight of the region's coal miners had become an object lesson in the shortcomings of the "affluent society" as petroleum challenged the supremacy of coal and operators introduced new machinery to mining. Covering the campaign, the journalist Theodore White wrote of mining operators who "automate their mines with the superb new machines of the postwar era."[10]

Much like the automobile industry, however, "automation" in postwar mining was largely a mechanized speedup. Coal operators invested in new apparatus, specifically the "continuous miner," a machine used mainly in room and pillar mining and first introduced in late 1940 in Marion Country, West Virginia, at the Carolina-Idamay mine.[11] Broad and low to the ground, the continuous miner's most notable feature was a large, rotating series of teeth that could chew coal from a face or seam as the machine advanced either on wheels or on crawler tracks. Said one miner in 1955, "Nobody likes the continuous miner. It has to be tended every second of the day. . . . Everything is on the fly now instead of just walking. . . . I've lost 30 pounds since I was put on this thing . . . the machine itself is a man-killer."[12] According to another miner in 1957, the relentless pace of the machine put workers in danger. "Since they keep it going all the time," he said, "they have the regular loading machine behind it. The loading machine loads loose coal the miner throws behind it into the buggies. The loading machine can stop. But not the miner. It keeps going." If the loading machines stopped while the continuous miner was in action, workers might find themselves buried alive. "Because it keeps going," this miner elaborated, "there are plenty of times when those guys on the miner are trapped there with the machine. They have put out so much coal that it is piled up to the roof, from rib to rib."[13]

Despite the speedup, White blamed "high union wages" for the unemployment and human misery that plagued coal country. Because "the union shoved wages up and up," White believed, operators had been left with no choice but to introduce the continuous miner. White was evidently unaware that the leaders of the United Mine Workers of America had themselves welcomed the introduction of new machines into the work process, despite incessant wildcat strikes and calls from the membership to stop the speedup. John L. Lewis, president of the United Mine Workers, considered the speedup an acceptable bargain in exchange for better wages and a welfare and retirement fund. "We've encouraged the leading companies in the industry to resort to modernization in order to increase the living standards of the miner and improve his working conditions," said Lewis. "It is better to have half a million men working in the industry at good wages and high standards than it is to have a million working in the industry in poverty and degradation." Between 1948 and the mid-1960s, three hundred thousand coal miners lost their jobs, although that was as much the result of a decrease in demand for coal as it was the new mining machines. (By the late 1970s, with an increase in the use of coal as a means to produce electricity, the number of coal miners would grow by one hundred thousand from its late-1960s nadir of about one hundred thirty thousand.) While wages improved amid the mid-century speedup, the miners' actual share of the wealth they produced fell. Between 1950 and 1967 coal operators increased production by thirty-six million tons while workers brought home $310 million less than they had before the introduction of the continuous miner. And despite Lewis's insistence on improved safety standards, the presence of a large reserve army of unemployed miners made it especially difficult for working miners to challenge management's degradation of the job. The speedup in coal mining led to more dangerous working conditions.[14]

The Kennedy administration understood high unemployment and poverty in places like Appalachia as largely the result of "automation." In 1961 Kennedy ordered the creation of the Office of Automation and Manpower to study the effects of "technological unemployment," which, he believed, were at least in part responsible for the relatively high unemployment rates of the late 1950s and early 1960s, and in May 1963, under the banner of The Nation's Manpower Revolution, Congress held a series of hearings to make sense of the new era. Those who testified before the Senate subcommittee acknowledged the inevitability and desirability of "automation." "It is urged, and properly," submitted Secretary Wirtz, "that full use must be made of automation to increase productivity, both in terms of improving efficiency and in terms of expanding the gross national product. We have no choice, if the economy is to grow at the rate it must, but to use every technological resource which is available." In what might have otherwise sounded like a contradiction, Wirtz then insisted, "It is no less important to use every manpower resource."[15]

The Kennedy administration, presenting itself as young, technologically savvy, and well prepared to lead the nation into the future, had no desire to question "automation." It considered recruiting into its ranks John Diebold, the so-called prophet of automation. That having come to nothing, Kennedy's advisor and lead speechwriter, Ted Sorenson, consulted with Diebold nonetheless. At a lunch in the summer of 1963, Sorenson met Diebold and told him that Kennedy had decided to ask Congress to consider the possibility of a looming railroad strike "in a wider context of general technology change." Sorenson suggested that the two of them go back to the White House and "draft some legislation for the President to send to Congress." Legislation concerning the rate or nature of technological change, or legislation that would call for an expansion of the welfare state, and with it a rise in taxes, was not what Diebold had in mind. "I protested," Diebold later reported, and, oddly, considering that the nation was supposedly in the midst of a "revolution," told Sorenson that "there was very little to legislate at this point." Kennedy was "really quite specific about wanting to send a Message to Congress on this," Sorenson replied. Diebold responded, "If something had to be done, it would be appropriate to study the question, and perhaps create a Presidential Commission to do so." Sorenson thought this was a rather good idea and asked Diebold to "send him some material describing what such a Commission might do."[16]

Kennedy did address Congress the following Monday, and instead of asking lawmakers to pass any specific legislation, he called for a special commission, drawing on what, as Diebold confided to his diary, were "the fundamental arguments I had been making for the past year or two to the effect that it was essential that the environment be created which allows for rapid technological change and that the human problems are considerably beyond the questions of immediate manpower and employment." Diebold need not have given himself too much credit. Willard Wirtz had been considering the possibility of a presidential committee on the subject of "automation" for the better part of a decade.[17]

Whether from Wirtz or Diebold, Kennedy took the advice. "We cannot stop progress," Kennedy told Congress. It would fall to the nation as a whole, Kennedy said, to ensure that the "public blessing" of "automation" did not become a "private curse" for individual workers. The commissioners were to be the "ablest men in public and private life." Their task, the president announced, was to identify the workers who would be made superfluous by the new machines and consider what overall social and economic consequences might result from their elimination from the workforce. Ultimately, this commission would advise lawmakers on the substance of a new law that would protect workers from the effects of technological change.[18]

Originally, the purpose of Kennedy's address to Congress had been to apprise lawmakers of the negotiations between the railroad companies and the firemen's and engineers' unions. That summer the nation was in the throes of the 1963 Railroad Work Rules dispute. On two separate occasions that year, deadlocked negotiations between the carriers and the unions brought the United States to the verge of a nationwide shutdown of freight and yard trains. The precipitating crisis had come in November 1959, when the nation's major railroads informed the unions that they would seek changes in work rules that would allow them to cut forty thousand jobs for yard and freight firemen, the people who, among other tasks, loaded coal into an engine's furnace. The railroads claimed that the switch from coal to diesel had made the firemen unnecessary. The president of the Association of American Railroads spoke of "wasteful and burdensome work rules" that "hang like an economic albatross around the neck of American progress."[19] The *New York Times* called the dispute "the classic modern example of the difficulty of adapting to technological change in the face of shrinking employment." The railroads claimed that with the firemen off the payroll they would save six hundred million dollars per year with no reduction in service. Was it the railroads' responsibility to maintain people who contributed nothing when technology had rendered them, objectively, obsolete?

Technics aside, the change from coal to diesel was an opportunity for the railroad companies to make sweeping changes to the character of train work, many of which had nothing to do with the combustive energy of a locomotive. Chief among them was an attempt to break down the existing job classifications in railroad operations so that fewer workers might be made to perform more tasks. Firemen performed duties other than stoking engines, and they claimed that their elimination would add a burden to engineers and brakemen. "The work in question," said the Brotherhood of Railroad Trainmen, "is not work which is no longer present. . . . The operating employees who have been performing this work would, under [the] carriers' proposal, be replaced with employees of another craft."[20]

The union representatives acknowledged that it was technically possible to make fewer workers do more work. The question for them was not the feasibility of the change but the justice of it. The current work rules, they maintained, were "a necessary regulation of the distribution of available work to the maximum number of employees which the employment opportunities will justify. This is consistent with our national policy in federal government and with our modern way of life." And the elimination of the firemen's positions turned out to be only one of the proposed changes the railroad companies hoped to implement under the guise of "technological" change. According to the Brotherhood of Railroad Trainmen, "The scope of carrier proposals is so broad that virtually every rule of the collective bargaining agreement on each railroad involved is either eliminated or drastically affected. . . . In the entire history of the railroads, there has never been such a large-scale demand for revision of the working agreements in effect on the nation's railroads placed before the parties." In fact, one of the union's single greatest complaints was the absence of technical specificity in the carriers' proposals. "The issues are so many and the proposed changes so drastic," the union said, "that the actual time used by the parties to date in negotiations has hardly scratched the surface." By 1963, both the railroads and the unions had dug in, with neither side willing to compromise on the definition of work rules.[21]

Rather than acknowledge the struggle as a consequence of the ongoing antagonism between workers and management, members of the press and the government interpreted the dispute as a result of the introduction of new machines. Hoping to avoid a nationwide railway strike, Kennedy called for the Interstate Commerce Commission to resolve the dispute. In August, and for the first time in the history of the United States, a peacetime Congress compelled management and workers to go to mandatory arbitration. In addition, seeking a technical rather than a political solution, Kennedy suggested that instead of passing legislation, the U.S. government undertake further study of the technical aspects of the problem.[22]

While Kennedy desired a technologically objective answer as to whether the firemen could keep their jobs, however, hundreds of thousands of Americans were at that moment traveling to Washington, D.C., in a March for Jobs and Freedom to suggest an alternative approach. Later remembered simply as the March on Washington, and most closely associated with the Reverend Martin Luther King Jr.'s "I Have a Dream" speech, the demonstration was originally conceived as a call for federal action to eliminate racist hiring practices in the United States. Organized by A. Philip Randolph, whose life as a labor organizer was inextricable from his career as a civil rights activist, as well as Bayard Rustin, the march was planned under the auspices of the Negro American Labor Council, a network of Black labor activists and union members. In order to tie labor demands in with civil rights activism, Randolph and King agreed to march under a banner reading "For Jobs and Freedom."[23]

But for Randolph, that pairing was not a compromise position. "We are the advanced guard of a massive, moral revolution for jobs and freedom," Randolph told the many thousands gathered on the National Mall. In both depression and boom times, racist exclusion from the job market had been the scourge of African American communities in the United States. Besides demanding civil rights legislation that would compel de facto recognition of the de jure rights of Black Americans, the organizers of the march also called for a government-sponsored public works program in the spirit of the New Deal's Works Progress Administration, an increase in the minimum wage, and an expansion of the Fair Labor Standards Act. They wanted the federal government to secure the right of all Americans to hold a good job and earn a decent livelihood, not simply to compete in an unregulated job market. Whereas the Kennedy administration believed that the economy, of its own accord, would create enough jobs to answer the need for full employment, Randolph took a different stance. People were not born to serve the economy, he insisted; the economy existed to serve the people.

Randolph, like practically all his contemporaries, believed that soon machines would abolish human labor—that "automation" was happening. But whereas for many the automation discourse promised an upgrading of the working class into middle-class professionals, Randolph's experience as an organizer of Black workers led him to distrust the unregulated labor market as a means to guaranteeing all Americans a good life. More to the point, he did not believe that work and freedom contradicted one another. His entire life as a labor organizer attested to that conviction. Facing racist exclusion earlier in the century by both employers and the American Federation of

Labor, Randolph's Brotherhood of Sleeping Car Porters, a Black-led union of Black workers, had in the late 1930s and early 1940s served also as one of the nation's most prominent organizations in the fight for Black equality. For Randolph, former editor of the radical *Messenger* and a socialist, worker power was an inextricable element in the larger program of Black liberation. That meant workers having a say over their work, not escaping it, and it was for that reason the Brotherhood of Sleeping Car Porters marched under a banner that made the distinction: "Service not Servitude."[24]

This was a crucial distinction. Black workers were pushed to the margins of the economy, forced to do jobs that the boosters of "automation" considered subhuman. The entire burden of Randolph's life of activism had been to help Black workers seize a meaningful measure of control over their lives by transforming otherwise degraded jobs into activities worthy of free people. It was for this reason that in their own communities Pullman porters were, in Randolph's words, "looked upon as sort of aristocrats of Negroes, you know. They made a lot of money, they dressed well and so forth." Randolph's idea of progress was to turn degraded jobs into dignified work, not by introducing a race of robot slaves into the workplace but through shop-floor democracy. Work, Randolph showed, became worthy of free people when those who performed it also controlled it.[25]

The activism of the Negro American Labor Council, including the March on Washington, was an extension of that same philosophy, which was why the organization insisted that the federal government create a public works program to place "all unemployed workers—Negro and white—on meaningful and dignified jobs at decent wages." Rather than hope that "automation" would work out for the best, Randolph demanded a fair division of the nation's resources and its powers in the present, right then. The problem of "automation" required a new level of government involvement in the economy, he argued. "It falls to us to demand new forms of social planning," he said before those gathered on the Mall in Washington, "to create full employment, and to put automation at the service of human needs, not at the service of profits—for we are the worst victims of unemployment." Yes, he continued, "we want a Fair Employment Practice Act, but what good will it do if profit-geared automation destroys the jobs of millions of workers, black and white?" Whatever "automation" was, he argued, the nation needed to direct it through the democratic process.[26]

Neither the Kennedy administration nor the Johnson administration shared Randolph's view. In 1962 Kennedy had supported the passage of the Manpower Development and Training Act (MDTA) and both the Kennedy and Johnson administrations intended the law as its main response to "automation." Likewise, the law's logic rested squarely on the claims of the automation discourse.

The purpose of the act was to provide the Labor Department with federal funds to offer on-the-job and vocational training to unemployed workers through both public and private institutions. Specifically, the law was to offer retraining to workers who had lost their jobs because of "automation" and provide them with the special skills that the new economy would soon demand.[27]

The shortcomings of the Manpower Development and Training Act revealed the effects of the automation discourse on government policy, and to a certain extent the shortcomings of what would become the War on Poverty's efforts to redistribute the nation's wealth to the neediest Americans. For the most part, policy makers behind the MDTA saw structural changes to the means of production as something beyond the scope of democratic governing. The MDTA did not take aim at reforming the structure of the economy. It was instead a means of playing catch-up, of manipulating the available human material to meet the needs of mechanization and the demands of a relatively unregulated labor market. Taking their cue from the Council of Economic Advisors, neither Kennedy nor Johnson agreed with progressive Democrats such as Wirtz, Senator Gaylord Nelson, and Representative Augustus Hawkins, who favored direct job creation. Certainly there was little conversation, if any, about the possibility of the nation democratically deciding how or what kind of machines should be used in the labor process. Instead of direct job creation, both Kennedy and Johnson chose tax cuts as their main tools of Keynesian adjustment, a position reflecting their belief that the postwar economy was a well-running machine that required only marginal directing. It might have seemed like a contradiction to some that Kennedy's administration would back a measure to provide for workers supposedly forced off the job by machines when, in the same year the MDTA passed, Kennedy also supported a capital investment tax credit as well as generous capital depreciation measures—providing employers with a government-backed incentive to invest in the new machinery that, his administration believed, threatened mass unemployment. But the automation discourse resolved this contradiction: The machines were progress, and workers needed to update themselves to meet the technological revolution.[28]

Although one of the key purposes of the MDTA had been to help "the unemployed, the underemployed, and those whose skills are endangered by automation," almost immediately the Department of Labor found itself catering not to recently unemployed industrial workers but to those who because of poverty and institutional racism were systematically excluded from the labor market entirely—people who were poor, old, mentally or physically handicapped, illiterate, incarcerated, or rural. A tacit confusion of means and ends reigned. In theory, the state hoped to provide vocational training so that individuals could provide for themselves through job holding and, as a result, keep the economy alive with their improved purchasing power. Yet it seemed to many Department of Labor officials that the government needed to offer the kind of support a welfare state would provide—a substantial living—in order to prepare people to compete in the job market. Its authors imagined the MDTA as a response to a new era in the history of industrial production, but like many previous job-training schemes the program assumed that the fundamentals of the economy were sound. They believed that systematic problems of unemployment were the fault of the most marginalized individuals, seeing them as personally ill prepared to share in the abundance created by society. This conviction became known as the "culture of poverty" thesis, and its influence on Johnson's War on Poverty was immense.[29] "Quite early in the program," said a Department of Labor official, "we found a disturbingly large number of unemployed persons who for any of several reasons could not participate in skill development activities." According to the culture of poverty thesis, the problem did not so much reside in the structure of industrial capitalism as it did within individuals who lacked the proper education to land a successful job or the "motivation" to sell themselves on the labor market.[30] In the words of J. B. S. Hardman, labor official and supporter of the MDTA, "without such training they will be lost in the backwash of progress and that progress may be seriously impeded."[31]

Very few MDTA programs managed to address the needs of industrial workers who lost their jobs because of changes in the means of production. In those that did, the purpose of the programs was to discover, as one official put it, "whether a radical change could be successfully made in a man's occupation." One such project, billed as an "experimental training course," was the Shapero School of Nursing's MDTA program at Sinai Hospital in Detroit, designed to turn laid-off UAW members into practical nurses. The question animating the experiment was best articulated by one of its designers: "Is it not a problem to turn a UAW man who's making very good money into a practical nurse who's making $15 a day? . . . Perhaps part of it would be adapting the teaching methods from teaching a nice little girl to teaching a factory hand . . . since you're taking people with great big calloused hands." Another member of the group answered, "It may be that we can evolve some kind of person who can fit the lower scores, to do a different job." Although in theory the purpose of MDTA projects was to upgrade industrial workers to white-collar professionals, these planners wondered whether the program was actually an experiment in job degradation. They expressed this concern along gendered lines, since it was making a job "normally thought of as a female occupation" one that might prove a job for "males, particularly men who have spent most of their working lives in an industrial setting," a setting coded as masculine and that was, often enough, unionized. The experiment had mixed results. Some of the men got along well enough. Others "felt they were being exploited."[32]

One million Americans would eventually receive at least some training thanks to the MDTA, and six hundred thousand of them would complete a full course of vocational study. Historians nevertheless regard the act as a failure; as one authority on the program argued in 1968, "There is no evidence that the unemployment rate is appreciably lower than it would have been had the program never existed."[33] A nationwide review of all MDTA projects in the late 1960s found that the program had not brought about the creation of either a broad middle class or a working class with improved bargaining power in the labor market.[34] Nevertheless, the program still made a significant if small difference. Institutional racism excluded many Black Americans from the chance to gain skills they could use to access the labor market; some civil rights groups applied and won MDTA funding to win access to skilled trades training for these workers.[35]

For Black liberation organizations, there were some advantages in subscribing, at least nominally, to the automation discourse, as Randolph had. When the National Urban League applied to the Department of Labor for MDTA money, it argued that because many Black Americans only had access to the most degraded and physically exhausting jobs, "automation" would hit them the hardest. Therefore, the leaders of the Urban League argued, Black Americans more than others needed "skilled" job training to meet the coming technological revolution. The demand for such training was as old as Booker T. Washington's Tuskegee Institute, but now, in terms of both the civil rights movement and the automation discourse, some Black Americans hoped to win a measure of federal support in their perennial struggle to make the labor market more just.[36]

Not until the late 1960s did the proponents of direct job creation amass the necessary political capital to pursue their agenda in earnest. President Johnson's Job Corps, another job-training program formed in 1964, suffered from the same conceptual handicaps as had the MDTA, placing the burden of the structural inequities of the labor market on individual shoulders. Secretary of Labor Wirtz had said as much to Sargent Shriver, director of the Office of Economic Opportunity and Johnson's War on Poverty tsar. The administration would need to create jobs by means of public programs funded through new taxes, Shriver told the president at a cabinet meeting in February 1964. A deputy of Shriver's who was present at the meeting described Johnson's reaction. "I have never seen a colder reception from the president. He just—

absolute blank stare—implied without even opening his mouth that Shriver should move on to the next proposal. We weren't even going to discuss that one. Whereupon Bill Wirtz, being the original proponent of jobs as a solution[,] chimed in and made the impassioned speech for jobs which the president completely ignored." Direct intervention in the labor market was out of the question for Johnson, who, advised by Gardner Ackley, chairman of the Council of Economic Advisors, believed that taxation to create jobs would not produce more employment but would simply shift jobs from the private sector to the public.[37]

In addition to resistance from their own leadership, opposition from conservatives and business groups prevented Democrats who favored direct job creation from making much headway. While the National Association of Manufacturers allowed for "the need for a greatly expanded program of education and training," its support of job training reflected its belief that workers should not possess any ownership of their jobs. As such, the association desired workers who commanded "the most fundamental skill of all: the skill to learn new skills quickly."[38] When push came to shove, businesses had no real love for government-funded vocational training. In 1964 Wirtz stood before an assembly of businessmen in Chicago to issue a jeremiad. "Gentlemen," he said, "if any one of you tried to run your business the way we're trying to run the Manpower and Development Program, you'd go bankrupt." The Department of Labor, Wirtz said, did not have the resources to collect data on how many people were out of work, the character of their needs, or the nature of the actual employment demands of the nation. "Do you know what the basic difficulty is?" he asked the businessmen. "Everybody is so afraid the government's going to start doing some planning in this country that they insist on our being unprepared. That's the root of the thing. And we simply can't proceed very successfully on a basis of that kind."[39]

Collective Bargaining and the Automation Discourse

While the automation discourse shaped the federal government's attempts to address the inequities of the labor market, another job-training program teetered on the verge of collapse, this one the creation not of law but of collective bargaining. Unlike many postwar CIO leaders, Ralph Helstein, president of the United Packinghouse Workers Union of America (UPWA), managed to steer his union through the troubled waters of McCarthyism without either purging its membership of Communist Party sympathizers or agreeing to contractual language that made it the responsibility of union leadership to crush wildcat strikes. "My position," Helstein said, "was that the purpose of the union treasury was for the union members and it seemed to me that when wildcat strikes occurred it was because people had some complaints. . . . That was not the time you denounced them." A friend of Martin Luther King Jr., he sat on King's "research committee," spoke at a Southern Christian Leadership Conference convention, and was a consistent opponent of racist segregation on the floor of UPWA meatpacking plants: "I would have shut down every God-dawn Armour plant over this issue," he insisted. As he said on one occasion when he defended the union's anti-segregation rules before white meatpacking workers at the Armour plant in Fort Worth, Texas, some having brought knives and guns to the factory in protest of the desegregation of the facility: "Our constitution requires this kind of behavior. You are either going to live by it or you can get the hell out of the union."[40]

Helstein's victory at the Fort Worth Armour plant, however, proved short-lived. In March 1962 Armour announced that it would close the factory. By June a thousand workers were laid off, and in December the plant was shuttered. Beginning in the 1950s and accelerating throughout the 1960s, plant closings, relocated shops, and mass layoffs became routine among the so-called Big Four of the meatpacking industry. By 1968 these practices would result in the effective destruction of the UPWA along with a vertiginous decline in working standards in the industry. The cause of this process, according to almost all the stakeholders, was "automation."[41] In response, the UPWA, along with the more conservative Amalgamated Meat Cutters and Butcher Workmen, negotiated in 1959 for the creation of the Armour Automation Committee. The committee consisted of four company representatives, two representatives from the UPWA, two from the Amalgamated Meat Cutters, and as chairman, George Schulz, future Secretary of Labor under Richard Nixon and later Secretary of State under President Ronald Reagan. As evidence of the seriousness of the experiment, none other than Clark Kerr, one of the minds behind the University of California system, held the position in 1961, and both Schulz and Kerr boasted significant laborite-liberal credentials.[42] The committee had $500,000 at its disposal, provided by Armour through a payment of one cent of every hundredweight of tonnage the company shipped. Armour was to use this money either to help workers resettle in jobs that the company had moved to other parts of the country or to offer them early retirement at age fifty-five at one-and-a-half times normal pension benefits.[43]

The Automation Committee was necessary because, like most other industrial unions at the time, the UPWA did not oppose mechanization in the labor process. Not seeing mechanical change as itself negotiable, the union demanded only that "progress should not mean enrichment of a few and misery for many."[44] As they had in other industries, managers and unions used the word "automation" to describe a constellation of material changes in the production process. In meatpacking, several upstart firms that would come to replace the Big Four and be known instead as the Big Three (Iowa Beef Processors, Excell, and Conagra) successfully challenged older methods of the industrial slaughter and butchering of animals in the years after World War II. In the process, they set off a race to the bottom. Companies moved away from the branch-house distribution system, in which highly trained butchers dressed meat to order, and replaced them with centralized meat cutters wielding power tools. Power tools allowed workers with less training to decapitate hogs and slice their bodies in half. Investment in heavy capital equipment such as the Anco Can Pak Puller enabled packers to keep cattle carcasses on a continuous chain while the machine skinned them, a task that had been the province of specially trained workers. Again, power tools helped eliminate highly paid positions, in this case those of floorsman and cattle splitter.[45]

The introduction of power tools, however, was in and of itself not enough to create the industrywide changes in mid-century meatpacking that would eventually undermine the UPWA as well as the Big Four. While firms moved production away from unionized northern urban facilities, they also degraded jobs. New factories were located in the countryside, not in cities, and specialized in the slaughter and packing of one kind of animal, instead of several. The concentration of certain labor processes in specific facilities and the decentralization of the industry as a whole across vast distances, along with the ability of managers to pay lower wages to rural workers, gave management the power to effect an industrywide speedup. The historian Roger Horowitz has argued that the postwar changes in the meatpacking industry constituted a return to the same "drive system" that Upton Sinclair condemned in *The Jungle*. "The dominating note of the drive policy is to inspire the worker with awe and fear of the management," said the mid-century economist Sumner Slichter, "and having developed fear among them, to take advantage of it." Considering the meatpacking industry at the end of the twentieth century, Horowitz observed that "inside the plants, the decline of unionism has been accompanied by a ferocious increase in the pace of work." The postwar changes to meatpacking, what interested parties referred to as "automation," had witnessed the degradation of what might have been seen in the 1950s as the "blue-collar middle class" to what by the 1990s Horowitz called "the working poor."[46]

Despite his vigilance, the UPWA's Helstein did not initially understand the nature of the changes taking place in the industry. Whatever was happening, he believed, was "automation." According to Eugene Cotton, the UPWA's general counsel during Helstein's tenure, "Clearly Helstein thought the changes in the industry [were] important, something big. I don't think he would have foreseen what eventually happened—the total decimation of the packinghouse industry, the breakup of the companies, which was not the result necessarily of technological advance, although it was a factor. It was a result of a whole new atmosphere in labor relations and I don't think there was evidence of his foreseeing that, or of anybody foreseeing that."[47] The managers of the Big Four had to fight to stay afloat, and, like the UPWA, they could not adjust quickly enough to survive. In the desperate search for profit, managers made whatever changes they could to stay in the black—they moved factories, they introduced new tools and machines, and they broke up or centralized production. For Helstein and his allies, these individual innovations seemed to add up to one large transformation: "automation," the abolition of work. Eugene Cotton described how he understood the alterations to the labor process over the course of the 1950s and 1960s. First, it appeared to begin with the introduction of power tools that managers used to effect a speedup of specific jobs. In response, the UPWA, like the UAW, initially fought for the integrity of job classifications and wage rates:

> For example, there may be no job loss initially, but you substitute a mechanical saw for a hand saw and there is an effort then to decrease the size of a gang working on a chain to do the same amount of work, or an effort to increase the volume of work that's expected, and so you get into an argument over rates or over job loads, because the technological improvement is used by the company as a means of trying to affect the job load.[48]

Under the sign of "automation," what the union had previously understood as a problem of reconciling new power tools to old jobs became something apparently much larger: "And then it became so widespread," said Cotton, "with the movement of whole plants, whole departments, or the reduction of whole departments, that that's when we got into negotiation of some sort of compensation, some sort of negotiation about what do you do about automation internally? And we set up the automation committee."[49]

Besides some resettlement funds and promises of a job in one of the new factories—should the worker's seniority make him or her eligible—the Armour Automation Committee bore the responsibility, according to the contract, of "studying the problems resulting from the modernization program and making recommendations for their solution." Again, the problem appeared to be "modernization," or, to put it another way, progress. This promise to study included a consideration of the vaunted "solution" to mechanized disruption that also informed the Manpower and Development Training Act: retraining.[50]

A year before Congress passed the MDTA, the Bureau of Labor Statistics had already filed a report on the outcome of the Armour Automation Committee's attempts to retrain "displaced" packinghouse workers. The bureau's conclusions were not encouraging. Perhaps, the report said, "careful advance planning" and "a carefully planned continuing education program" could help laid-off workers prepare for an advantageous entry into the labor market, but "no amount of contact or promotion is likely to produce any significant number of jobs in a period when unemployment is steadily rising." When a plant laid off hundreds or thousands of workers at one time, no one could expect the labor market, spontaneously, to produce enough jobs to compensate, and it certainly could not provide enough "good" jobs. "The closing of a plant creates extreme hardships for the workers who are involved," the report said, "particularly if unemployment is already high. In such a period, discrimination in hiring on the basis of age, sex, and race becomes more evident." Moreover, "those who find new jobs are likely to suffer a substantial drop in earnings." Plant closings hit hardest those already systematically excluded from full participation in the labor market: older workers, women workers, and workers of color. After an Armour plant in Oklahoma City shut down, the Oklahoma Employment Service advised that 65 percent of those out of work had the best chance of finding jobs "in manual labor." Had there existed thousands of unfilled specialized positions—the promised skilled jobs to be brought about by "automation"—perhaps retraining would have provided laid-off workers with the means to sustain themselves. But as Helstein himself observed, "What you were doing was training people so that they could be unemployed at a higher level of skill, because they couldn't get jobs." Eight months after the Oklahoma City plant closed, only 40 percent of the laid-off workers had found any employment.[51]

Schulz reported similarly unimpressive results after the Fort Worth closing. Although retrainees had some advantages on the labor market compared to those who had not undergone retraining, the jobs available to them generally proved worse than those they had held at Armour. Whatever the retraining was, the new skills did not provide a step up into the middle class. This was precisely what the national assessment of the MDTA concluded five years later—people who underwent retraining did not move up the ladder of pay or respectability. The Armour study explained why: There were too few skilled jobs available for retrainees, and employers continually refused to fill the jobs that did exist with workers of color. Schulz noted that while Black Americans and Latino/a workers had somewhat more success securing employment after retraining than their white counterparts, the jobs they landed required fewer skills and paid less than those they had held at Armour. "It seems likely," concluded Schulz, "that the poorer employment record of the whites is attributable, in part, to the white males' reluctance to accept low wages."[52] Retraining individuals, it seemed, could not on its own produce skilled jobs or abolish racist hiring practices.

By 1963 Helstein and the UPWA had had enough of the Armour Automation Committee. On pulling out of the committee, the UPWA said that from the beginning it had been nothing more than a bad-faith gesture, a "façade of humaneness and decency that would conceal a ruthless program of mass termination of employees of long service and cynical manipulation of the natural fears of its employees to accomplish drastic cuts in wages and working conditions." The union accused Armour of discouraging workers with seniority from making use of the agreement's guarantee of the right to transfer to new plants. When senior workers transferred, Armour put them on the payroll and, after a grace period, laid them off. On October 3, 1963, six days before Helstein traveled to Princeton, New Jersey, for a meeting of the Ad Hoc Committee on the Triple Revolution (a gathering that would propose that Americans receive a government-provided guaranteed income), he and the UPWA declared a nationwide strike against Armour to demand that the company accept worker transfers at six of its new, ostensibly automated plants. The strike lasted two weeks before Armour folded. It marked the last major victory of the UPWA. Armour agreed to make 80 percent of the new plant jobs available to transfer workers. But that success alone could not compensate for the UPWA's loss of control of the shop floor. At best, the strike won a reprieve for workers without addressing the central difficulty: management's ability to change the nature of the job by invoking "automation" as a requisite stage in the development of human history. As long as managers could persuasively argue that technological progress, not exploitation, led to the chaos of degraded jobs and closed factories, collective bargaining and strikes would not remedy it.[53]

Not all unions that faced dramatic material changes to the labor process, however, suffered the same fate as the UPWA and the Armour Automation Committee. Some managed to secure a living for their members without contesting management's changes to the labor process or the premises of the automation discourse. The most notable example was the 1960 Mechanization and Modernization Agreement (known as the M and M agreement) of the International Longshoremen's and Warehousemen's Union (ILWU) on the Pacific coast.

The introduction of the shipping container posed a serious challenge to dockworkers across the United States. In 1934 longshoremen had gained almost total control of the hiring process on West Coast docks. Workers, not shipping operators, decided who would work and when. Since the 1950s, shipping operators had been experimenting with containerization as a means to take that control away from workers. When fully implemented, container shipping would change the face of dockwork around the world. Harry Bridges, head of the ILWU, hoped to get out ahead of it. In return for a free hand in the introduction of the shipping container—along with the accompanying paraphernalia of cranes, redesigned ports, new ships, specialized storage facilities, trains, and trucks—employers agreed to compensate currently employed longshoremen. The companies paid out a total of five million dollars a year to the union. Workers with more than twenty-five years on the job who retired at age sixty-five received a $7,920 severance payment plus a pension of $100 per month. Workers between the ages of sixty-two and sixty-five received $220 a month if they retired early. Remaining workers with full seniority, known as A-men, enjoyed a guaranteed thirty-five-hour-per-week income, regardless of whether they worked the full thirty-five hours.[54]

Some rebelled against the M and M agreement. One Hawaiian dockworker remembered the Pacific Maritime Association's first test of containerization in Hilo: "When we began to see the results of automation in about 1956, we raised so much sand that Harry [Bridges] flew over for one of our meetings. We told him, 'Wherever the containers go, even if it's to a supermarket uptown, we want to follow it and do the unloading.' He said, 'Now wait a minute you Pineapples, it's not going to work like that.'" The workers suggested making the security of their jobs the precondition of any changes to the means of production. Bridges, however, saw containerization in terms of the automation discourse. "Do you want to continue our present policy of guerilla resistance to the machine," he asked union members in 1957, "or do we want to adopt a more flexible policy in order to buy specific benefits in return?" Rather than defend jobs, Bridges believed it was more realistic to sell them for a price. The Hilo dockworkers were among the first to experience this exchange: "I was in the first bunch let go," remembered one. "That was 1958. They called us the 'First Phase.' They gave us all 850 dollars to get ourselves and our families to a West Coast port. I [have] been here now seventeen years. . . . In this port it's the same bad joke."[55]

In the present, however, the M and M agreement and the "automation" of dockwork meant speedup, for the deal in fact preceded the widespread introduction of containers to shipping by more than a decade. The union having sacrificed the right to negotiate over the character of the work, "massive productivity gains came from sweat, not automation," in the words of the historian Marc Levinson. "On the first day that the mechanization agreement went into effect," remembered the historian, intellectual, and West Coast dockworker Stan Weir, "hold men found themselves working sling loads of hand-handled cargo that were double the weight of those that had been hoisted in and out of hatches the previous day. Thus, the first change to be felt was the elimination of the work rule that had for twenty-five years limited man-made sling loads to 2,100 pounds." In 1960 container shipping made up less than 2 percent of West Coast cargo tonnage. Until 1973 the majority of cargo coming into American ports still arrived outside containers, in the traditional form known as "break bulk."[56]

In preparation for eventual containerization, Bridges and the leadership of the ILWU created a second class of dockworker. The A-men were full union members; they were the ones who would benefit from the M and M contract. In 1959, just as the two sides finalized the terms of the M and M agreement, shippers and union leadership initiated the first cohort of so-called B-men. These workers were not full union members. When they attended union meetings they were required to sit in a segregated area of the meeting hall and did not enjoy the same protections. The new work rules officially cut gang size from eight to four. But because eight workers were still required to accomplish the task of working in the hold of a ship, the other four members of an eight-person gang were no longer considered full members of the shift but were instead "swingmen" who could be summarily fired. In effect, the union sold its control over dockwork and forced B workers to pay the price with sped-up and precarious human labor. The first step in "automation" on West Coast piers was the degradation of the job of dockworker—all before a single new machine was installed. "While these changes in relations between supervisors and workers on the job were being made," Weir remembered, "there was little change in the nature of cargo handling methods. Despite the negotiation of a so-called 'automation' contract." For the better part of the 1960s, dockworkers labored without the benefit of the work rules they had fought to win decades earlier. "Production almost doubled," Weir wrote. "Thus, the longshoremen were directly subsidizing the purchase of the very machines that would kill over half their jobs by 1980." This situation led in 1963 to the irony of Bridges demanding faster mechanization from shipping companies. "We intend to push to make the addition of machines compulsory," Bridges announced. On the East Coast, Teddy Gleason and the International Longshoremen's Association never achieved a unionwide settlement for the introduction of shipping containers to dockwork, although in New York and Philadelphia longshoremen won a guaranteed annual wage in exchange for smaller gang sizes—again, in exchange for a speedup.[57]

The benefits of the M and M agreement only applied to A workers, not to those who might work in the future and not to the B-men whose intensified labor paid for the containerization of shipping. Still, old-age pensions and a privately won guaranteed annual income figured as about the best settlement any American workers managed to win in the postwar United States in exchange for surrendering control of their jobs. If a union's responsibility was only to protect its members, then the M and M agreement largely achieved that end, even if it came at the cost of future generations' job security and an immediate speedup for current workers. If all parties agreed that historical progress forbade workers from controlling work, the union reasoned, then at least workers should command a right to live. The M and M agreement stands as perhaps the only example in the postwar period of a union's embrace of the automation discourse actually paying off for at least a few working people. But for the vast majority of workers in the late twentieth and early twenty-first centuries, including many dockworkers, the UPWA's experience would be their future. In abandoning a meaningful say over the nature of work, they found themselves consigned to underemployment or unemployment, while those still in the workplace worked harder for less.

The Automation Commission

So it was that in 1963, as the Armour Automation Committee crumbled, as thousands of Americans packed the National Mall in the name of jobs and freedom, and in the midst of what could become a nationwide halt to all railroad freight traffic, President Kennedy entertained the possibility that something more comprehensive than vocational retraining might be required in response to "automation." The president called the existing measures of the MDTA "too limited to provide the full answer to a program of this magnitude." He continued: "The problems of manpower displacement, of which automation is only one cause, should not be settled primarily by the use of private economic power and pressure, or discussed only on the picket lines. Their solution is of importance to the entire nation which now enjoys all the benefits of economic progress but, except when it is part of the employe [*sic*] group affected, now bears very little of its burdens."[58] Instead of developing any kind of legislation, however, as Sorenson said the president had originally intended, Kennedy's administration proposed the creation of a commission to study the effects of technological change on employment. Its purpose was to inform lawmakers, showing them exactly how to legislate the nation's response to material changes in industry, something that managers and boosters such as John Diebold did not want. Legislation might lead to regulating how, when, and why an employer could introduce new technology into the labor process. More likely, it would justify an expansion of the welfare state. Several Republican members of the subcommittee that conducted hearings on the MDTA bill feared "federalizing the entire unemployment compensation system," or in other words, a dramatic expansion of unemployment benefits, higher taxes, and a more heavily regulated labor market. Rather than fight that battle on the ground of values, the stuff of political contest, the Kennedy administration saw the problem in terms of the automation discourse. In subscribing to its terms, Kennedy addressed the deeply political issue of the expansion of the welfare state into a question of apolitical technics: The characteristics of machines would decide what the U.S. government owed American workers.[59]

Over the course of the seven months that followed congressional hearings regarding the possible changes facing the nation's workforce, where once again Diebold testified, three different bills were introduced onto the House floor calling for the creation of Kennedy's commission on automation.[60] While it was under consideration, the arbitration board established by Congress to resolve the railway work rules dispute decided that 90 percent of the striking firemen were "unnecessary." Although firemen performed "lookout" functions on freight and yard trains, the arbitration board ruled that it was not an undue burden to ask brakemen to take on that responsibility. Forty thousand jobs were to be eliminated as firemen quit, died, retired, were dismissed for cause, or were reassigned.[61] If anyone was disturbed by this turn of events, he or she need only have looked to Congress, which was in the process of establishing Kennedy's automation commission. Some relief might come from that quarter. The round of bills calling for the commission led to yet another set of congressional hearings in the spring of 1964 ("and here we are again," Elmer J. Holland of Pennsylvania, chairman of the hearings, said to Secretary Wirtz), until finally, in November of that year, President Johnson named fourteen members to the newly formed National Commission on Technology, Automation, and Economic Progress.[62] The commission was composed of some of the most recognizable representatives of business, labor, and the academy, including the titan of Detroit, Walter Reuther, the head of IBM, Thomas J. Watson Jr., and the sociologist and public intellectual Daniel Bell.[63]

The commission met regularly for a year; its mandate, to determine the impact of technology on the country in the past, present, and future. Congress handed the commission the daunting task of evaluating the effects of technological change "on the Nation's economy, manpower, communities, families, social structure, and human values." Beyond this, the group was to indicate areas where technology had failed to meet certain "community and human needs," to advise on how to apply new machines to meet those needs, and then to recommend what actions labor, management, and government, state and federal, should take to support technological development while easing the burden it would place on working Americans. It was a tall order.[64]

The commission had a million dollars at its disposal and access, according to Bell, to "a dozen government agencies to assemble whatever data it needed."

Over the course of eleven months the group of experts heard testimony. Robert Theobald, of the Ad Hoc Committee on the Triple Revolution, spoke to the commissioners, as did the eccentric inventor of the geodesic dome, Buckminster Fuller, along with members of the Council of Economic Advisors and three representatives of the CIA who briefed the commissioners on the state of Soviet "cybernetics." The commission ordered reports prepared for its consideration that, in Bell's opinion, taken as a whole constituted "what is probably the most comprehensive set of materials on technology and the American economy ever assembled." The commissioners worked hard. By the winter of 1965, the group's four academic members were ready to prepare its final report.[65]

Some controversy lay in store. A few days before Christmas, news leaked that the commission's labor representatives were outraged by the final draft of the commission's report. Walter Reuther, president of the UAW, Joseph Beirne, president of the Communications Workers of America, and A. J. Hayes, former president of the International Association of Machinists, took exception to one of the report's central findings: that "automation" had not eliminated many jobs. According to the draft, the commission had "seen no evidence to indicate that there has been a sharp break in the continuity of technological progress, and concludes that for the next decade, at least, no radical disruption of past trends is likely." It blamed the high unemployment of the late 1950s and early 1960s on slow economic growth, not technological innovation. "It ignores people," a spokesman for one of the commission's labor representatives said of the report. He went on to claim that the commission was dominated by business interests. Referring to the common demand of the rank and file within the labor movement for a thirty-five-hour work week, the report held that "increased leisure" should be "a matter of choice" instead of "relying on the shorter work week as a solution to the problem of unemployment." One of the labor leaders reading the report drew a large question mark next to the line "leisure as a matter of choice" and wrote in the margin, "What does this mean?" According to a journalist, "the labor members of the panel feel these suggestions do not meet the basic threat of automation."[66]

A flurry of rewriting followed, but in the end the substance of the report remained the same. According to Bell, while the labor members of the commission had "every reason" to be satisfied with the final report's recommendations, given that those recommendations "dealt with the considerable gaps and flaws in the operation of a genuine welfare state," the finding that "automation" was not a threat to full employment "undercut the 'ideological' basis of many trade union arguments."[67] In the same year Bell published an article in which he called "automation" a "bogey." This was an about-face for the thinker who nine years earlier had written that "automation" would "revolutionize the social topography of the United States as a whole."[68] When the final report was published in early 1966, the labor leaders and their allies on the commission included by way of dissent a "General Comment" in which they held that "the report lacks the tone of urgency which we believe its subject matter requires and which its recommendations reflect."[69] Union leaders remembered the origins of the commission, now almost three years distant, when President Kennedy had worried about the prospect of forty thousand fired firemen, a nationwide railway strike, and a welfare state incapable of adequately protecting working people against the ups and downs of the labor market. A very specific fear had inspired the Kennedy administration to call for an expansion of unemployment protections and benefits: the possibility of a future in which technological change and full employment were irreconcilable. In the absence of that threat, on what basis was labor to demand increased federal support? "There has not been and there is no evidence," the report announced, "that there will be in the decade ahead an acceleration in technological change more rapid than the growth of demand can offset, given adequate public policies." Despite the many prophecies of impending revolution, the commission found nothing to indicate that the nature of work in the United States was on the verge of radical change. Machine action would not abolish human labor any time soon.[70]

Instead of considering the possibility that either the rate or the nature of mechanization might be made subject to democratic decision making, the commission advocated a larger welfare state to lend assistance when new technics "displaced" workers. Had anything come of the commission's recommendations, Americans in the second half of the twentieth century might have enjoyed a welfare state more in line with the model of western European nations. The commissioners called for a "program of public service employment," in which the government would be "an employer of last resort," finally fulfilling "the promise of the Employment Act of 1946." They recommended a guaranteed floor under family income and "a broader system of income maintenance for those families unable to provide for themselves." They suggested that all Americans have access to fourteen years of free public education and that the government provide "lifetime opportunities for education." The commission wanted a nationwide job-matching database to help people find work. Employment services that were currently state-administered should be centralized under the federal government. Relocation assistance for workers forced to leave home to follow a job should become a permanent government service. The commission wanted to see an end to all "social discrimination" in hiring practices, as well as a program of affirmative action "to compensate for centuries of systematic denial." It asked employers to "humanize" the workplace by, among other measures, "eliminating the distinction in the mode of payment between hourly workers and salaried employees." This was, in short, a program in tune with the most progressive wing of the New Deal Democratic coalition.[71]

But little came of the commission's report, and even less of its recommendations. By 1966 the political situation had changed. The Great Society was in retreat as Johnson escalated the war in Vietnam and uprisings broke out in American cities. Bell called the Johnson administration's reception of the report "curious indeed." Originally, the commissioners were to present the report to President Johnson in person. First, White House staff pushed back the day of the presentation. Then, four days later, Johnson's press office called the executive secretary of the commission to inform him that the report would be released that very afternoon. And so, at the end of a regular press conference, Johnson's press secretary informed the press corps of the report, according to Bell, "in desultory fashion" and "with no member of the Commission on hand to answer questions." The White House buried the report. The urgency had eased for new, sweeping legislation of the kind the commission recommended. The railroad work rules dispute was over, President Kennedy was dead, and unemployment was down.

The "private reason" for the White House's attempt to dismiss the report, as Bell learned, "was that the report was thought to be too 'controversial,' and that the White House did not want to become identified too directly with some of the proposals that had been put forward by the Commission." One is left to wonder which specific recommendations troubled Johnson, architect of the Great Society. Certainly, the deepening quagmire in Vietnam diverted funding away from ambitious domestic programs, and the high employment of a wartime economy muted anxiety about "automation." But Bell, considering the commission that had finally served its purpose after a two and a half years of bills, hearings, and reports, was not particularly concerned with the proposals themselves or even "the graceless manner in which the White House brushed them temporarily under the rug." Rather, he wondered about the nature of commissions in general. Instead of a public debate in Congress about a law that might have aimed either to enlarge the welfare state or regulate mechanization, the issue of "automation" and unemployment had been cloistered for two and a half years behind closed doors. Instead of lawmakers fighting over the meaning of work and technological change, a committee of unelected experts had sought to come dispassionately to an objective answer. The issue had been largely depoliticized. Considering this, Bell wondered why "so crucial a social problem had been turned over to a Commission in the first place."[72] The answer was to be found in the word "automation" itself.

5. Machines of Loving Grace

The New Left Turns Away from Work

I like to think
(it has to be!)
of a cybernetic ecology
where we are free of our labors
and joined back to nature
returned to our mammal
brothers and sisters,
and all watched over
by machines of loving grace.
—Richard Brautigan, 1967

For a brief period in the middle of the twentieth century, more than a few serious people on the American Left thought that history would end in 1964. If it was ironic that the automation discourse led not only the federal government but also union leaders to see the degradation of the workplace as inevitable, another irony in the career of "automation" was that it encouraged many on the postwar Left to call the denigration of work a "revolution." The eponymous 1964 pamphlet *The Triple Revolution* testified to that irony.

The pamphlet's progressive pedigree was exquisite. When the *New York Times* ran a front-page, above-the-fold article on the event of its publication in March 1964, *The Triple Revolution* bore the signatures of a Nobel Prize winner (Linus Pauling) and a brigadier general (Hugh B. Hester). A leader in the civil rights movement and one of the organizers of the 1963 March on Washington, Bayard Rustin, put his name to it, as did A. J. Muste—labor organizer, pacifist, civil rights activist, and co-founder of *Liberation* magazine. Household names in leftist causes added their signatures: H. Stuart Hughes, Michael Harrington, Gunnar Myrdal, and Irving Howe. But while for a brief moment it might have commanded the attention of the nation, *The Triple Revolution* does not deserve our scrutiny because of its insight, which was minimal, or because of what it directly caused to happen, which was, perhaps, almost nothing. Remarkable instead was the broad consensus behind the document.

The authors of the pamphlet called themselves "The Ad Hoc Committee on the Triple Revolution," and they wrote of three intersecting historical developments that, they believed, made the year 1964 a critical time in the history of the world: the Human Rights Revolution (the civil rights movement), which could eradicate racism in the United States; the Weaponry Revolution (the nuclear standoff with the Soviet Union), which made the outcome of another world war so cataclysmic that the stage was now set to abolish the institution of war altogether; and the Cybernation Revolution, "the combination of the computer and the automated self-regulating machine," which was already reorganizing the economy away from human labor. The newspapers covering the publication of the document dwelt on this last "revolution," in particular the Ad Hoc Committee's suggestion as to how the United States should respond to it. "The problems posed by the cybernation revolution are part of a new era in the history of all mankind," said the committee. It meant nothing less than "a basic reordering of man's relationship to his environment." Very soon, the committee prophesied, industrial society would no longer be able to make use of the vast majority of its people in the task of production. Job holding, therefore, no longer served as a rational means of distributing income. Until the country divorced income from job holding, industrial society would not be able to move on to the next stage of civilization; it would act "as a brake on the almost unlimited capacity of a cybernated productive system." This analysis, the committee continued, explained the current "historical paradox" of a wealthy America in which millions of people lived in poverty. To seize the future, therefore, the United States needed to provide every citizen with a guaranteed annual income.[1]

Speaking at a UAW convention in Atlantic City, New Jersey Secretary of Labor W. Willard Wirtz responded, "I think the analysis is right but the prognosis and the prescription is wrong. . . . I don't believe that the world owes me a living and I don't believe it owes anyone else a living."[2] On the campaign trail, Barry Goldwater was more adamant. "Our job as Republicans," he said, "is to get rid of people who will even listen to those who say we should pay people whether they work or not."[3] Editorials ran the gamut from strongly supportive to venomous, but few disagreed with the pamphlet's historical claims. Even the New York intellectual Irving Kristol, teetering on the edge of cold war liberalism and about to take the plunge into what would become known as "neoconservatism," agreed with the Ad Hoc Committee that the inevitable drift of technological change would result in a country that no longer needed workers. The economic slump of the late 1950s and early 1960s, Kristol wrote, had not been merely the result of another cycle of insufficient demand, as the Keynesians maintained. "There really is such a thing as technological unemployment," he said. "The larger corporations in America today are, on the whole, 'cash rich.' They are using their money to replace their workers by one or another form of 'automation.'"[4]

The Triple Revolution was the result of a meeting that took place over the course of three days in October 1963 when a group of ten people representing a broad swath of America's progressive intellectual and political life gathered in J. Robert Oppenheimer's Princeton office to discuss the beginning of the end.[5] Among the attendees was James Carey, the one-time secretary-treasurer of the CIO and president of the anti-Communist International Union of Electrical, Radio, and Machine Workers. So was Gerard Piel, editor of *Scientific American* and the driving force behind the magazine's 1947 revival. The budding student movement had its representatives, the current president of Students for a Democratic Society (SDS), Todd Gitlin, and one of its principle architects, Tom Hayden. Ralph Helstein, president of the United Packinghouse Workers of America, helped organize the meeting, along with the futurist Robert Theobald (who six months earlier had been called before a Senate subcommittee to testify on the subject of the changes to the country's workforce), and W. H. "Ping" Ferry, emissary of the intellectual Left as well as vice president of the Center for the Study of Democratic Institutions, a progressive think tank.[6] James Boggs attended as well. Oppenheimer, chain smoking and saying hardly a word, allowed this company, which would be known as the October Group, to meet in his office, his only condition being that no one leak to the press that he was in any way involved.[7] Still cagey a decade after his appearance before the House Un-American Activities Committee and the loss of his security clearance, he ordered the telephones removed from the room on the assumption that they were bugged.[8]

Ferry, Theobald, and Helstein called the meeting because as far as they were concerned it appeared as though the world stood on the threshold of the future, the last stage of history already upon them. "In mid-1963," they wrote in the invitations they sent out to prominent activists and critics, "the evidence is accumulating that many of the postulates of the American socioeconomic system are no longer valid. A major crisis is likely. The crisis may well develop within the next year or two and appears certain to occur within the next Presidential term." They predicted a disaster on the scale of the Great Depression if not worse, "the genuine prospect of a breakdown," one that would "shake all institutions and may well cause the collapse of the social order within the United States; and perhaps even a collapse of international economic, political and social relations." They listed several indications that the center could no longer hold: the mobilization of African Americans in the civil rights movement, the persistence of poverty in a supposedly affluent age, a growing sense of "purposelessness, represented by such words as alienation, anomie, delinquency, and irresponsibility," and the reliance of the economy on what Dwight Eisenhower had three years earlier named the military-industrial complex. But first among all these signs of apocalypse stood one troubling certainty: Unprecedented unemployment was on the way as a result of "automation." In hindsight, these predictions sound unduly alarmist, even allowing for an unemployment rate that since the 1958 recession had swung between 5 percent and 7 percent (nowhere near the 25 percent unemployment rate of 1933). What in other times might have appeared as yet another turn in the unending cycle of bust and boom now seemed more significant. This was not just another downturn; it was the end. Ferry, Theobald, and Helstein arrived at this conclusion not because they had lost faith in the institutions of the United States but, rather, because those institutions appeared to them to be working all too well. "The American system has succeeded in one of its basic goals," they wrote. "It has demonstrated its ability to provide enough goods and services for all those within its borders and also to help those outside them. It is this very success which poses the present problems but which opens up, at the same time, totally new potentials which depend solely on learning to use abundance wisely." These were the birth pangs of a truly abundant society, they argued, the preconditions of utopia.[9]

In the years leading up to the meeting Ferry had made "automation" the central concern of the Center for the Study of Democratic Institutions. In 1962 the center published *Cybernation: The Silent Conquest*, in which Donald Michael coined a synonym for "automation" that gained widespread rhetorical purchase. Michael had previously testified before the Senate subcommittee on the manpower revolution and explained the word "cybernation" to lawmakers.[10] Michael found that in the current literature there was confusion as to whether "automation" meant replacement of the human body by the use of servomechanisms or replacement of the mind by way of electronic digital computers. He disliked the distinction, saying, "We invented the term 'cybernation' to refer to *both* automation and computers."[11] He wanted a word that would include all machines, an understandable impulse when, since the late 1940s, the automation discourse had represented all the latest technological developments, regardless of their technical character, as producing the same result: no more work, the final stage in the history of industrialization. When the October Group met at Princeton, they used "automation" and "cybernation" as synonyms, as would most who spoke on the subject for the rest of the decade.

Ferry had published a book of his own in 1962, *Caught on the Horns of Plenty*, in which he asserted that "automation and its technological cousins may prove to be the main destroyers of what is left of capitalism." He predicted the growth of a "liberated margin," those "permanently liberated" from the need (or opportunity) to work, whether they liked it or not. In Ferry's analysis this liberation was not a question of politics or of the meaning of work—it was an objective technical reality to which governments needed to adapt.[12] As for Theobald, his 1963 *Free Men and Free Markets*, like many books before it, described the postwar period as "a new revolutionary era" in which "the *power of the machine is combined with the skill of the machine* to form a productive system of, in effect, unlimited capacity." Because "Western societies" now possessed a seemingly infinite supply of everything anyone could want, and all of it soon to be produced automatically, it only made sense that governments guarantee their citizens the right to life. Theobald claimed that it was "the coming of abundance," secured through automatic machines, that "allows and requires that we provide everybody with the resources they need to live with dignity; in short, it allows and requires that we develop the good life."[13]

Ferry's and Theobald's take on "automation" was typical of their moment. "I think it significant that consensus at the meeting was so extensive," wrote Todd Gitlin of the October meeting. "Also auspicious, given the diversity of our experiences, stations, indeed our politics."[14] This auspicious consensus that the end of work meant freedom, however, was new in the history of the United States. From the far Left to the center, thinkers came to agree on what only a few decades earlier would have been anything but a truism: that work meant only the toil of the body, that machines would abolish it imminently, and that these fateful developments constituted the preconditions for a political revolution, one that would result in a truly democratic society.[15]

The Autoworker from Alabama

Those on the American Left who sympathized with the automation discourse and its ideal of freedom as liberation from work found ample justification for their views in the work of Karl Marx.[16] In the midst of postwar abundance and technological optimism, Marx's Aristotelian tendencies stood out more prominently than they had only a few decades earlier, and they received no better advocate than James Boggs.

Organizer, revolutionary theoretician, and sometime correspondent with Bertrand Russell, James Boggs was the only participant at the Princeton meeting who was also a full-time autoworker. For twenty years until he retired in

1968, Boggs woke at five o'clock every morning to drive a jitney at Chrysler's Jefferson Avenue assembly plant in Detroit. He wrote when he came home, lying on the floor and filling notepad after notepad. It would not be an overstatement to say that for the second half of the twentieth century, the rented house James Boggs shared with his wife and fellow organizer, Grace Lee Boggs, was an unofficial center of radical politics in the city of Detroit. Labor militants, civil rights activists, radical intellectuals—it seemed everyone had sat on their couch. The Boggses were relentless organizers: Instrumental in the hundred-thousand-strong civil rights march down Woodward Avenue, they also proved indispensable in putting together the Northern Negro Grassroots Leadership Conference.[17]

The same year he came to Princeton, Boggs published *The American Revolution: Pages from a Black Worker's Notebook*. It was perhaps the most original and idiosyncratic rereading of Marx ever produced in the United States. In it Boggs argued that the combination of industrial plenty and racism had pushed the American working class out of its historical role as the agent of the revolution. "Automation," specifically, he wrote, had changed all that. "The workless society," Boggs asserted in a bold contradiction of a key premise of Marxist thought, "is something that can only be brought about by actions from outside the work process." It was traditional Marxist labor organizers, Boggs argued, those who fought "automation," who were the most mistaken, for they failed to accept "the inevitability of the workless society." Because of this refusal, he wrote, "these militants who are so advanced are really behind the average worker who has reconciled himself to eventual oblivion." He claimed that material changes in the means of production had positioned a new class to lead the communist revolution in the United States—unemployed Black Americans.[18]

In reinterpreting Marxism, Boggs brilliantly accounted for the problem of racism in the formation of the American working class. At the same time, however, at the heart of his approach lay "automation" and its definition of freedom as the escape from work. Presuming the inevitability and even the desirability of the industrial abolition of work, Boggs, a lifelong organizer, found himself embracing the same changes to the means of production as those advocated by executives of the Ford Motor Company. It was a supreme irony, and one that would have been unthinkable had it not been for the persuasiveness and power of the automation discourse.

Boggs's reinterpretation of Marxism relied on two assumptions, both typical of the automation discourse on the American Left in the postwar period: First, that "automation" was the last and inevitable stage in history, and second, that freedom meant liberation from the activity of answering the demands of one's biological condition. *The American Revolution* grew from Boggs's 1961 "State of the Organization, State of the Nation," a paper he circulated among the Correspondence group, the revolutionary Marxist-Humanist organization then under the leadership of the West Indian philosophe C. L. R. James, whom the U.S. government had deported at the height of the McCarthy-ite purge. Boggs began by asking what Marx meant by "socialism." As was common in their marriage, he sought out Grace, the first English translator of the *Economic-Philosophic Manuscripts of 1844* and holder of a PhD in philosophy from Bryn Mawr. Grace provided James with the standard mid-twentieth-century interpretation of Marx: that he had understood socialism as a stage between the fall of capitalism and the rise of Communism, that socialism would arise when the workers seized the helm of the state, and that the emancipated workers would then use their newly gained political power to develop, as quickly as possible, the productive powers of humanity toward the end of creating "the abundance that would make possible Communism."[19] According to Marx, Grace told James, this industrial horn of plenty was the material precondition of Communism. Once achieved, Communism would follow, an age when each contributed according to his talents, and all received according to their needs.[20]

With that, Boggs hit upon the central premise of his book, a reinterpretation that would split the Correspondence group and make him a minor celebrity. The present, he argued, was faced with an obvious contradiction. The technical apparatus for Communism already existed in the United States, yet by no means could any leftist call mid-century America a classless society. Cause and effect were reversed; the mode of production that should have in theory belonged to an emancipated people had anticipated emancipation itself. Marx's analysis seemed to fall short. The workers were not in power, and yet the tools that they were supposed to have developed after their liberation had preceded the revolution. James Boggs had a name for this revolutionary technical apparatus, the one that should have provided the material basis for a Communist society. He called it "automation." His definition was simple, if vague: "an advanced form of technology which replaces individual human controls with electronic controls." With that, he came to a startling conclusion: the members of Correspondence could no longer rely on Marx's projection of the coming of Communism.[21]

In *The American Revolution* Boggs took this idea even farther, premising not only Communism but also Black liberation on the "automation" of American industry. Picking up the argument from Harold Cruse's seminal 1962 essay "Revolutionary Nationalism and the Afro-American," Boggs argued that African Americans were essentially a superexploited colony of the United States.

The high quality of life attained by many members of the nation's industrial working class was, Boggs argued, like the material privilege enjoyed by the working classes of European imperial powers, bought with the wealth stolen from colonial subjects. In the case of the United States, those colonial subjects lived within the national borders of the mother country. For centuries, Americans of African descent—slaves, sharecroppers, tenant farmers, domestic workers, casual laborers, and lumpen proletarians—had toiled under some of the most abysmal working conditions of modern times, only to have the lion's share of their labor's value taken from them. As W. E. B. Du Bois had argued in the wake of World War I, and as Frantz Fanon concluded in the midst of his revolutionary activity in Algeria, Boggs held that racism allowed one part of the working class to rationalize and accept the degradation of its other part. The old battle cry of the CIO, "Black and White, Unite and Fight!" missed the point, he argued. The majority of white American workers benefited from racism; they had an existential stake in perpetuating it. Racism allowed some workers to escape the wide array of "scavenger" jobs (a term he coined with Grace) on which the U.S. economy relied. These privileged workers could count themselves fortunate, because while employers degraded work, there existed an African American working class to perform degraded jobs. This tectonic fissure running through the working class, argued Boggs, meant that the working class in the United States would not make the revolution.[22]

Boggs's contribution to the New Left's use of the automation discourse lay in how he adapted it to the Black liberation movement. "Automation," he believed, was destroying all but the most highly skilled industrial jobs, jobs that white workers, with the collusion of employers, had denied Black Americans. The destruction of semiskilled and unskilled work, Boggs held, would effectively exclude Black workers from regular employment. Unmoored from the U.S. economy, Americans of African descent, "on whom has fallen most sharply the burden of unemployment due to automation," would find themselves "just as expendable as the Jews were in Nazi Germany." Still, with their exile from industrial production and their alienation from the means of production by racism and "automation," Black workers would also be the catalyst of revolution given the changing structure of the political economy of the United States. "It is this exclusion," Boggs wrote, "which has given the Negro struggle for a classless society its distinctive revolutionary character." The end of labor, supposedly brought about by "automation," would be both the ends and means of this revolution, and Black Americans its vanguard.[23]

Boggs did not see "automation" as management's word. It was, he claimed in *American Revolution*—as had Norbert Wiener, Daniel Bell, John Diebold, Walter Reuther, and the executives at the Ford Motor Company—"a new stage of production." Soon, "man as a productive force will be as obsolete as the mule," he wrote. "The fact has to be faced. Automation is the greatest revolution that has taken place in human society since men stopped hunting and fishing and started to grow their own food." In his view, "automation" was not simply another term for mechanization, decentralization, and speedup. He saw it, instead, as a result of the unfolding logic of industrialization. "Whereas the old workers used to hope they could pit their bodies against iron and outlast the iron," he said, "this new generation of workless people knows that even their brains are being outwitted by the iron brains of automation and cybernation." Trying to roll it back would be the same as "telling a man in the big city that he should hunt big game for the meat on his table." It would be sadistic to send people to factory work unless it were absolutely necessary: "It is like sending them to prison to punish them. Because that is what the factory is: a prison."[24]

Boggs knew that it was management that made the factory a prison, not machines. He was keenly aware that the UAW leadership's postwar compromise on production standards, not the installation of transfer machines, had allowed management to usher in a new regime of speedup. "After 25 years," he said, "the UAW has given back to management every right over production won in the movement of the 1930's and the war years. Today the workers are doing in eight hours the actual physical work they used to do in twelve." He also recognized the disruption caused by decentralization: "The work force in the old plants was broken up and sped up, requiring fewer workers but also scattered to the new plants," he wrote. "Thus the machine shop work which had been done by 1,800 at the old Chrysler-Jefferson plant was now being done by 596 in the new Trenton, Michigan, plant which supplies not only the old plant with machined parts but all the other plants of the corporation." Finally, he even acknowledged that after decentralization "layoffs followed by the hundreds as more was being produced not only by the new automated machinery but by forcing workers to tend more of the old machines—man-o-mation." What Boggs called "man-o-mation," in other words, labor-intensifying speedup, activists in the League of Revolutionary Black Workers would in 1969 call "niggermation."[25]

Boggs gave statistics for Chrysler's Jefferson plant because since 1940 he had worked there driving an engine jitney. His position was on the motor line, the very process that Ford executives targeted for heavy mechanization. When Boggs began working there, production workers built engines from rough engine blocks that were cast elsewhere. Beginning in the early 1950s, Chrysler converted all plants concerned with both manufacturing and assembly—like the Jefferson plant—to pure assembly. By the mid-1950s, all engine production had moved from Jefferson Avenue to a "state-of-the-art" engine factory in Trenton, Michigan, beyond the Detroit city limits.[26]

The change must have appeared stupendous. Though Boggs recognized "man-o-mation," he also watched as the engine line at the Jefferson plant withered and eventually disappeared. He no doubt heard that the new "automated" engine plants hired fewer workers. With his own eyes he saw daily the completed engine sitting in his jitney, while he considered how twelve hundred fewer workers had made it. The jobs remaining at Jefferson were not the skilled jobs of engine machining but semiskilled assembly work. The implications of this change were too stark, too overwhelming. If one part of the labor process could be so heavily mechanized, one can imagine Boggs concluding, surely the rest of it could be as well. That these "automated" motor lines were inflexible yet still demanded a great deal of labor, that the heavy capitalization of all other work in automobile manufacturing would have been prohibitively expensive—these considerations must have weighed less with James Boggs than what he had witnessed. The mechanization of engine building seemed so dramatic that surely enormous, unprecedented powers lay behind the changes. It was this power that the revolution would need to seize.

Despite seeing with his own eyes how management increased its exploitation of workers under the aegis of "automation," Boggs nevertheless called for a "crash program," not to reduce "automation" but to speed up its supposed takeover of American industry. In doing so, it was necessary that he articulate his understanding of a full human life as one in which an individual was free from the activity necessary to maintain his or her biological survival. Revolutionaries needed to "make [their] objective maximum automation so that full *un*employment can be realized, giving man his first opportunity to be free from the fear of want and from the injustice of unnecessary work, and thereby, both in the struggle around this program and in the achievement of it, developing man for his most important human task of making responsible social decisions." The fact was, he continued, that "this society has reached the stage where it is no longer a question of improving these conditions but of doing away completely with the working condition itself."[27]

Boggs's definition of freedom as a condition opposed to work was inextricably bound in the sharp division he made between human flourishing and mere animal life. "Just coming out of your mother's womb does not make you a human being," he was fond of declaring.[28] He juxtaposed the right to "live like a man" against that of "working like an obsolete animal."[29] People would not "regain their membership in the human race," he argued, until they made politics, rather than material goods. As he put it in 1963: "The struggle for human relations rather than for material goods has become the chief task of human beings."[30] Freedom and full individual authenticity were possible only given the vital precondition of "abundance," if one were no longer bound to biological necessity, the work that "someone" had to do. "Worklessness," he wrote, was not an alien condition. It was the end point of the "natural development" of the species. "Man's whole history has been a search for means to do things more efficiently so as to reduce the efforts that he had to make to produce."[31]

Having committed himself to the automation discourse, Boggs's definition of history had come to ring less of Marx than of the 1961 Ford Motor Company Management Brief that described the history of American capitalism and "automation" as the "manifestation of the search for ways of doing things better, doing them more efficiently, doing them more effectively, that has long characterized American business . . . an evolutionary process that started centuries ago."[32] For Boggs, a full human being did not work. He or she dwelled in the political world, the only place where the uniquely human function of reasoning was possible. In an astonishing conclusion for a Marxist, even a Marxist-Humanist, James Boggs came to believe that work and politics were exclusive of one another. It therefore paid, argued one of the most active of worker-revolutionaries in American history, to commit one's revolutionary energy outside the workplace.

From Affluence to Post-Scarcity

In his analysis of modern working conditions, Boggs was one of a constellation of leftist thinkers who wielded great influence over the theoretical development of the New Left. His argument that the working class had ceased to serve as the agent of the revolution was also, for example, that of C. Wright Mills in his 1960 "Letter to the New Left." There, the author of *White Collar* argued that the working class was no longer "*the* historic agency, or even the most important agency" and that "such a labour metaphysic" was "a legacy of Victorian Marxism that is now quite unrealistic."[33] In the importance he granted "automation," Boggs also had much in common with Herbert Marcuse, who in *Eros and Civilization*, and later in his 1964 *One-Dimensional Man*, argued that the imposition of unnecessary work was a means of social domination. The solution was not for workers to increase their control over their jobs but, rather, to escape work completely. "To be sure," wrote Marcuse, "this form of drudgery is expressive of *arrested, partial* automation, of the co-existence of automated, semi-automated, and non-automated sections within the same plant." Under these conditions, he claimed, modern industrial working conditions exhausted not muscles, but the nervous system. For Marcuse, freedom from oppression meant freedom from all necessity. "Thus," he wrote, "economic freedom would mean freedom *from* the economy—from being control by economic forces and relationships; freedom from the daily struggle for existence, from earning a living."[34]

A minority of postwar Marxist-Humanists, however, disagreed with the claim that "automation" was the technological precursor of working-class revolution. Raya Dunayevskaya, who with C. L. R. James had for a time collaborated with Grace Lee Boggs in the Correspondence Group, wrote that "*the* fundamental problem of true freedom" lay not in the question, How can we abolish work? but, she asked, "What type of labor can end the division between 'thinkers' and 'doers'?" The divorce of mind from body was, she held, one of the most alienating characteristics of capitalism. True liberation would seek to bring mind and body back together, or to put it more concretely, to allow individuals to direct their own actions. This meant answering necessity according to one's own design, not escaping necessity altogether.[35]

While Marcuse and Boggs believed that liberation meant the complete divorce of people from the means of production, what they understood as "automation," Dunayevskaya held that workers' control, or a *closer* relationship between workers and the means of production, would end the division between thinking and doing. "The workers," she wrote, "the American workers, made concrete *and thereby extended* Marx's most abstract theories of alienated labor and the quest for universality. Marx was right when he said the workers were the true inheritors of Hegelian philosophy." In light of the technological optimism of the postwar period, however, Dunayevskaya's argument sounded backward and out of touch. Material reality in the form of "automation" appeared to have consigned her and the other proponents of the old labor metaphysic to the dead past.[36]

While James Boggs used the term "abundance" when writing of the political possibilities of a society freed from the natural world, by the mid-1960s leftist intellectuals began to adopt a new term. "Post-scarcity" invoked the same meanings as "affluence" and "abundance" but without the assumption so often accompanying "affluence" that all already shared equally in the industrial wealth the United States produced. Thinkers calling on post-scarcity wished to discuss industrial potential, rather than fact. It was the Left's answer to capitalist consumerism, but its invention nonetheless assumed the automation discourse.

"Post-scarcity" served a crucial function on the American Left in translating the terms of the automation discourse from capitalist fantasy into socialist utopian program. The honor of its invention lay with environmental anarchist Murray Bookchin, who coined the term sometime in the mid-1960s.[37] A former organizer and shop steward for the United Electrical Workers, and like Boggs at one time an autoworker and member of the UAW, Bookchin today is remembered by scholars and activists for his synthesis of anarchist thought and environmentalist criticism. Scholars have credited Bookchin with almost singlehandedly reinvigorating the anarchist movement in the United

States by means of his collection of essays written in the 1960s, *Post-Scarcity Anarchism*. In that volume he argued that the damage done to the natural environment stemmed from the same will to dominate that encouraged the exploitation of people for profit. "Capitalism," Bookchin wrote, "is inherently anti-ecological."[38]

Unlike most in the budding environmentalist movement who criticized the devastating effects of industrial capitalism on the natural world, Bookchin was an enthusiastic supporter of the productive powers of postwar industry. "The technological revolution, culminating in cybernation, has created the objective, quantitative basis for a world without class rule, exploitation, toil or material want," he wrote. "The means now exist for the development of the rounded man, the total man, freed of guilt and the workings of authoritarian modes of training, and given over to desire and the sensuous apprehension of the marvelous." For him, "work" was a stable category tripping down through the centuries. It meant, simply, activity undertaken to answer the demands of the body. Unfortunately, Bookchin wrote, "the world of necessity has subtly invaded and corrupted the ideal of freedom" [for] "to view the word 'post-scarcity' simply as meaning a large quantity of socially available goods would be as absurd as to regard a living organism simply as a large quantity of chemicals." Bookchin had read Marx-the-humanist closely. The ideal of freedom meant more than well-fed slavery. It meant an end to alienation. "Post-scarcity society, in short," he wrote, "is the fulfillment of the social and cultural potentialities latent in a technology of abundance."[39]

The new technology, what Bookchin called "cybernation," would allow for decentralized communities to produce for themselves much of what they needed.

> That freedom must be conceived of in human terms, not in animal terms—in terms of life, not survival—is clear enough. Men do not remove their ties of bondage and become fully human merely by divesting themselves of social domination and obtaining freedom in its *abstract* form. They must be free *concretely*: free from material want, from toil, from the burden of devoting the greater part of their time—indeed, the greater part of their lives—to the struggle with necessity.[40]

People must live in small, local settlements, Bookchin held, where all would interact face to face. Multipurpose, programmable machines would allow these humble, intimate communities to develop. Machines would facilitate the downfall of hierarchy. And what did Bookchin consider an example of successful cybernation? The "automation" of the Ford Motor Company's engine line.[41]

Though Bookchin called for freedom from natural necessity, he also insisted on a greater intimacy with the natural world. The goal of the eco-anarchist revolution was to make humanity's dependence on nature explicit. "To bring the sun, the wind, the earth, indeed the world of life, back into technology," he wrote, "into the means of human survival, would be a revolutionary renewal of man's ties to nature." He distinguished between "work" and "toil," but he never went into great detail about the finer points of the differences between the two, other than to say that work was "pleasurable" and toil "onerous." Certainly one was alienated, the other not; one spontaneous and expressive of individuality, the other routine and expressive of nothing but mere biology. But there was a problem. Bookchin considered any bodily experience of the natural world through labor as manifestly unacceptable. "How to achieve this transformation," he asked, "without imposing 'painful toil' on the community[?] How, in short, can husbandry, ecological forms of food cultivation and farming on a human scale be practiced without sacrificing mechanization?" He answered that machines would remove the toil while simultaneously allowing the "artistic completion" of a task to fall to the human being.[42]

Bookchin wanted the power of industrial capitalism without the social form of industrial capitalism. Like Boggs and Marcuse and much of the New Left, he marveled at the inconsistencies of modern industrial power; the tools of liberation were at hand and yet freedom failed to materialize. "The decay of the American institutional structure," Bookchin wrote, "results not from any mystical 'failure of nerve' or from imperialist adventures in the Third World, but primarily from the over-ripeness of America's technological potential."[43] Industrialization had created immense wealth for some and hard poverty for others. Post-scarcity thinkers wished to resolve the contradiction, hoping, as traditional Marxists had, that if they could simply turn to other ends the machines developed under the social form of capitalism, a system built to accrue private profit would become a tool to create universal liberation.

The New Left would come to embrace both James Boggs's belief that "automation" had deprived the working class of its historical role, and that post-scarcity was a material precondition for revolution. Both convictions would hold fateful consequences for the movement.

The New Left and the Denigration of Work

Like the older generation of thinkers whose books they read, many members of the New Left also adopted the automation discourse's denigrated meaning of work. They founded their notion of revolution on the assumption that meeting biological necessity was incompatible with freedom. Take, for example, Todd Gitlin. When he attended the meeting on the Triple Revolution in the fall of 1963, Gitlin was twenty years old. He had recently been elected president of Students for a Democratic Society (SDS), which over the course of the decade would grow into the most visible organization representing the student movement. Still in college when W. H. Ferry invited him to the October meeting in Princeton, he was rooming with twenty-three-year-old Tom Hayden, one of the leaders responsible for the transformation of SDS from a quiet association of college leftists into a major political force of the 1960s.

At the time SDS was suffering from an identity crisis. It was a student group, but the individuals leading the organization wondered if perhaps the future of American politics lay beyond the gates of the college campus. Just as Mills, Marcuse, and Boggs had before them, SDS members now asked themselves who would become the agent of revolution. If it was the students, and student activists themselves were not at all confident it was, did their revolutionary potential come from their activism on campus, or should they apply their efforts somewhere else? In this frame of mind, Gitlin and Hayden took their seats in Oppenheimer's office.

Throughout the spring and summer of 1963 "automation" had figured as a growing concern for SDS. In June a conference in Nyack, New York, gave rise to the National Committee for Full Employment, in truth little more than a letterhead under which Stanley Aronowitz, with orders from Bayard Rustin, helped persuade unions such as the UAW and the UPWA to participate in the March on Washington for Jobs and Freedom. The presence of numerous members of SDS at the Nyack meeting led to the dissemination in the organization of arguments typical of the period, in this case made by Ray Brown, an employee of the Federal Reserve System, who read a paper titled "Our Crisis Economy: The End of the Boom." The labor force "will expand by a million and a half each year in the coming decade," Brown said. "Add to this demand for jobs the number of jobs destroyed each year by automation (estimates range from one to one-and-a-half million), and the problem takes on monumental proportions."[44]

Taking the advice of Stokely Carmichael, the conference decided that while the Student Nonviolent Coordinating Committee, one of the most active organizations in the civil rights movement, would organize Black working people, SDS members would go to the streets of the urban North to reach unemployed white workers, the young in particular. That September, with a five-thousand-dollar grant from the UAW, SDS formalized its plan for the Economic Research and Action Project (ERAP). This project signaled not only a departure from SDS's previous organizing strategy but also a readiness to entertain a different understanding of the political importance of work. In drafting the Port Huron Statement a year earlier, SDS members had hoped to redefine work away from its degraded industrial meaning to one consistent with full democratic citizenship. Work, they wrote, should involve incentives worthier than money or survival. It should be educative, not stultifying; creative, not mechanical; self-directed, not manipulated, encouraging independence, a respect for others, a sense of dignity, and a willingness to accept social responsibility, since it is this experience that has crucial influence on habits, perceptions and individual ethics; . . . the economic experience is so personally decisive that the individual must share in its full determination; . . . the economy itself is of such social importance that its major resources and means of production should be open to democratic participation and subject to democratic social regulation.[45]

Surely, this was a definition of work far different from that promoted through the automation discourse. It showed the influence of C. Wright Mills, who in *White Collar* had argued that "work has no intrinsic meaning," good or bad, and that the meaning of work was essentially ideological, and therefore political.[46] More directly, the Port Huron Statement's understanding of work drew on the thought of another prophet of the New Left, Paul Goodman, author of the 1960 surprise bestseller and manifesto of the youth rebellion, *Growing Up Absurd*. Poet, philosopher, playwright, novelist, teacher, pacifist, and hardly a youth in 1960, the forty-nine-year-old Goodman did not share the era's technological optimism, nor did he blame scarcity for the travails of history. He wanted "a more sensible abundance," one that satisfied not only empty stomachs but spiritual hunger. Modern society, he argued, was "lacking enough man's work." In short, he wrote, "There are not enough worthy jobs."[47] Rather than abolish work, Goodman hoped to "make industrial technology humanly important for its workmen." As Arendt had two years earlier, Goodman demanded the reconciliation of freedom and necessity. "Necessity," he wrote, "gives justification."[48] A healthy community offered its young people authentic necessities, real jobs, and genuine duties—not just a mission, but a noble mission. In Goodman's masculinist language: "If there is little interest, honor, or manliness in the working part of our way of life, can we hope for much in the leisure part?" If people decided to, he believed, they could make factory jobs good jobs. If people had a meaningful say over their work, a job would become "man-worthy," whether the necessity was the composition of a poem or the repair of an automobile.[49]

As much as Goodman's line of thought might have informed the authors of the Port Huron Statement, for most of the 1960s only a sliver of the young New Left still saw the industrial shop floor as the decisive battleground of the revolution. Mills's criticism of the "labour metaphysic" held sway. By 1963, Goodman's analysis of work had ceased to persuade the SDS leadership. The automation discourse seemed a better description of reality, especially when authorities on the Left from Galbraith to Marcuse insisted that humanity now possessed the technological capability to eliminate all industrial labor and replace it with either leisure or professional white-collar employment. If in 1962 the Port Huron Statement had hoped to restore "a sense of dignity" to work, a year later both Gitlin and Hayden represented the new take on the subject.[50] The "era of scarcity" was at an end, Gitlin wrote in October 1963. "Now," he continued, "the replacement of human machines by automated machinery makes possible the freeing of men for employment as full persons in the making of society." With the new machines, he argued in the same vein as Ferry and Theobald, "we can be entire unto ourselves. The economic necessity of a crippling constriction is lifted; men become free to assume the general and integrative role of citizen. We will be able to instill liveliness and meaning into the political life of the nation, and to act with effect as individuals."[51] Because machines would labor like slaves to produce biological life, he reasoned, all Americans could finally become full citizens.

Gitlin and Hayden left the October meeting convinced that the United States stood on the verge of a grave economic crisis and that SDS should plan to organize around it. Assuming that "automation" would imminently throw hundreds of thousands of white Americans out of work, organizers flocked to the cities. James Boggs had argued that automation would determine the material preconditions to make Black Americans the agents of historical change in the United States, but SDS leadership believed mass unemployment would make possible an interracial movement of the poor. Black and white Americans both, they hypothesized, would feel the sting of technologically produced unemployment. In 1964 SDS set up thirteen semi-autonomous ERAP cells across the country, with the Chicago, Newark, Boston, and Cleveland cells the most successful and enduring. The organizers had high hopes. "I think most of us had the mass movement idea of change," remembered Cleveland ERAP organizer Dave Strauss. "The Civil Rights Movement . . . the Russian Revolution, sitdown strikes of the '30s. That's how you change things." Because of "automation," argued a working paper authored by Hayden and fellow member of SDS Carl Wittman, "unemployment very definitely is a chronic *threat*, if not yet a reality, to whites." While unions might have protected some of their members from losing their jobs, "automation," Hayden and Wittman believed, meant that "opportunities for youths entering the labor market are completely cut off." These young unemployed people were "the most invisible of the invisible poor." When the "automation" disaster hit the workforce, SDS would be on hand to organize them.[52]

Unfortunately, "automation" failed to arrive at its appointed hour. The masses of unemployed industrial workers kicked off the job by machines did not show up. "We failed, and are still failing, to make a case for the *quantitative* impact of cybernation," Gitlin wrote to the Ad Hoc Committee after a year of organizing with ERAP in Chicago. The Chicago cell had established itself in the hopes of organizing the meatpackers supposedly on the verge of being "automated" out of existence. The president of the packing workers' union, Ralph Helstein, had gone so far as to supply a paid organizer to the ERAP's Chicago settlement in addition to the labor of his own daughter.[53] The current economic reports, Gitlin continued, did not "suffice to indicate the coming of a 'revolution.'" In fact, now that he was on the ground putting the assumptions of the Ad Hoc Committee to the test, he was no longer certain what "automation" meant. "We fail to note how much the new machinery is in fact in the tradition of industrial innovation—as I understand most of the 'automation' in the packing industry is. . . . I suspect," he went on, "we *cannot* make a convincing case for the *existence* of the cybernetic trend." But rather than call it quits for the Triple Revolution right there and then, Gitlin advised that the Ad Hoc Committee shift from making factual claims about the mechanization of work and instead "consider making the *normative* one—men should not be beasts of burden, leisure properly defined and exploited is not useless indolence, etc." In other words, work *should* be abolished, and in theory packinghouse workers should call for more "automation" of their jobs. If, a year earlier, the ERAP contingent in SDS had given up on the meaning of work defended in the Port Huron Statement because of the seemingly inevitable development of industrial progress, now Gitlin argued that activists should *begin* from the point of view that work was incompatible with freedom.[54]

There remained a problem: The poor people whom Gitlin and other members of ERAP hoped to organize did not respond well to promises of mechanized liberation, not when they were, in Gitlin's words to the Ad Hoc Committee, "afflicted with the Protestant ethic so egregiously." They said they wanted to work. Gitlin had expressed as much to Boggs the previous month. "I am more puzzled than you seem to be about the meaning of the Protestant ethic," he wrote, "though not at all about its ugliness, costliness, wastefulness. . . . After spending the summer attempting to organize white unemployed on the North Side of Chicago, I have little doubt that most of these victims of economic frustration want *jobs, not income.*" As far as Gitlin was concerned, these unemployed people suffered from a bad case of false consciousness. "Generally," he said, "work in the old sense is degrading. But that doesn't solve the *organizing* problem when men want jobs." How, he asked, could they counter the Protestant ethic? "How does one transmit the new cultural standard, new definition of work, and new possibility, etc. that must inform the movement? After a summer of work I have no answer beyond the superficial one that we need to develop new forms of political education among the deprived and de-privable."[55] In asking the question, he answered it: Organizers must inform the masses that the definition of work had changed, that the demands of biological necessity were no longer consistent with liberation, and that they clung to a false idol. The sentiment did not quite gibe with SDS's mantra, the imperative that ran on the masthead of *New Left Notes*: "Let the People Decide."

If working people and the unemployed still found meaning in work, it behooved organizers to deal with the institutions that workers already found meaningful, which was precisely what they did. By the end of 1964 ERAP in Chicago, as well as throughout much of the country, moved away from a focus on unemployment and instead, like the settlement house movement of the turn of the twentieth century, organized to compel municipal and state agencies to serve these decidedly underserved communities. Rather than unemployed men forming the backbone of community organizations as JOIN (Jobs or Income Now) had intended, activists discovered that women fighting for the basics of welfare and city services became by and large the most effective leaders. Rather than JOIN, many organizers spoke of GROIN (Garbage Removal or Income Now).[56] By the end of the decade the two extremes would meet and women would come to argue that their work as mothers demanded proper compensation from the state, as we will see in the next chapter.

While many SDS members continued to organize among the poor and unemployed in Northern cities, the escalation of the war in Vietnam drew much of the New Left's attention away from the problem of unemployment and "automation." Running under ideal conditions—the production of war—American industrial capitalism no longer seemed ready to collapse. As an article in *New Left Notes* put it in 1966, "Prosperity of a sort can be bought with Vietnamese and American blood. The war may indeed prevent automa-tion from creating mass unemployment—for a while at least."[57] The campuses exploded as young men vulnerable to the draft fought to save themselves and the country from the quagmire in southeast Asia. The movement splintered along fault lines of race, sex, and revolutionary zeal.

What remained of SDS rallied as best it could. The authors of the "Port Authority Statement" of 1967 intended the document as the successor to the Port Huron Statement, and for a brief period the manifesto seemed to of-fer a theoretically rigorous alternative to the ready-made political analyses imported wholesale from the European Left. But *plus ça change*. Typical of mid-century American thought, it presumed a world of material abundance and insisted that the mechanized abolition of labor was the precondition of freedom, that "automation" was the latest and perhaps last stage in history. In this "new working class theory," the agents of the revolution became college-educated middle-class professionals. While Boggs believed that "automation" would transform unemployed Black Americans into revolutionary agents, the authors of the "Port Authority Statement" contended that "automation" would put the levers of industrial society into the hands of the best-educated. For all intents and purposes, the new working class theory was a left-wing version of the older claim that "automation" would upgrade the entire workforce into white-collar professionals. "Of the issues radical politics is concerned with," said one SDS member, "automation is one most likely to affect us in our daily lives—not for the few years we spend in school, but for the next ten, twenty, thirty years we will spend working for a living."[58] "More and more of them will find their road to the suburbs blocked by an IBM/360 computer," wrote one SDS activist of college students on the path to middle-class employment.[59] For SDS, the new working-class theory raised campus activism to the place of authentic political activity. Increasingly, ideas that had been current through the automation discourse took on the language of Bookchin's "post-scarcity" and even "post-industrialism." Gitlin wrote in support of the new working class theory along these rhetorical lines:

> *Either* the post-scarcity Left comprehends its own unprecedented identity as a social force, grasps its caused-ness, elaborates that identity into vision and program for its own trajectory on the campus and in youth ghettos, uses its reality as a strength from which to encounter anti-colonial and working-class energy to devise common approaches; *or* it turns from its identity, throws the vision out with the narrowness of the class base, and seeks a historically pre-packaged version in which students and déclassé intellectuals are strictly appendages to really 'real' social forces or are either the vanguard or the tail of the really real.[60]

Once again, the assumption that progress meant the mechanized abolition of labor did heavy rhetorical lifting. But now, Gitlin and the authors of the "Port Authority Statement" used a new term to capture the spirit of this phase of human development. Rather than "affluent" and "abundant," they called their world, using Murray Bookchin's formulation, a "post-scarcity" society. Although the enemy might be capitalism, humanity's first adversary was Nature. "Nature imposes limitation over men's capacity to create their own conditions of fulfillment and control their own lives. . . . In this kingdom of necessity, neither liberty nor equality, nor fraternity, were possible." This argument relied entirely on the assumption that the introduction of automation, along with other forms of industrial "rationalizing," would make possible "the social complexion of post-scarcity. The language of post-scarcity is the language of the fulfillment of all social needs and of non-compulsive labor." Whereas the

Port Huron Statement had argued that participatory democracy meant the sharing of meaningful and worthy work, the "Port Authority Statement" dismissed that possibility out of hand. The authors, avowedly more sophisticated than their forbears in 1962, quoted André Gorz's *Strategy for Labor*, attesting to "the social origin and nature of human needs and of the necessarily social character of their satisfaction," but went on to endorse the same story John Diebold had told members of Congress in 1955. "Automation" (or its rhetorical New Left equivalent, cybernation) replaced bodily labor; it destroyed "bad" jobs and created skilled positions in their place. The entire labor force would need to spend more time in school. The dreams of 1950s liberalism returned. "A change that will affect the entire labor force will be increased educational requirements," according to the Port Authority Statement.[61]

Had its leaders not been so quick to accept the automation discourse's denigration of labor, SDS might have had to reconsider its decision to organize outside the labor movement and away from the workplace. Some on the Left had a different idea. Looking at the problem through the maelstrom of the Black freedom struggle, Martin Luther King Jr., for one, was not ready to abandon the meaning of work. Like his contemporaries, King believed that "automation" was a term of technics, not politics. Addressing the Illinois AFL-CIO in 1965, he referred to "automation" as a "destructive hurricane," one that was "sweeping away jobs and work standards." But as others dreamed of a world where a race of robot slaves served human masters, King fostered a different vision of the good life. A liberation theologian immersed in the Social Gospel as well as a lifelong critic of capitalism, King held that "everyone can be great, because everyone can serve." That had been one of Christ's most radical contentions: that to love is to serve. No definition of work could have been farther from the tacit Aristotelianism of the automation discourse, in which the superior being commanded the labor of the inferior so that he might be free of any obligation. Believing that indeed "automation" was on a path to "grind jobs into dust as it grinds our unbelievable volumes of production," still King could not dismiss the activity of work as essentially subhuman, especially when the labor market forced Black Americans into the worst jobs available. Influenced in no small part by Bayard Rustin, King called for both good jobs and a universal basic income; if "automation" did create mass unemployment, King concluded, people at least should have the means to live. But that did not mean work was necessarily the task of the unfree. Instead, King argued, work was unworthy of people only when workers had no power on the job.[62] This was King's message when he flew to Memphis in 1968 to support striking sanitation workers. "You are demanding that this city will respect the dignity of labor," he told an assembly of people who handled garbage for a living:

FIGURE 7. Striking Memphis sanitation workers in 1968, © Dr. Ernest C. Withers, Sr. Courtesy of the Withers Family Trust.

So often we overlook the worth and the significance of those who are not in professional jobs, of those who are not in the so-called big jobs. But let me say to you tonight that whenever you are engaged in work that serves humanity and is for the building of humanity, it has dignity and it has worth. One day our society will come to respect the sanitation worker if it is to survive, for the person who picks up our garbage, in the final analysis, is as significant as the physician, for if he doesn't do his job, diseases are rampant. All labor has dignity.[63]

For post-scarcity thinkers, nature as much as capitalism was the enemy, and industrial "progress" the road to victory. As long as that conviction persisted, so did the automation discourse. While much of the New Left claimed that it was always beneath the dignity of a human being to work, King died defending a different belief—that politics, not biology, made socially necessary tasks inhuman. The sanitation workers themselves insisted as much. In a true democracy, they held, a necessary task became a fully human task. They marched with signs that read, "I *Am* a Man."

6. Slaves in Tomorrowland

The Degradation of Domestic Labor and Reproduction

As the automation discourse forced the New Left to consider the definition of man, it encouraged others to revisit what it meant to be a woman.

In 1951 Robert Heinlein moved the third Mrs. Robert Heinlein, Virginia "Ginny" Gerstenfeld, into the new house he had designed for them. Although he was already recognized as an important writer, the books that would seal Heinlein's legacy as one of the twentieth century's greatest authors of science fiction—*Starship Troopers*, *Stranger in a Strange Land*, *The Moon Is a Harsh Mistress*—all lay ahead of him. His first major speculative venture was, instead, the planning and construction of this house. By training an engineer, not an architect, Heinlein designed the single-story, flat-roofed home to do work. "A House to Make Life Easy," *Popular Mechanics* called it.[1]

"Heinlein's house runs itself with a minimum of maintenance and housework," the magazine reported. Almost all the furniture in Heinlein's house was "built-in," a phrase William Levitt had introduced in 1947 to sell houses in Levittown by offering special features like refrigerators, washing machines, and television sets fitted into the frame of the house.[2] Heinlein preferred the built-in technique, he said, to reduce the amount of time necessary for cleaning, which now would never take more than an hour. In building a home that would make life easy, Heinlein had dictated step by step the work processes that would go on within it, quite literally laying his understanding of housework into the foundation of his home. "The house is sealed," he announced. No one could violate the logic of its original design, not without physically damaging it. Not even the windows could be opened.

Its layout fixed for all time from the moment the first concrete block was laid, Heinlein's house-of-the-future epitomized the trend toward heavy capi-

FIGURE 8. Virginia Heinlein hard at work in a house designed to "make life easy." From Stimson, "A House to Make Life Easy."

talization that became the ruling conception of single-family housing in the postwar period. Arguably the most carefully designed element of the Heinlein house was its kitchen. It connected to the living dining room by means of a communicating interior window. Ginny could set the dining table from the kitchen, dish out the food, and fill the water glasses inches away from the site of their preparation. Then, right from where she stood, she could pass the entire assembly into the dining area. Meal over, one of the Heinleins would send the table floating back to the kitchen, where Ginny could transfer the dishes "directly to the dishwasher." Robert had even built an office for Ginny, "in a corner of the kitchen," where *Popular Mechanics* took a picture of her. In that photograph she holds a telephone receiver to her ear while she rests a hand on a small fold-out desk dominated by a typewriter, a page of loose-leaf already looped into the carriage, next to an oven where one could easily imagine a dinner was cooking that she would place on the dining table and roll away toward up to seven comfortably seated guests. Evidently in the house designed to make life easy Ginny Heinlein was still working hard, although now she worked according to the ingenious design of her husband.[3]

Just as in factories and offices, the automation discourse described house-work and even reproduction as an essentially degraded and degrading activity. Here the automation discourse found itself navigating choppy ideological waters. Those marketing the highly mechanized postwar home depicted housewifery as a woman's natural condition, a healthy expression of her womanhood, while also arguing that the labor of raising children and keeping house were forms of toil from which housewives required technological relief. The attempted resolution of this tension held that if modern machines could remove the drudgery from domestic labor, women could then perform their "natural" functions as household servants joyously. Domestic labor would be pleasant. But for many women performing unpaid domestic service in their homes, the physical reality of those tasks in the postwar period was remarkably similar to that experienced by industrial laborers. Mechanical innovations in the labor process intensified the human labor required to do the job so that now one worker did the job of many, improving productivity while also degrading the activity itself by making it less visible as work.

Like Heinlein, John Diebold devoted a great deal of attention to exactly how labor in his home should be performed; like Heinlein he saw home "automation" as something more than the installation of specific gadgets. When applied to the automobile factory, Ford vice president D. S. Harder had called automation "a new concept—a new philosophy—of manufacturing." For Diebold the same was true of the "automation" of domestic labor, which was, he said, "as much a matter of concepts and philosophies and methods as it will be equipment." The reigning assumption in Diebold's understanding of "automated living" was that domestic work, especially any labor that went toward maintaining bodily survival, was incompatible with a worthwhile human life. According to him, the "automated" home was one where labor processes were built into the structure of the house, making the home itself responsible for the reproduction and maintenance of the family. Practically speaking, this meant Taylorization by another name, the further division of housework into smaller and more overdetermined tasks. But Diebold was right when he said that, when applied to the postwar home, this process signaled a move in the ongoing contest over the "concept" of social reproduction, what it meant in the United States, and how that labor was valued. Diebold's official biographer summed up Diebold's philosophy this way: "Automation in the home, therefore, is more than just mechanization. It is an entire philosophy of living, dedicated to the belief that families have far more important purposes in life than simply attending to all of the little details that sustain them from day to day."[4]

In imagining a home designed to relieve a housewife of domestic labor, Diebold tacitly asserted a view of social reproduction as a task that was necessarily servile. Because "automated" living was still years away, or so he believed, Diebold wrote and had bound several copies of a book for his own home titled

Household Procedures, which he insisted "all his household help" read. The book was a masterpiece of micromanagement. Diebold informed his servants precisely how they should clean, dust, lay out clothing, polish silver, lock the door, set the table, arrange flowers, care for a model ship he had hung on his wall, talk to the other staff in the building, take action in case of fire, report a theft, respond to an accident, serve wine, welcome guests, and act when legal papers were served at the residence. Just as Heinlein designed his home under the assumption that Ginny's efforts were essential to make the kitchen of the future do work, Diebold's conception of the automated home assumed it would operate as though it were a house maintained by a staff of servants all acting according to his detailed instructions. Until household automation could be achieved, Diebold's servants would act as though they were equivalent to what his biographer called the ideal of home automation: "Robot Housekeepers."[5]

Both Heinlein's and Diebold's visions of the future were more products of their own time than prophecies of the future. In 1948 Siegfried Giedion had argued that the mechanization of the home, specifically the single-family home, was fundamentally changing housing design and, consequently, the culture of the house. Looking at the work of utopian visionaries like Buckminster Fuller and the more sober if no less visionary designs of architects writing in *Architectural Forum*, Giedion claimed that the problem of the future would be creating housing plans flexible enough to respond to local needs that still adopted the principle of the "mechanical core," a mechanized center around which the rest of the house would be built. In the postwar period no home could be considered complete unless it boasted certain mechanical amenities. Fuller's idea was to democratize labor-saving appliances by building prefabricated, all-in-one houses that could cheaply and easily be transported anywhere. Giedion was horrified. "Communication with outer space," he wrote, "through a protracted zone (porch), is one of the most attractive features of the American house." With Fuller's mechanical core, the "freedom to alter the ground plan or add to it is abolished, the dweller being imprisoned within the rigid uniform shell. Why? Because in the center, within the mast, sits a robot, the mechanical core, tyrannizing the whole structure." This core, he wrote, "is a token of full mechanization." Designers, therefore, would have to find a way to reconcile freedom, contingency, and adaptability with a mechanized work process that allowed for little deviation from a predetermined pattern. That, argued Giedion, was difficult when the ideal of social reproduction presumed that domestic work was essentially degrading.[6] Taking a slightly less pessimistic view, in a 1955 promotional film sponsored by *Woman's Home Companion* to sell kitchen appliances, the filmmakers called this set-up "the fifth freedom maybe: freedom from unnecessary drudgery. Freedom to go shopping when the urge hits you, or when there's a sale going on."[7] Or as Nancy Reagan, in a televised advertisement for General Electric, confessed to her husband, GE spokesman and future President of the United States of America: "My electric servants do everything."[8]

The immediate postwar period witnessed a housing boom and the explosion of suburban America. The highly mechanized single-family home became the symbol of middle-class arrival. Mechanical contrivances developed during the interwar period and marketed as labor-saving began to find their way into the homes of a majority of Americans. Taking only one major appliance as an example, between 1940 and 1950 the percentage of households boasting a mechanical refrigerator jumped from 44 percent to 80 percent. Homes mass-produced to answer the postwar housing shortage and subsidized by the federal government were now more uniformly embedded in telephone, gas, transportation, and electrical networks. Having gained access to these overlapping grids of power and motion, along with the wages and credit structures to access them, American homeowners introduced ostensibly labor-saving machines to their houses: refrigerators, dishwashers, washing machines, vacuum cleaners, and sundry appliances. But just as Robert Heinlein designed his mechanical home with the presumption that Mrs. Heinlein would be there to do the work, the postwar home became more fully mechanized on the basis of a model that presumed the services of an unpaid housewife ready to operate the new machines. And at the same time builders mechanized millions of homes on that assumption, women were entering the labor market in ever-increasing numbers, jumping from 29 percent to 40 percent of the workforce between 1950 and 1975.[9]

In other words, there remained human servants in the mechanized, "servantless" household. Of course, the isolation of women in the so-called private sphere and the devaluation of their labor there was by no means new to the postwar period. The removal from the home of production for the market that took place over the course of the industrial revolution had done much to code the home as a place of nonwork, despite the near-constant labor of both paid and unpaid workers, usually women. Taking their cue from the industrialization of other forms of labor and its tendency to break up and distribute productive tasks, what Dolores Hayden has called the "material feminists" had, from the end of the nineteenth century and into the 1930s, seen the socialization of domestic labor as crucial to women's liberation. The "grand domestic revolution" they envisioned would have included wages for housework, the collectivization of many basic domestic tasks, community child-rearing, and women's control of their labor. But with the rush to the suburbs and the rise in the price of hired domestic help that began in the

1930s, Americans witnessed the adoption of a different idea of the organization of domestic labor. Rather than women sharing and controlling their remunerated labor, the new home placed the entire burden of housework on the shoulders of a single unpaid woman. Losing sight of an alternative vision of industrial progress in which the material feminists had imagined ways to redefine domestic work—to change the character of the job by socializing it—postwar traditionalists and feminists alike came to believe that the mechanized, single-family home was the inevitable and indisputable next stage of industrial civilization.[10]

The Postwar Robot

The automation discourse functioned in the home as it did in the factory, asserting that the degradation and devaluation of labor constituted progress. As both Susan Strasser and Ruth Schwartz Cowan have argued, despite the promises of the glossy magazines and department store display kitchens, the interwar and postwar mechanization of the home did not free women from housework. Rather, it increased their productivity.[11] At the same time, what Betty Friedan would call the "feminine mystique" took shape, a body of expectations that held that domestic labor was synonymous with femininity and that women should expect to realize their true selves by performing it. But the feminine mystique sat uneasily with the quite different assumption that the arc of history bent toward the full mechanization of the tasks of a housewife. If women were naturally happy homemakers, why mechanize the home at all? At the same time that society excluded women from positions of authority outside the home, the automation discourse coded social reproductive labor as inherently degrading. And, like industrial wage earners who desired meaningful jobs, women who sought to find satisfaction in domestic work struggled against the loss of autonomy that came with mechanization: isolation, loss of control over the labor process, and a monetary and psychological devaluation of the work they performed.

The automation discourse perpetuated the assumption that domestic work was a menial activity. Some, like two-time Democratic Party presidential nominee Adlai Stevenson, saw women's domestic labor as something that saved men from household drudgery. "We are fast approaching the time," said Stevenson, "when machines will perform pretty much every other form of drudgery. . . . Destroying the machine will not halt the march. It never has, not since Adam discovered the advantages of putting a rib to work for him."[12] The prospect of an "automated" home threatened to disembody housework from the body of the housewife. Without the celebration of women's labor in the home, the only meaning of housework that remained in the patriarchal understanding of social reproduction was drudgery. Ray Bradbury expressed the danger the automation discourse posed to the traditional understanding of the patriarchal family in his 1950 short story "The World the Children Made," in which an entirely automatic house, "The Happylife Home," turns a family's children against its parents. "That's just it," says the now useless housewife, Lydia. "I feel like I don't belong here. The house is wife and mother now, and nursemaid."[13] At the story's end the automated house eats the parents. The children, who have come to see the house as their mother, don't care. The mechanization of household drudgery, at least for Bradbury, obviated the necessity of the mother's body and, by extension, the family itself.

The assumption that household labor was in essence a degraded activity found its clearest postwar metaphorical expression in the image of the robot. By means of this mainly literary creation, moderns had discovered a way to represent not only the degraded meaning of domestic work but the beings best suited to perform it. For some, the line between literature and reality tapered to an almost microscopic thinness. Futurist Robert Theobald embraced the prediction made by a professor of engineering who had suggested that "it will be possible during the 1970s to buy an efficient robot 'housemaid' for $2,000, which will set the table, make beds, push a vacuum cleaner, and do other household chores." Daniel Bell, doyen of postwar liberal thought, looked forward to the possibility that by the year 2100 robots would be common, in the words of a study by the RAND Corporation, as "household slaves."[14]

Bell and Theobald were by no means alone in looking forward to the arrival of a race of natural slaves who would perform social reproductive labor. Science fiction, the far from respectable though increasingly popular cultural pulp of the century, expressed these concerns with remarkable insight, and the image of the happy robot house-slave became a staple of the genre. The immediate origins of the robot—the machine as bound worker—lay in the 1920 play *Rossum's Universal Robots*, or *R.U.R.*, by Czech writer Karel Čapek, which received its American premiere in New York in 1922. Čapek coined the word "robot" from the Czech word "robota," meaning forced labor, which traced its origins to the word "rab," or slave.[15] Čapek intended the robot as a metaphor for exploited human workers in an industrial society. His robots were made, not of metal, but engineered flesh, and in *R.U.R.* they rise up and kill their masters.[16]

If in the 1920s the robot served as a metaphor for the dignity of labor and the endurance of the human spirit in the face of industrial exploitation, by the end of World War II it had come to represent the exact opposite. Now the robot symbolized the inherent justice of hierarchy and the essential degradation of bodily labor. As it transformed itself from resentful worker to happy slave, the robot lost its rebellious flesh and became a creature of obedient metal. It was along these lines that Isaac Asimov introduced the three Laws of Robotics in his classic 1950 short story collection *I, Robot*, the first of which was that "it is impossible for a robot to harm a human being" or allow through inaction for a human to be harmed. The two additional laws spell out the fantasy of any humane master of slaves: A robot must obey all orders except when they may result in harm to a human, and a robot must protect its own existence, representing as it does a sizable capital investment.[17]

Asimov's robot stories were thought experiments that elaborated on his three laws, portraying a world made better by the invention of a race of natural slaves constitutionally incapable of rebellion. The negative implications that came with enshrining natural slavery as an ideal did not concern Asimov. In that he was not alone. Newly submissive, classic robots of the golden age of American science fiction proved excellent house servants. The first chapter of *I, Robot* introduced Robbie, a metal nursemaid who was perfect at his job, without a will of his own, and utterly loyal. Likewise there was Robby the Robot from Disney's 1956 film *Forbidden Planet*, who, also made of metal, cared for Dr. Morbius's house on the planet Altair IV—"Why, it's a housewife's dream," remarks a visitor. *The Jetsons*, an animated sitcom of the early 1960s, also boasted a metal robot servant, Rosey, built not only to labor but also to speak like a proletarian maid-of-all-work. In the world of robot servants, human women remained as supervisors, organizing the labor of their mechanical help and themselves fulfilling the role of ideal mothers, sex objects, and gracious hostesses.

For adherents to the automation discourse, the fantasy of the house-slave robot—the combination of a labor-saving, mechanized home and a woman naturally constituted to perform nothing other than household labor—expressed the contradiction between the degradation of domestic labor as an activity befitting only a slave and the expectation that middle-class women would happily perform it. The automation discourse never successfully overcame this contradiction. On one hand, the prospect of the complete mechanization of household labor threatened to make women's traditional role in the home obsolete. On the other, it held out the promise that women might find that same role, now freed from its drudgery, pleasant. An architectural innovation expressed these concerns in that ubiquitous artifact of mid-century suburbanization: the open-plan, ranch-style house.[18]

Just as Heinlein built his house to reduce the work necessary to maintain it and also to make that work the sole responsibility of his wife, the open-plan house hoped to collapse natural womanhood into domestic work. In doing so, it could obscure the value of domestic labor as work behind a veneer of spontaneous, unalienated, feminine expression. In the mid-1930s Frank Lloyd Wright began designing homes that effaced the boundary between the kitchen and living room, best exemplified by his 1940 Gregor Affleck House, built just outside Detroit. According to Siegfried Giedion, the abolition of the border between living space and what Wright called the "work space" implied that domestic work was no longer something shameful, that "cooking need no longer be done behind closed doors, hidden from the eyes of the family or from guests."[19]

Under other circumstances, this acknowledgment of domestic labor might have proved a step forward in the realization of its democratization. But in coding the activity as essentially feminine, ironically, the open-plan house could also perpetuate the notion of that work as something other than work. In the most immediate and literal sense, revealing the kitchen to the rest of the house could become a tacit assertion of sexist presumptions that the domestic work now visible was not an activity for which a person should receive paid compensation. Rather, that labor could now be read as the spontaneous and natural expression of a respectable, feminine woman living the good life. For example, in 1945 the architect Raymond Fordyce saw only convenience in the open plan, which made "the kitchen an active center of household life, where a family can work, play, eat, and spend 90% of its working time and where, most important, a housewife can watch children and entertain without leaving her work."[20] Betty Friedan described the innovation differently: "The open plan also helps expand the housework to fill the time available. In what is basically one free-flowing room, instead of many rooms separated by walls and stairs, continual messes continually need picking up." Visiting a friend who had once been a writer but had given it up to become a full-time housewife, Friedan thought "the gorgeous mahogany and stainless steel of her custom-built kitchen cabinets and electric appliances were indeed a dream, but when I saw that house, I wondered where, if she ever wanted to write again, she would put her typewriter."[21] If only Friedan had read *Popular Mechanics*, she'd have been familiar with the Heinlein home and would have known: It could be stuck in a corner of the kitchen.

Critics in the 1950s regarded the mechanization of the American house—its transformation into a node plugged into the many power networks of industrial production—as a radical redefinition of the home's meaning. Rather than question how domestic work could be reorganized so that it was consistent with freedom and personal satisfaction, those who took for granted the inevitability of technological development instead lamented that the degradation of housework appeared to be an inevitable byproduct of progress. According to this logic, the most serious burden of living in the postwar house was bearing with its meaninglessness, for no inherently valuable activity took place inside the home. In the early 1950s the landscape critic J. B. Jackson provided a vivid expression of this line of thought. Whereas the American home had once served as the locus of socially valued activity, and work in particular, Jackson argued, now it functioned only as a place where individuals in a nuclear family stopped temporarily to recharge their vital energies before re-emerging into the outside world where meaning might still be found. To that end Jackson called the modern house a "transformer." A transformer, he explained, neither increased nor decreased the energy in a system but merely changed its shape. With domestic labor understood as mere drudgery toward the end of sustaining mere physical perpetuation, Jackson argued, the postwar home "demands no loyalty which might be in conflict with loyalty to the outside world." Humane, meaningful activity took place outside its walls: the "earning of daily bread"; the education of children; medical care; and the production and preparation of food. Rather than blame the political conditions surrounding domestic work as degrading, the new conception of household labor presumed that the work of making a home was, in essence, beneath human dignity.[22]

Ironically, the mechanization of the single-family home did not seem to Jackson actually to reduce the amount of work a housewife performed. Instead, it simultaneously intensified and degraded it. Even when sumptuously appointed, the home meant only the bare minimum. Of course, many middle-class women of the period, as Betty Friedan so eloquently documented, sought to prove their worth to themselves and the world by domestic labor, seeking to make their lives meaningful by dedicated service to their families. Some did so successfully. Others could not. Their efforts to find satisfaction through labor in a house that appeared to them as Jackson's "transformer" led to acute psychic anguish. The anomie engendered by the methods of social reproduction built in to the single-family mechanized home likewise inspired literary protest. Books denouncing the supposedly soul-crushing conformity of suburban life such as John Keats's 1956 *Crack in the Picture Window* and Richard Yates's 1961 *Revolutionary Road* gained increasing cultural purchase. And a new cliché began to take root in American cultural life: the freestanding suburban home as meaningless hell.[23]

Liberal and Radical Feminists Adopt the Automation Discourse

The same assumptions about meaningless work in meaningless homes informed feminists who called for rebellion, foremost among them Betty Friedan. Although the 1963 publication of *The Feminine Mystique* inspired a

generation of feminists, more recently Friedan's articulation of women's liberation has come in for criticism on the grounds that the vision of freedom she
imagined applied only to middle-class white women. The "problem that has
no name," the plight of the middle-class housewife, was not quite the same
as that faced by working-class women who both cared for their homes and
also worked for wages, or women of color who, besides suffering carceral
working conditions on the job and at home, lived under the oppression of
American racism. The explanation for Friedan's privileging of the privileged
has been that she only cared about the difficulties of educated, white suburban
women. Perhaps. Some have also wondered whether the former journalist for
the communist United Electrical Workers, like many postwar liberals, denied
her earlier enthusiasm for proletarian liberation either because she was disillusioned or to save herself from the witch hunts of McCarthyism. Also likely.
But there is a tendency within Friedan's argument itself that explains the small
tent of her feminism, one bound up in the automation discourse's dismissal
of bodily labor as incompatible with freedom.[24]

Friedan's feminist criticism remained searing and revolutionary within its
limits, and at first blush *The Feminine Mystique* reads as a defense of meaningful work in an age dedicated to its abolition. Sexist hiring practices had closed
off the middle and upper levels of the labor market to women, Friedan argued;
sex disqualified women from holding positions of power. Women's liberation
meant a good job outside the home. It seemed as though Friedan rejected
the equation of "freedom" and "leisure." This made sense, for if any class of
people in the postwar period came anywhere close to living the "leisure" life,
it was white middle-class housewives. And yet, according to Friedan, it was
awful. "I'm looking for something to satisfy me," one housewife told Friedan.
"I think it would be the most wonderful thing in the world to work, to be useful." Another confided, "I feel so empty somehow, useless, as if I don't exist"
One housewife admitted, "At times I feel as though the world is going past my
door while I just sit and watch." True, Friedan said, many housewives were
overworked, but none of their work was "quite as real, quite as necessary" as
it seemed. For those she interviewed, Friedan wrote, "the problem seemed
to be not that too much was asked of them, but too little." In other words,
"housewifery expands to fill the time available."[25] Perhaps this was why the
report of the President's Commission on the Status of Women, published the
same year as *The Feminine Mystique*, suggested that as part of an education
in home management young women should study subjects such as "the uses
of family leisure," so that they might know what to do with their empty free
time.[26] Housework was like junk food, Friedan argued. It had no real value. It
could not satisfy. But because housewives lived in a world that allowed them

no other activity, they continually tried to gain some measure of satisfaction by creating more make-work for themselves, by gorging on emptiness.

Often lost in the standard glossing of *The Feminine Mystique* is Friedan's argument that technological progress was to blame for making domestic work obsolete for middle-class housewives. She saw the postwar mechanization of the home as progress, and therefore "to live according to the feminine mystique depends on a reversal of history, a devaluation of human progress." Housework was no longer necessary, Friedan implied, and it was wrong for women to answer the call of necessities that machines now handled. This argument was a commonplace at the time. "To the extent that women who want jobs to combat boredom will not be able to get them," wrote Donald N. Michael a year earlier in his much-publicized *Cybernation*, "there will be a growing leisure class that will be untrained for and does not want the added leisure . . . they will have less and less to do at home as automated procedures further routinize domestic chores." The "scientific advance" that Friedan and many liberal progressives believed would save women from domestic drudgery also appeared to them to increase its meaninglessness. Deprived of a "function in society at the level of her own ability," Friedan concluded, the mechanized home left women "without any function at all."[27]

In addition to Friedan's understanding of technological progress, her definition of work was likewise typical of the postwar period. For her, the source of the problem that had no name was not that the organization of domestic labor went unrecognized and unremunerated but, rather, that all housework in and of itself was incompatible with freedom. Both the space of the home and the domestic labor that occurred within it, Friedan believed, were beneath the dignity of a full human subject. Instead, she argued that housework was suited for undeveloped human minds and cited an old study affirming that "housework was suited to the capacities of feeble-minded girls. In many towns, inmates of institutions for the mentally retarded were in great demand as houseworkers, and housework was much more difficult then than it is now." Friedan believed that social reproductive labor was beneath women, not because it was organized to accommodate patriarchy, but because in essence it was a subhuman task.[28]

While a certain kind of meaningful work spelled freedom for Friedan, she did not necessarily mean industrial wage work. She was not so bold as to call the wage work performed by many working-class American men freedom, because, she argued, "work that does not fully use a man's capacities leaves in him a vacant, empty need for escape—television, tranquilizers, alcohol, sex." Middle-class men, however, seemed engaged in meaningful work, "work that demanded ability, responsibility, and decision." An ungenerous reading of *The Feminine Mystique* would understand Friedan's position as a demand that privileged women be allowed to benefit more fully from inequality, just as privileged men were. But when Friedan compared the futility of housework to more worthwhile activity, she did not celebrate the chance to reign at the top of the social hierarchy. Instead, she understood worthwhile work as what Pieper or Bell would have called, ironically, the fruits of leisure, leisure in the Aristotelian sense—activity that was an end in itself, beyond the mere making of life, or as Friedan put it: "splitting atoms, penetrating outer space, creating art that illuminates human destiny, pioneering on the frontiers of society."[29]

If middle-class housewives had too little to do, why couldn't they make more of their leisure? Certainly the millions of women who entered the labor force in mid-century America, like millions of men, did not spend their days splitting atoms or building rocket ships or composing symphonies. If Friedan was correct and middle-class housewives had too much time on their hands, why weren't they all busy giving life to masterpieces of Western civilization, as the leisure theorists said they should have been? Why were they instead trapped in a "comfortable concentration camp"? Because, we may conclude, it was not biological necessity that oppressed them, but injustice. It was not housework that kept women from "free participation in the world as an individual," but the sexist organization of housework that reduced their entire being to a set of chores whose necessity appeared beyond question. Central to the sexist organization of housework was its degradation to the activities befitting a robot or a person who was intellectually challenged, along with the reigning assumption that anyone who performed this work could perform *only* this work, rather than share it equally with men and children so that all could likewise share the advantages it produced. Or, even more radically, decide that the chore should not exist at all.[30]

Friedan's denigration of housework had serious consequences. In writing off domestic labor as subhuman work, she also disregarded the people not fortunate enough to escape that labor. In her contribution to the 1970 anthology *Sisterhood Is Powerful*, Beverly Jones made precisely this point: "If, as is often said, women are being automated out of the home, it is only to be shoved into the car chauffeuring children to innumerable lessons and activities, and that dubious advantage holds only for middle and upper-class women who generally can afford not only gadgets but full-or part-time help." Now, "as always," Jones wrote, comparing women's household labor under patriarchal conditions to the actions of a robot, "the most automated appliance in a household is the mother."[31] The shortcomings of Friedan's approach remained clear by the century's end as American women continued to find themselves shouldering the double shift of wage work and housework, the first often poorly compensated and the latter not at all. Except, of course, when the two were the same, and domestic workers, for the most part women of color, continued to fight an uphill battle by means of unions and legal protections for recognition of the fact that housework should be properly valued.[32] Friedan, not unsympathetic to the travails of working-class women, still could not bring them along in her program of liberation, not when the oppressor was as much work as it was sexism.

That definition of work, perpetuated across political allegiances by means of the automation discourse, appealed not only to liberal feminists like Friedan but also to a growing cohort of self-proclaimed radical feminists. Along with Kate Millet's *Sexual Politics*, Shulamith Firestone's 1970 book *The Dialectic of Sex* served as one of the movement's keystone theoretical works. No one could mistake the radical feminist movement of the late 1960s and early 1970s for the liberal feminism of Friedan and the organization she helped found, the National Organization of Women (NOW). Friedan's NOW hoped to reform the existing institutions of American lawmaking and moneymaking so that both might become true meritocracies, fair hierarchies based on honest appraisals of individual merit, regardless of sex. The radical feminist movement, however, coming out of the cultural and political ferment of the civil rights and student movements of the previous decade, called instead for a truly equal society. Liberal feminists saw sexism as an aberration, a grievous contradiction in American values. Radical feminists argued the opposite: Sexism, like racism, went right to the heart of modern society and implicated every major institution. While many feminists on the Left believed sexism was a product of capitalist exploitation, one that would wither away with capitalism's overthrow, radical feminists understood sexism as a deep-seated phenomenon in and of itself that worked in tandem with capitalism to oppress women. As Ellen Willis described it: "The American system consists of two interdependent but distinct parts—the capitalist state, and the patriarchal family."[33]

Firestone was one of the pivotal theoretical architects of radical feminism. For three crucial years in New York she helped lay the foundations of the movement as both an intellectual tradition and a political program. In her often frustrated search for an organization that would bring together a materialist explanation of sexism and disciplined political action, she established New York Radical Women with Pam Allen in 1967, Redstockings with Ellen Willis two years later, and at the end of 1969 the New York Radical Feminists with Anne Koedt. She never found what she was looking for. By the end of 1970, at the age of twenty-five, she was out of the movement. But though she might have walked away, on her way out she left something behind, *The Dialectic of Sex*. Part philosophical treatise, part manifesto, the book remains an ambitious attempt to reinterpret the history of modernity by placing sexism at its core. If Marx flipped Hegel on his head, Firestone turned Marx inside out. Capitalist oppression did not lead to sexism, she argued; capitalist oppression was the *result* of sexism. The first division of labor between man and woman had served as the model for every other division of labor that followed, as well as every other form of exploitation. The family, she agreed with John Stuart Mill, was the first school of injustice. To set all people free, she concluded (unlike John Stuart Mill), revolutionaries would need to overthrow the family. While liberal feminists hoped to bring women into the major institutions of the United States by making them equal to men, and while the cultural feminists wanted to celebrate femininity as superior to masculinity, Firestone wished to destroy the usefulness of the distinction of sex altogether. In an equal society, she argued, men and women would not be equal. Indeed, the terms "man" and "woman" would cease to hold any political meaning whatsoever. Maleness or femaleness would be as politically significant as a person's shoe size.[34]

When he testified before Congress in 1955 on the subject of "automation" in the automobile industry, Walter Reuther had told lawmakers: "You know, you can automate the production of automobiles, but consumers are still made, thank God, in the old-fashioned way. This is our trouble, this is our trouble, this is our trouble."[35] The Congressmen laughed. Fifteen years later Firestone agreed that the old-fashioned way of making consumers was her trouble too, but she saw nothing funny in it. The cause of women's oppression, she asserted, was biologically determined. Specifically, it was women's child-bearing capacity that made them vulnerable to exploitation. It followed inexorably that men took advantage of this vulnerability. Therefore, the only way to liberate women from oppression was, she wrote, "to free humanity from the tyranny of its biology."[36]

While it might have seemed an unacceptable concession to sexists for Firestone to argue that women were by nature subject to masculine domination, from the point of view prevalent in 1970 Firestone's biological determinism made a certain sense. In 1969 Redstockings had taken up the legalization of abortion as its first major cause, distinguishing itself from the liberal pack by demanding a woman's unequivocal right to choose. Redstockings took a strong line, claiming that a woman had an uninfringeable right to control her own body, full stop. "Our first target," Ellen Willis remembered, "was the 'reformers' who sat around splitting hairs over how sick or poor or multiparous a pregnant woman had to be to deserve exemption from reproductive duty.'" And "duty" was precisely how Firestone understood biological reproduction. It was work, or, not to put too fine a point on it, labor.[37]

For a woman to be free, Firestone argued, her body needed to belong to her. But as long as the survival of the species required that women bear children, women's bodies would always remain a social rather than a private resource. For this reason, she wrote, pregnancy itself was "barbaric." Not merely an unwanted pregnancy, she argued, but the very capacity to become pregnant rendered a woman uniquely vulnerable to oppression. "Pregnancy," she said, "is the temporary deformation of the body of the individual for the sake of the species." As Aristotle had argued two thousand years earlier, Firestone assumed that the patriarchal family was the natural, basic unit of the species. Only when reproduction took place outside a woman's body, then, only when it was "automated" and the labor left to machines, would society have the practical ability to do away with women's oppression. A revolutionary generation needed to seize control of the means of both production and reproduction, Firestone argued, and use machines to do away with all forms of labor: "The division of labour," she wrote, "would be ended by the elimination of labour altogether (through cybernetics). The tyranny of the biological family would be broken." Escaping biology would lead to the dissolution of the patriarchal family, for Firestone assumed the two to be the same, and with its destruction would go the taproot of all injustice. Only by leaving the demands of the human body behind through "cybernation," Firestone held, would humanity clear the way for "a fully human condition."[38]

Firestone was not alone among radical feminists in her belief that machines would allow women to gain freedom by escaping the demands of the body. A year before she put a bullet in Andy Warhol, Valerie Solanas demanded in her self-published *SCUM Manifesto* (the treatise of the Society for Cutting up Men) that society "institute complete automation and destroy the male sex."[39] Half in jest, one imagines, half in dire earnest, Solanas demanded that the bottom rail be put on top. While it remains unclear what precisely she meant by the "automation" of the male sex, Solanas anticipated much of the "cybernetic communism" that Firestone would flesh out three years later in which not only human reproduction but all work was achieved by machines:

> The elimination of money and the complete institution of automation are basic to all other SCUM reforms; without these two the others can't take place; with them the others will take place very rapidly. The government will automatically collapse. With complete automation it will be possible for every woman to vote directly on every issue by means of an electronic voting machine in her house. Since the government is occupied entirely with regulating economic affairs and legislating against purely private matters, the elimination of money and with it the elimination of males who wish to legislate "morality" will mean that there will be practically no issues to vote on.[40]

For Solanas, the "automation" of men also spelled escape from the female body for women themselves. She urged that "the female" should "condition away her sex drive, leaving her completely cool and cerebral and free to pursue truly worthy relationships and activities." When the female "transcends her body, rises above her animalism" Solanas wrote, "the male, whose ego consists of his cock, will disappear." Not all radical feminists agreed that sexism arose as a necessary consequence of sexual reproduction, but at the Sandy Springs meeting of radical feminists in August 1968, Roxanne Dunbar, of Boston's Cell 16, read passages of the *Manifesto* aloud and said it was "the essence of feminism."[41]

Unlike many other postwar advocates of "automation," however, Firestone was no technological determinist. The mere ability to mechanize human reproduction would not itself usher in the revolution. Rather, the technological capacity to do so was an indispensable precondition of revolution. The revolution that Firestone imagined would culminate in a socialist "cybernetic" economy where the proletariat would seize the machines and then "redistribute drudgery equitably, but eventually eliminate it altogether." From then on, Firestone wrote, "cybernation would take care of most domestic chores."[42] Rather than schools, people would attend "non-compulsory 'learning centres'" staffed by "teaching machines," a goal she shared with R. Buckminster Fuller, who in 1961 had told the planning committee of the Southern Illinois University, Carbondale, that students would ideally learn by means of "impersonal tools" that would convey knowledge that was "decontaminated," freed of a human teacher's prejudice, knowledge that would be "piped" directly into a student's home so that he or she would have no need to risk the influence of other people. ("I am quite confident," Fuller said on that occasion, "that humanity is born with its total intellectual capability already on inventory and that human beings do not add anything to any other human being in the way of faculties and capacities.")[43] Firestone's utopia was a hyperindividualistic world practically without any society at all, one where no one owed anything to anyone. "Each individual would contribute to the society as a whole," she wrote, "not for wages or other incentives of prestige and power, but because the work he chose to do interested him in itself, and perhaps only incidentally because it had a social value for others." Firestone called this "healthily selfish." Rather than imagine a way to make socially necessary activity also personally rewarding, to open the definition of social necessity to negotiation, she had in mind a static understanding of certain kinds of work as essentially demeaning. In a cybernetic communist world, she imagined, "Work that had only social value and no personal value would have been eliminated by the machine."[44]

Firestone saw little distinction to be made between workers' control and the escape from work. She did not consider the possibility that a society committed to equality could organize the labor of reproduction so that the burdens of childbearing could be made consistent with a free subject. Like Friedan, she relied on the possibility that a technological solution would eliminate the usefulness of the sex distinction, politically and biologically. As radical as Firestone's analysis was, it relied on the same understanding of work that was common across much of the American political landscape after World War II. Her biological determinism lay just as much in her ideas of the meaning of work as it was in her understanding of sex. She did not argue that mechanized pregnancy was one way among many to organize the labor of reproduction equitably. There is no reason to disagree with Firestone that a society could mechanize reproduction as one means of achieving universal freedom and equality. For her, it was the only way. In her analysis, bodily necessity rather than politics was the source of political oppression. No combination of rewards and privileges, no system of rights and prerogatives could ever result in a society where the necessity of childbearing did not contradict the possibility of a world both equal and free.

Defending the Value of Labor as a Means to Achieve Women's Liberation

Not all critics of the postwar organization of domestic work subscribed to the automation discourse and its devaluation of social reproductive labor. In the late 1960s and early 1970s an alternate understanding of labor and women's liberation came to the fore, one that was more reminiscent of the material feminists of the turn of the twentieth century and that aimed to reconcile the demands of necessity with political freedom. Unlike the feminists looking for a technological fix to sexism, the women receiving public assistance who made up the membership of the National Welfare Rights Organization (NWRO), most of them of African descent, did not believe that the labor of reproducing the species was a subhuman task.

With its founding in 1966, the NWRO had sought to organize mothers on welfare to help them gain better access to the benefits of citizenship. Since the New Deal, Aid to Families with Dependent Children (AFDC) had provided welfare assistance to impoverished families, primarily mothers. As welfare rolls expanded in the mid-1960s with the worsening economic crunch of the late postwar period, state governments faced the increased financial strain of providing for rising numbers of recipients, and soon enough virtually all interested parties agreed that welfare required reform. Since the mid-1960s, a government-provided guaranteed income had been the welfare reform of choice among many critics of the welfare system, appealing to intellectuals as different as Robert Theobald of the Ad Hoc Committee on the Triple Revolution and neoliberal Milton Friedman. By the late 1960s the NWRO, too, called for a guaranteed annual income. As women came to constitute a larger share of the workforce, welfare policy aimed to push them more aggressively into the labor market by connecting welfare benefits to work requirements. With divorce rates on the rise and people of color in the urban North increasing their representation among welfare recipients (although they were not the majority), the state began to make its welfare policies more punitive.

For example, the 1967 Social Security Amendments federalized the morality and sexuality qualifications for welfare that were present in many states and which gave government officials the power to deny aid to women they perceived as failing to meet their standard of feminine virtue. Repealed in 1969 before they could go into effect, the amendments nevertheless signaled a sea change in American welfare policy. Also in 1967, Congress passed the Work Incentive Program (WIN), which stipulated that to continue receiving benefits, women in AFDC with school-age children had either to take a job or go through job training. With these changes, AFDC began to make manifest for welfare mothers a tension present in all wage relationships under conditions of capitalism, in which commodified labor must be bartered in a market. Degraded work could not persist where men and women had alternative, less exploitative means of subsistence. Historically, the threat of utter immiseration pushed vulnerable people into the worst jobs. Cutting off subjects from the sources of life (as in, for example, the progressive alienation of people from farming and the land over the course of the century) had pushed people from self-directed subsistence into degraded and exploitative wage labor. Work requirements for welfare recipients wrote that de facto reality into law. It was for this reason that the National Welfare Rights Organization organized: to divorce welfare from employment.[45]

Although contemporaneous with Firestone's *Dialectic of Sex*, the NWRO's alternative vision of women's liberation was radically different. Instead of calling for "automation," it focused its activity on the Nixon administration's proposed welfare reform package, the Family Assistance Program, a plan that, had it ever been passed into law, would have provided a family of four a guaranteed annual income of $1,600. The plan dissolved the distinction between "dependent" families and the "working poor." Why precisely Nixon, a Republican, supported FAP is a subject of much historical controversy. However, had it gone into effect it most likely would have been an important first step toward removing the stigma from welfare benefits in the United States.[46]

Nevertheless, even as Nixon called on Congress to replace AFDC with a guaranteed annual income, he hoped to assuage the suspicions of Republican conservatives by demonizing welfare recipients and by associating welfare with racist stereotypes. On the Right, employers who relied on cheap labor feared that a government subsidy to the working poor would allow exploited workers to abstain from selling their labor on the market. The executive vice president of the U.S. Chamber of Congress wrote to Nixon in 1970 that he feared that "work incentives would be weakened" if workers had a source of income that was not a wage.[47] In other words, bad jobs would have to become better jobs if they were to attract workers, or those jobs would cease to exist. It was along just these lines that Senator Russell Long of Louisiana exclaimed, "I can't get anybody to iron my shirts!" and, in a similar vein, Georgia representative Phillip Landrum complained: "There's not going to be anybody left to roll these wheelbarrows and press these shirts. They're all going to be on welfare."[48] In the hopes of calming the right wing of his own party, Nixon returned again and again to the inviolability of the work ethic. In his Labor Day speech in 1972 he warned, "We are faced this year with the choice between the 'work ethic' that built this Nation's character and the new 'welfare ethic' that would cause that American character to weaken."[49] Or as he said in the privacy of the Oval Office when discussing with his chief of staff and domestic affairs advisor how to portray the reform to the American people: "But it's work, work. Throw them off the rolls. That's the whole deal."[50]

The Family Assistance Program, like AFDC, contained work requirements. But while Nixon invoked the sanctity of work as a way to limit welfare benefits, those who would have been the direct beneficiaries of the Family Assistance Program, namely, poor mothers, invoked work as a meaningful practice in order to argue for *more* benefits than the reform provided. The NWRO's members stood at a disadvantage in a labor market committed to both sexist and racist exclusion, and the work requirements of welfare shone a light on a mechanism of social control that usually remained obscure: that to access the means of life, the state required a worker to enter a hierarchy, often at the bottom rung.

The life and activism of Johnnie Tillmon, chairwoman and executive director of the NWRO, testified to the injustices that underlay the normal functioning of the American labor market. Born to sharecroppers in Scott, Arkansas, at the height of the Jim Crow era, she had performed the labors demanded of a poor, rural Black woman: She picked cotton and took in laundry for a white man. Arriving in California in the late 1950s, she found work ironing shirts. She joined the labor movement, organizing her co-workers, who then elected her their shop steward. It was only after an illness and unexpected hospitalization that Tillmon was forced to consider the politics of welfare. Unable to work and needing to take care of her daughter, she encountered a welfare system designed to degrade and shame its ostensible beneficiaries.

Tillmon's experience was typical. Caseworkers went through her refrigerator and demanded an accounting of when and why men visited her home. The price of welfare was humiliation.

Applying the craft of organizing that she practiced in the labor movement, Tillmon began organizing welfare recipients. A few years later, as the NWRO's leader, she explained how the designers of welfare intentionally tailored it to be both demeaning and insufficient. "There are some ten million jobs that now pay less than the minimum wage," she wrote, "and if you're a woman, you've got the best chance of getting one. Why would a 45-year-old woman work all day in a laundry ironing shirts at 90-some cents an hour? Because she knows there's some place lower she could be. She could be on welfare." For Tillmon, welfare needed to be embarrassing, hard, and terrifying in order to discipline a degraded workforce. "Society needs women on welfare as 'examples' to let every woman, factory workers and housewife workers alike, know what will happen if she lets up, if she's laid off, if she tries to go it alone without a man." For that reason, the NWRO argued that welfare should be a right regardless of a recipient's job-holding status. It should have no work requirement. Otherwise, it became a stick with which state authorities drove people into exploitation.[51]

Opponents of welfare reform, and even some of its allies, like Nixon, publicly shamed welfare recipients for lacking the proper work ethic. In response, defenders of welfare recipients' moral integrity went to great lengths to prove that poor Americans wanted to work, by which they meant, to hold waged employment outside the home. The Brookings Institution's 1972 volume *Do the Poor Want to Work?* argued that poor people desired formal employment as much as middle-class professionals did. Less important to the statisticians who came to this conclusion was whether mothers on welfare *already* understood themselves to be working.[52]

To that end, NWRO mothers took a different tack, arguing that the work requirements of both AFDC and FAP were actually employment requirements. They were especially onerous because mothers on welfare, though not always employed, were in fact currently working, and working quite hard. They maintained their homes and raised children, labor that society either ignored entirely or took for granted as the consequence of a woman's natural essence. Either way, that work went undervalued. "Motherhood—whether the mother is married or not—is a role which should be fully supported, as fully rewarded, as fully honored, as any other," argued a group of welfare activists in Boston. Johnnie Tillmon called for the President of the United States to issue "a proclamation that women's work is *real* work." She insisted that mothers should be paid "a living wage for doing the work we are already doing—child raising and housekeeping." Cassie Downer, chair of the Milwaukee County

Welfare Rights Organization, explained: "A guaranteed adequate income will recognize work that is not now paid for by society. I think that the greatest thing that a woman can do is to raise her own children, and our society should recognize it as a job. A person should be paid an adequate income for that."[53]

This was a far cry from Betty Friedan's description of the home as a comfortable concentration camp fit only for the mentally handicapped. She had defined domestic labor as essentially meaningless. The mothers of the NWRO, on the other hand, defined it as deeply meaningful because it contributed to the reproduction of society. "Up until now," wrote Johnnie Tillmon in *Ms.*, "we've been raised to expect to work, all our lives, for nothing. Because we are the worst educated, the least-skilled, and the lowest-paid people there are. Because we have to be almost totally responsible for our children. Because we are regarded by everybody as dependents." The reason mothers worked for nothing, Tillmon argued, was not that the activity of mothering and keeping a house was worthless or a less-than-human task, as Friedan and Firestone had maintained. Rather, women received nothing for it because society had systematically oppressed and degraded them so that they were not in a position to demand that their contribution receive its proper recognition. Biological necessity did not stand between Tillmon and freedom, she argued. Politics did. Other people did.[54]

Some left-wing theorists followed the lead of the welfare rights movement. Joan Jordan, a white, working-class member of the Socialist Workers' Party and a contributor to leftist publications like *Radical America*, expanded on the NWRO's call for a guaranteed annual income. In order to make household labor and reproduction consistent with freedom, she argued, women needed access to free public daycare, legalized abortion, planned parenthood centers, a shortened workday for both mothers and fathers, and three to five years of guaranteed parental leave for both parents (during which time parents would work in the public daycare centers that supported their own children), as well as the "reorganization of home chores by application of mass production methods," just as textile production had been removed from the home and industrialized. Above all, wrote Jordan, women needed a paycheck for the work of motherhood, "making it as important as any other form of labor. . . . It would recognize that having children is a part of the socially necessary labor in the reproduction of life."[55] Rather than "automate" away the labor of motherhood and maintaining a family, some radical feminists sought to humanize the labor—to organize the political and material conditions surrounding that necessity so that it would be consistent with freedom.

Silvia Federici's 1975 "Wages Against Housework" constituted the most notable theoretical effort along these lines. Federici, a participant in the Marxist

Autonomist movement arising from Italian *operaismo* communism, a movement emphasizing the importance of worker militancy as a source of radical change, had since the early 1970s organized with the International Wages for Housework Campaign. In order to achieve women's liberation across the board, Federici wrote, household labor and caring for a family needed to be more highly valued, not less. Tillmon had made this argument three years earlier when she called the mothers of the National Welfare Rights Organization "the front-line troops of women's freedom." Federici wanted to abolish certain social roles. Just as the "job" of being a slave had been abolished in the nineteenth century, so, too, should the position of "housewife" cease to exist. Simply demanding wages for housewifery, Federici argued, would help achieve this aim: "It is the demand by which our nature ends and our struggle begins," she wrote, "because just to want wages for housework means to refuse that work as the expression of our nature, and therefore to refuse precisely the female role that capital has invented for us." Demanding the appropriate valuation of labor was the first step, ironically, in refusing it, "because the demand for a wage makes our work visible, which is the most indispensable condition to begin to struggle against it, both in its immediate aspect as housework and its more insidious character as femininity." Valorization through recognition, rather than alienation by way of "automation," would be the means to make women's labor in the United States consistent with political freedom. Until the question of social necessity was visible as a controversial issue, political actors could not negotiate over it. This was not the feminine mystique by another name. Far from a cynical ploy to force women into servitude, the demand to respect social reproductive labor was a way to redefine the very meaning of social necessity.[56]

In many ways, Federici's conception of the meaning of domestic labor opposed that held by many rank-and-file members of the NWRO. In the pursuit of a wage for their labor, mothers on welfare could invoke the sanctity of motherhood and family life, and no doubt they often found the sentimental justification of motherhood meaningful.[57] Federici, on the other hand, believed that identifying oneself as a housewife was a fate "worse than death." But with the intensifying economic pain of stagflation and a rise in worker militancy across the industrialized world in the mid-1970s, the automation discourse was on the wane. By 1975 the "automation" of housework no longer appeared imminent or even possible. Doubts concerning technological progress and the all-too-visible activism of workers themselves, like the mothers of the NWRO, no longer allowed attentive feminist theorists to assume that the mechanized home would soon do all the work. Workers had made their hitherto invisible labor publicly obvious. Thinkers concerned with winning women's liberation needed to imagine a way to make domestic labor consistent with a full human life.

The automation discourse, with its assumptions of technological progress and its denigration of work, had a crucial theoretical influence on the postwar women's movement. Both the liberal Freidan and the radical Firestone premised women's liberation on escape from domestic work and the labor of the body. Believing that the inevitable tendency of industrial society was the mechanical abolition of all bodily labor and blaming biological necessity for women's oppression seemed consistent with a program of universal liberation. These pivotal works of both liberal and radical feminism premised their visions of autonomy on the understanding that a free person did not perform bodily labor and perhaps was also free of all demands of social necessity. In embracing the automation discourse, Friedan and Firestone saw no way to reconcile necessity and freedom, no way to be free here and now or to hold oppressors accountable through redistributing present rather than future powers. In subscribing to a program of liberation that left behind the burdens of the body, they inadvertently left behind the women, many of them people of color, still performing low-wage and unpaid labor. Not until the mid-1970s would it become apparent that behind "automation" human beings continued to labor, that all too often Robby the Robot, far from a being of unfeeling metal, had remained all along a creature of flesh and blood.

7. Where Have All the Robots Gone?
From Automation to Humanization

Paul Goodman took heart in 1970 when he observed that the people walking the streets of New York were still human beings and not robots. They did not seem, he wrote, "less human, less people, than when I was an adolescent nearly fifty years ago. . . . They do not look the least bit more robotized." At the time, this counted as something of a discovery. For years Goodman had been one of a chorus of thinkers who criticized modern life as "dehumanizing."[1] When in 1959 C. Wright Mills sought a metaphor to describe the effects of modern industrial society on the human personality he hit upon the metaphor of the cheerful robot. The cheerful robot would be a happy slave, Mills argued, rational but unable to rebel because bureaucracy and affluence had eliminated the desire to be free. "The society in which this man, this cheerful robot, flourishes," he wrote, "is the antithesis of the free society—or in the literal and plain meaning of the word, of a democratic society."[2]

While throughout the postwar period critics on the Left and the Right in American politics argued that the working class had been tamed into a machine-like submission, by 1970 this assertion clearly no longer described reality, not when the United States found itself in the midst of a nationwide workers' rebellion. Acts of minor sabotage and absenteeism shot up. The year 1970 witnessed the largest strike wave in America since 1946. Almost two and a half million workers put down their tools in protest against speedup, insufficient pay, and what they considered unjust conditions on the shop floor. Thirty-four individual "work stoppages" that year involved at least ten thousand workers, including an illegal wildcat strike in which two hundred thousand postal workers walked off the job.[3]

In the late 1960s and early 1970s, rank-and-file organizations challenging both management and traditional union leadership sprang from the fertile ground of the antiwar, civil rights, and women's liberation movements: the League of Revolutionary Black Workers in the auto industry, Miners for Democracy, Steelworkers Fight Back, the Coalition of Labor Union Women, the Coalition of Black Trade Unionists, 9to5 among clerical workers, and Teamsters for a Democratic Union. Evidence of the continuing presence of hard physical labor gained nationwide attention through the organizing efforts of thousands of Chicano farm laborers and the United Farm Workers. Nor was the rebellion a passing phenomenon. Worker activism continued throughout the decade, driven in no small part by women and African Americans seeking to gain access to the fullest expression of American citizenship available to working-class people, membership in a labor union. In 1979 eleven strikes took place in which at least ten thousand workers participated, including a strike of two hundred thousand Teamsters.[4]

For nearly three decades robots had loomed in the middle distance representing the supposedly inevitable, apolitical, and technologically driven degradation of work. The metaphor of the robot stood in for a definition of work as an essentially nonhuman practice, fit only for slaves and nothing more than the activity of subsistence. But by the turn of 1970 there was no longer any denying that human beings remained on the job, not when daily they idled the factories, fields, offices, and highways of the nation. "Now American working people are stirring again," said left-wing activists Staughton and Alice Lynd.[5] Personnel executives at the Ford Motor Company complained of a new "people problem," with absenteeism, turnover, and "disciplinary cases" all doubling since the previous decade. "We see a potential problem of vast significance to all industrial companies," one senior vice president for General Electric announced at a stockholders' meeting. "This involves the slowly rising feeling of frustration, irritation and alienation of the blue collar worker. . . . It involves a gut feeling on their part that industrial society has left them with the dull, hard, dirty jobs—and doesn't care."[6] In response to the threat, President Richard Nixon formed the National Commission on Productivity in 1970. Two years later and the worker rebellion still not checked, he ordered the creation of the National Commission for Industrial Peace.[7] The robot invasion had quite obviously failed to materialize, and as the pair of social scientists wondered in the title of their 1972 book on the worker insurgency, Americans now asked themselves: *Where Have All the Robots Gone?*[8]

The question carried a double meaning. Not only had the figurative human robots failed to appear at their appointed hour, neither had the labor-abolishing machines. If since the 1950s it had been practically common knowledge that "automation" stood on the verge of eliminating nearly all industrial workers and many more besides, by the early 1970s it seemed that, in fact, "automation" had never happened at all. "The basic problems facing workers have not changed over the last thirty years, nor have their attitudes basically changed," said an official of the International Union of Electrical, Radio, and Machine Workers. "Automation, or the less exotic mechanization, has not reduced the hard slog of work for many people."[9] "For a long time there seemed to be the promise that technology would eliminate many undesirable jobs," testified New York's Deputy Manpower Commissioner at a Senate hearing. "I would suggest that has not happened at nearly the rate that was predicted 15 or 20 years ago. Many really bad jobs are still with us."[10] A government report came to a similar conclusion, noting, quite simply: "The automation revolution that was to increase the demand for skilled workers (while decreasing the need for humans to do the worst jobs of society) has not occurred."[11]

It was not only the wave of worker militancy that led Americans to question the substance of "automation." As the postwar order began to collapse in the late 1960s, the reality of economic, imperial, technological, and environmental limits asserted themselves in a series of crises: a falling rate of profit (especially in manufacturing); the loss of global market share to the industrial powers of Europe and Japan, now rising phoenix-like from the ashes of World War II; the failure of American military power to effect its will abroad, specifically in Vietnam; a simultaneous increase in unemployment and inflation, so-called stagflation, something that Keynesianism could not explain; the loss of credibility among many of the nation's established authorities in the wake of the feminist, civil rights, and antiwar movements; and a growing understanding of the environmental degradation caused by modern technological society.

"Automation" had been a credible description of reality because of the widespread faith Americans had placed in industrial society itself, but as events cast doubt on the future or even the benefits of the industrial apparatus, "automation" came to seem ever more like a fantasy. At the 1972 White House Conference on the Industrial World Ahead, Nixon could vouchsafe little confidence in the future of progress: "For a long time in America we were able to take productivity increases for granted. . . . We rather imagined a sort of technological cornucopia that promises increasing abundance every year without any extra effort on our part. . . . But now the new situation in the world has changed all that."[12] The nationwide humbling undermined much of the power of the automation discourse. If work could not be escaped, then arguments that dismissed socially necessary activity as essentially slave-like no longer sounded like a program for universal liberation; they were a defense of the exploitation of human beings.

The powers at its disposal having proved less decisive than hoped, the country faced the possibility that perhaps it could not escape the demands of the body and the activity of meeting bare life. In a remarkable turnaround, nature and the necessities of the human body became the preconditions of liberation, rather than slavery. The earlier desire to make industrial methods of production as inhuman as possible—literally bereft of human beings—now stood as a rebuke against modern civilization. "Industrialization was a battle with 19th century ecology to win breakfast at the cost of smog and insanity. Wars against ecology are suicidal," said the Diggers, an anarchist guerilla theater troupe who staged impromptu productions in the streets of San Francisco. "No Pleistocene swamp could match the pestilential horror of modern sewage."[13]

As a sign of the change in attitude, three years later Nixon, not exactly an ally of anarchist guerilla theater troupes, called in his 1970 State of the Union Address for a cease-fire in the war on nature: "The great question of the '70s is, shall we surrender to our surroundings, or shall we make peace with nature and begin to make reparations for the damage we have done to our air, to our land and to our water?"[14] The political condition of freedom, as well as a meaningful life, demanded reconciliation with the natural world and embodied existence. That meant a reconciliation with the activity of meeting social necessity—with work. "The notion that automation gives any guarantee of human liberation is a piece of wishful thinking," Lewis Mumford wrote in 1970. "No machine, however complex its nature or however ingenious its human inventor, can even theoretically be made to replicate a man, for in order to do so it would have to draw upon two or three billion years of diversified experience." Organic life, the life of the body, did not stand in the way of the good life, Mumford argued. It *was* life. "Surely the time has come to reconsider the abolition of work," he concluded. "As for the eventual assemblage of a completely automated world society, only innocents could contemplate such a goal as the highest culmination of human evolution."[15]

As the limits of industrial society came into sharper focus, and the politics of the workplace found their way into the politics of the nation, the value of the laboring human body became more visible. Although a few years earlier union leaders and managers alike had looked forward to the "automation" of work, by the early 1970s they called instead for its "humanization." Rather than perfect the worker's alienation from the means of production, it became the mission of a humane society to reform the workplace so that it could accommodate, rather than function in the absence of, a human being. Because labor possessed worth, so too must the embodied condition; because the natural world was not the enemy of society, society should not evict the demands of the human body from its definition of freedom. For the United States to be a free country, freedom and work demanded reconciliation.

The Meaning of Work

With the turn of 1970 the meaning of work became an explicit topic of national discussion. *New York Magazine*'s "Confessions of a Working Stiff" would have been a remarkable essay at any time if for no other reason than its author was also a cargo loader at Kennedy Airport. More remarkable still, the substance of the story was nothing more than an account of a cargo loader's average working day. After decades of talk about "automation," the fact that physically difficult jobs still existed was news. The work was hard, the article's author, Patrick Fenton, recounted. It was unrewarding, exhausting, carceral, dead-end, boring, and profoundly physical. Workers "pushed 8,000-pound pallets with their backs. Like Egyptians building a pyramid, they will pull and push until the pallet finally gives in and moves like a massive stone sliding through the sand."[16] It was likewise newsworthy that workers employed in physically grueling jobs did not enjoy a middle-class life of leisure. As the *AFL-CIO American Federationist* reported: "Workers were never as affluent as John Kenneth Galbraith once thought they were."[17]

The call for a discussion of the meaning of work crossed ideological and political boundaries. Books appeared with titles like *The Meaning and Demeaning of Work*, written by left-wing journalist Barbara Garson, and *Creating More Meaningful Work*, authored for the American Management Association by a Harvard Business School professor. After interviewing dozens of workers employed in low-wage jobs, Garson found that "people passionately want to work." They went to great lengths to "put meaning and dignity back into" their daily activities. "The crime of modern industry is not forcing us to work," she concluded, "but denying us real work." No less a figure of the counterculture than Charles Reich lamented, "America lacks a meaningful concept of work," and Nixon's Secretary of Health, Education, and Welfare confessed: "One cannot help but feel that however deeply we have cared in the past, we never really understood the importance, the meaning, and the reach of work." Assistant Secretary of Labor Jerome M. Rosow's 1970 report, a memorandum that gained some public notice as the "Rosow Report," advised that "efforts should be made to enhance the status of blue-collar work." He considered the possibility of bestowing national awards for craftsmanship, as well as issuing postage stamps that portrayed workers in a heroic light.[18]

Because it no longer appeared reasonable to expect that industrial society might escape the embodied condition, work needed to regain its values if it was to be at least theoretically consistent with freedom. Responding to the nationwide worker rebellion, in the summer of 1972 Ted Kennedy chaired Senate hearings in support of a bill he co-sponsored: the Worker Alienation Research and Technical Assistance Act, a bill that was never passed into law but which asserted, "It is in the national interest to encourage the humanization of working conditions and the work itself[;] . . . work should be designed to maximize potentials for democracy, security, equity, and craftsmanship."[19] For Kennedy, the first step in giving work a more "human" definition was to recognize the human body as capable of producing value, and therefore as itself valuable. To do this, Kennedy argued, the body needed to be visible. "The Nation marvels at the impressive speed of the automated equipment in the Nation's modern plants," he said. "Unfortunately, it is as if the Nation's institutions were mesmerized by the industrial machine and unable to see the man behind the machine." Kennedy had expanded on this point at the UAW's annual convention earlier that year. A human being had a will; a human being worthy of the name demanded a say over his or her life. Fairness and decency, said Kennedy, "means an effort to make it possible for workers to live not just as robots or machines, but as men and women who are human beings. Admittedly, making the assembly line more human and humane is a large and difficult task, but it is at the heart of anything we mean by social justice in America."[20]

While only a few years earlier liberal critics had portrayed work and freedom as mutually exclusive, now in a remarkable turnaround they said that ideally one implied the other. The much-publicized 1973 government report commissioned to explain the workers' rebellion, *Work in America*, told the American public that to reduce social upheaval, work needed to become more "meaningful." The report understood work as "an activity that produces something of value for other people." Not the curse of Adam, this definition denoted a thoroughly *social* necessity, activity recognized and valued by society. A mere "job" was activity undertaken solely to sustain life. "Work," on the other hand, meant meaningful activity, at least somewhat self-directed, personally satisfying, and woven into the fabric of society. The final conclusion was obvious: A truly human life was a life of meaning, and meaning lay in making a contribution to society that was both appropriately valued and intrinsically rewarding. For that reason, the authors of the report asserted that "work probably defines man with the greatest certainty." Freedom from work would therefore be freedom from a human life, and not real freedom at all. Not going so far as to endorse the principle of workers' control of production, *Work in America* nevertheless argued that for work to be consistent with a fully human life, workers needed a certain degree of real power on the job: "When it is said that work should be 'meaningful,' what is meant is that it should contribute to self-esteem, *to the sense of fulfillment through the mastering of one's self and one's environment*, and to the sense that one is valued by society."[21] In the mouths of striking workers, this "sense of mastery" would mean shop-floor democracy.

The Origins of "Humanization": The Counterculture, Vietnam, and Environmentalism

Considering that the word "automation" originated in the automobile industry, it was fitting that its antithesis, "humanization," emerged there as well. But while "automation" came down from the boardroom to describe postwar retooling and speedup, "humanization" rose up from the shop floor. When in 1964 a little-advertised strike wave washed over American industry at the local level, rank-and-file auto workers initiated their own grassroots drive to sway union leadership to negotiate more substantively over working conditions, many of which the 1949 "production standards" clause had excluded from collective bargaining. Taking their lead from several Detroit locals, they launched their campaign under the banner "Humanize Working Conditions."[22]

The demand for a humanized factory was one element in a broader intellectual movement that, beginning in the mid-1960s, called into question the legitimacy of industrial society. Among the most influential of these elements was the growing counterculture. The same year Detroit auto workers demanded that working conditions be humanized, students participating in the Berkeley Free Speech Movement depicted the human organism as the practical and symbolic antithesis of modern technological society. That December, undergraduate Mario Savio stood in front of Sproul Hall and announced, "We're human beings." For Savio, the solution to the inhuman mechanism of the modern university, what he called "the machine," was to sabotage it with the body itself: "You've got to put your bodies upon the gears and upon the wheels, upon the levers, upon all the apparatus," he said, "and you've got to make it stop." Another student carried a sign that provided a taste of what would become a commonplace of the anti-technological, anti-industrial thrust of much of the counterculture. Borrowing the warning that accompanied punch cards fed into a digital computer, the sign read: "I am a UC student. Please don't bend, fold, spindle or mutilate me."[23]

At the heart of the counterculture's criticism of industrial society lay a philosophy of historical change widely shared across the political spectrum.

According to this view, neither great men nor class struggle caused events. Rather, technological development itself was the decisive agent of history. In the late 1960s John Kenneth Galbraith, the face of American Keynesianism, Harvard economist, and advisor to four American presidents, celebrated this world-historical entity as the "techno-structure."[24] As the counterculture grew increasingly disillusioned with the many wonders of industrial society, it sought out thinkers who could provide intellectual weapons with which to attack the liberal faith in a technologically produced utopia. Answering that need, in 1964 W. H. Ferry, one of the lead organizers of the Ad Hoc Committee on the Triple Revolution, lobbied to have translated into English what became an intellectual lodestar for the counterculture, Jacques Ellul's 1954 book *The Technological Society*. What Galbraith would go on to call the techno-structure Ellul had already lambasted as "technique," a force that sacrificed all humane values on the altar of technical efficiency, leading to a world that was "less than human."[25] In 1966 Lewis Mumford denounced this historical tendency as the "megamachine." Not nature but the megamachine, he argued, made work a "curse."[26] By the late 1960s Charles Reich blamed the "technological society" for the anomie of America's youth, while in his 1969 *The Making of a Counter Culture*, Theodore Roszak accused the "technocracy." In opposition, both asserted the value of the human organism, or as Roszak put it, "the joy of being this human animal so vividly alive in the world." The "apparatus of power," Reich wrote, needed to be brought under "human control."[27]

In addition to the influence of the counterculture, the demand to humanize work on the shop floor also drew rhetorical strength from the antiwar movement. Since the end of World War II, military might and industrial power had presented different facets of the same phenomenon, Progress, with the United States its vanguard. The nation could assert its will abroad because of its productive capacity and technological know-how. As Henry Kissinger put it: "A scientific revolution has, for all practical purposes, removed technical limits from the exercise of power in foreign policy."[28]

By the late 1960s, however, American military power appeared to have encountered its technical limits. American warplanes dropped more tons of bombs on Vietnam than they had on Europe and Japan combined during World War II, and still success did not materialize. Other capital-intensive measures miscarried just as spectacularly. Operation Igloo White, the latest in digital computing warfare, scattered sensors along the Ho Chi Minh Trail that relayed erroneous seismic and acoustic data to computers in Thailand that then forwarded inaccurate target coordinates to bombers in the air. Despite great expense and the loss of more than three hundred U.S. aircraft, the operation did little to stanch the flow of North Vietnamese soldiers and supplies into

South Vietnam.[29] Smaller failures were no less disturbing. The general-issue U.S. rifle, the M-16, was notoriously prone to jamming. As one soldier wrote his congressional representative: "We left with 250 men in our company and came back with 107. Practically every one of our dead was found with his rifle torn down next to him." A congressional investigation found the Army's conduct in the matter bordering on "criminal negligence."[30]

At the time, critics saw the moral shortcomings of the war as inextricably linked to its technical failures. "In the particular case of the Vietnamese bombing system," wrote John McDermott in his seminal essay "Technology: The Opiate of the Intellectuals," published in 1969, the "political goals of the bombing system clearly exclude the interests of the Vietnamese."[31] From foreign battlefields workers brought their disillusionment with technocracy home with them. Incompetence and moral culpability were two sides of the same coin. "Here again it's the rich getting richer," said Theo Hochheimer, veteran and auto worker at Lordstown, Ohio. "And they have such power they can get the government to put slobs like me in uniform, and we're dumb enough to think that we're fighting for freedom and democracy, when we were really fighting for American business interests."[32]

The combination of moral and technological failure—the sense that limits had been reached—informed not only antiwar protest but also the growing environmentalist movement. When the poet and social critic Wendell Berry sought to convey the magnitude of the domestic environmental degradation caused by strip mining, he compared it to the war in Asia. "Whole mountain tops have been torn off and cast into the valleys. And the ruin of human life and possibility is commensurate with the ruin of the land. It is a scene from the book of revelation. It is a domestic Vietnam."[33] Berry was only one of a growing troop of public environmentalists who were radically critical of industrial society. "Progress," wrote Barry Commoner, was the word Americans used to describe what was in actuality a "global catastrophe," and the cause of the environmental emergency was all too clear: "the sweeping transformation of productive technology since World War II."[34]

In 1950, the image of a swiftly receding planet taken by an Aerobee rocket had served for Robert Oppenheimer and the editors of *Scientific American* as a metaphor for humanity's imminent liberation from the demands of the natural world.[35] In 1969, the same year the Cuyahoga River caught fire and the Environmental Protection Agency was founded, a trip to the moon, often billed as proof of humanity's new life beyond the curved horizon of the Earth, now looked quite different, at least to some. "The landing of the first two astronauts on the moon was not the beginning of a new age of cosmic exploration, but the end," wrote Lewis Mumford. In the moon he saw "a satellite as uninhabitable as the earth itself will all too soon become."[36] In their way, the first travelers to the moon agreed. After entering lunar orbit, Commander Frank Borman of *Apollo 8* radioed back to Houston: "The moon is a vast, lonely, forbidding-type existence, or expanse of nothing. It looks rather like clouds and clouds of pumice stone, and it certainly would not be a very inviting place to live or work."[37]

Lordstown

By the early 1970s the call to humanize working conditions was ubiquitous. In language reminiscent of the unnamed Berkeley student who demanded that he be not bent, folded, spindled, or mutilated, in 1972 John French, professor of psychology at the University of Michigan, testified before a Senate subcommittee that "humanized work . . . should not damage, degrade, exhaust, stultify or persistently bore the worker." After conducting a survey of worker satisfaction, French concluded that a humanized job should also interest the worker. It should satisfy him. It should demand the use of his skills and help him foster new ones. Humanized work would not make the worker sick, he said. Nor would it conflict with his social roles, including that "of citizen." It would pay enough.[38]

Auto workers in the 1970s generally agreed with many of the elements of French's definition of humanized work, but they also found it lacking in one key respect. Humanized work, they held, gave workers power over their jobs. It gave them control.

This brings us to Lordstown. The strike from February to March 1972 at the General Motors Vega plant in Lordstown, Ohio, was not the biggest strike of the era, nor the longest. Neither a great success nor a resounding defeat, it directly touched fewer lives than did the airline mechanics' strike of 1966, and it did not win as much national sympathy as the grape boycott of the late 1960s called by the United Farm Workers. Still, if it became the symbol of the worker uprising of the 1970s it was because the strike seemed to reflect in miniature how the signal accomplishments of postwar American industrial society had in the sequel become its failures. The workers there were relatively well-paid among industrial laborers. They seemed to represent the affluence promised by the postwar period. In that they were young, they reflected the rebelliousness of 1960s youth. Because the workforce was integrated, its existence could be read as a victory of civil rights organizing and the country's ability to overcome its racist history. In addition, according to management, the facility was the most "automated" auto factory in the world. It was a marvel of technological advancement, producing the latest in automobile design.

So when workers called a strike on the grounds that a job at Lordstown was little better than a prison sentence—85 percent of the workforce participating in the vote and 97 percent voting in favor—it was as if they were rejecting nothing less than the postwar industrial order itself.[39] "[T]he Lordstown plant is a sort of laboratory," a writer for *Workers Power* observed. "It offers us a trial run of the class struggle of the 1970s." Or in the words of another article from the same paper: "GM's vanguard plant has turned out to have a vanguard workforce."[40] As Lordstown became the focal point of a national discussion about the meaning of work in industrial society, the press called the country-wide rank-and-file rebellion the "Lordstown syndrome." The primary demand of the workers was not more money but more control over their work and their working conditions. For Gary Bryner, union president at Lordstown, the central problem was that the character of labor in the factory did not respect the realities of existence as an embodied human being. Management, in its relations with the worker, "did not step up to his needs as a worker or as a human." He said of GM, "If they could put the human guy's rights in front, they would win in the long run. But you cannot convince them, and it only further alienates people."[41]

In the context of Lordstown, "automation," instead of setting workers free, now described highly regimented labor conditions. "Automation was supposed to relieve back-breaking drudgery on the assembly line while improving manufacturing efficiency and product quality," wrote *Business Week*. "But it has only accentuated the monotony of such labor—and in the view of union critics—'dehumanized work.'" The *New York Times* called the Lordstown strike the "Revolt of the Robots," and according to the paper of record, the strike that "shut down the world's fastest assembly line is a symptom of widespread rank-and-file rebellion against the dehumanizing effects of automation."[42]

Stumping on the campaign trail, Democratic presidential nominee George McGovern paid a visit to Lordstown and declared, "We don't want workers to be treated like robots or machines."[43] The Nixon administration's answer to the nationwide worker rebellion, *Work in America*, likewise used the Lordstown strike to criticize "new technology" for degrading work without releasing human beings from the labor process. "Early in 1972," it said, "workers there went on strike over the pace of the line and the robot-like tasks that they were asked to perform. This event highlights the role of the human element in productivity: what does the employer gain by having a 'perfectly efficient' assembly-line if his workers are out on strike because of the oppressive and dehumanized experiences of working on the 'perfect' line?" And according to the report, this dehumanized experience was by no means isolated to one factory in Ohio. "As the costs of absenteeism, wildcat strikes, turnover, and industrial sabotage become an increasingly significant part of the cost of doing business, it is becoming clear that the current concept of industrial efficiency conveniently but mistakenly ignores the social half of the equation."[44]

Production at Lordstown was part of a larger effort by General Motors to overcome the crisis in profitability afflicting not only the auto industry but U.S. manufacturing generally. In competition with the industrial powers of Japan and Europe, the United States saw its rate of profit in manufacturing fall 40 percent between 1965 to 1973, with the profits of private business falling 30 percent in the fourth quarter of 1969 alone.[45] Hoping to counter these trends, GM launched a media blitz to promote its latest model, the Vega, a relatively small automobile meant to win back the American consumer from the fashionably petite European and Japanese cars capturing an increasing share of the domestic market. To produce the little car that was to reassert American industrial hegemony, in 1970 GM handed over the management of the Lordstown plant to the General Motors Assembly Division, or GMAD (pronounced Gee-Mad). Its mission was to win back for GM its high rate of profit by introducing new machinery and cutting labor costs. To that end, four months after taking over, GMAD laid off between five hundred and eight hundred workers, breaking up their jobs and adding them to the tasks of those who remained on the line. In addition, GMAD increased the speed of the line. Whereas before the change in leadership the plant had produced 60 cars per hour, the industry standard, under GMAD management workers turned out 102 automobiles every hour. With good reason, workers and management alike claimed that the assembly line at Lordstown was the fastest in the world.[46]

At first, both the media and General Motors depicted increased production at the Vega factory in the style they had for most of the postwar period: as evidence of technological innovation, not speedup. Journalists and auto executives spoke of Lordstown as the most technologically advanced automobile assembly plant anywhere. The *Wall Street Journal* reported that "GM resorts to aggressive automation" in order to "be able to wring about 10 percent of the normal labor costs of producing an automobile." A month before the strike, Richard Gerstenberg, GM's chairman, said of Lordstown, "Every attempt was made to design out costs in the assembly process." *Time* wrote: "Its assembly line is the most highly automated one in the industry."[47]

This time "automation" centered the gaze on several material innovations, the most spectacular of which was the introduction of twenty-six Unimate robots. The first industrial robot, the Unimate was patented in 1961, the same year General Motors installed several of them in a New Jersey auto plant. At Lordstown, GM used the Unimates to weld car bodies. Writer Emma Rothschild took a tour of the Lordstown plant and described them this way: "The

Unimates are unmistakable, white and contoured on a dreary iron line. They even move like science fiction automata—or, as one small boy who had joined the tour with his father and grandfather put it, 'like little animals, nibbling the cars.'"[48] Besides the Unimates, Lordstown also boasted two new computer systems that the company advertised as "automation": the Assembly Line Production and Control Activity, or ALPACA, which assigned to workers the type and number of jobs they should perform, and the Product Assurance Control System, PACS, which consisted of sixteen optical scanners located along the line to perform quality control inspections that would catch production problems early.

As they had since the late 1940s, workers in the factory described "automation" as a speedup. It was the "Vega speedup," and the strike was "Lordstown's revolt against speedup."[49] "They treated us like animals, human robots," said one worker of his job in the paint shop. "They set the speed they want you to work and if you can't do it they put you on notice. I would miss about half of the added work." Said another worker installing weather strips after management cut gang sizes from seven workers to five, "That made it impossible to do at a normal pace. . . . I couldn't keep up on the line. . . . The foreman and the general foreman were standing around watching. 'Hurry up. Come on. Quit your stalling. Don't talk on the job.'" Nor was speedup the only issue. Despite management's portrayal of the factory as state-of-the-art, the facility wanted for basic safety protections. Testifying before Congress, Lordstown assembler Dan Clark said that in summer workers recorded temperatures of 120 degrees Fahrenheit in the plant. Lacking appropriate safety equipment, Clark stuffed cotton in his ears against the din in the body shop where workers and Unimates welded the Vega. Ventilation in the plant was poor, and GM did not provide protective breathing gear. "You will have fumes like smoke or something like that come on over," he said, "and dust and fumes and smoke coming out, and they do not have anything for that either."[50]

As with earlier technological innovations in the auto industry, "automation" at Lordstown did not lessen the amount of human labor necessary to produce an automobile. The purpose of ALPACA was not to reduce human labor but to exploit it to the fullest, using algorithms to fill each worker's day with as many jobs as possible. Joseph Godfrey, head of GMAD, acknowledged as much: "If a man works sixty minutes an hour, that's full productivity. That's how I measure it." He elaborated, "Within reason and without endangering their health, if we can occupy a man for 60 minutes, we've got that right." In response, Irving Bluestone, head of the UAW's GM department, said of working conditions under GMAD: "A worker has to work harder to produce the same amount.

This is simple speed up." Speaking of another plant that GMAD ran under similar conditions, Bluestone claimed that where once nineteen workers had installed a windshield, now only nine did. "The job wasn't made easier," he said. "Yet they insist the rest of the men do the job." Neither did PACS relieve the workers of labor. If it had functioned as hoped it would have been an aid to managers in checking up on the consistency of the workers' output and spotting production errors. It did not. Workers said that they were the ones who informed management of production problems on the line. As for the impressive Unimates, *Fortune* reported that they also did not reduce human effort. If anything, they created more arduous and monotonous tasks for human beings. Although the Unimates took over some welding, a job considered skilled labor in the hierarchy of factory employment, the machines still required human assistants. "At Lordstown," said *Fortune*, "people pick up the sheet-metal panels and clamp them into position in the welding fixtures. At one time GM considered robotizing this job too. But the panels would have to be presented to the robot's clutching hands exactly the same way every time, and the machinery to accomplish this was judged prohibitively expensive." The machines also had the tendency to break down.[51]

Striking workers saw a direct connection between GM's ability to introduce machinery to the shop floor and its capacity to impose its will on line workers. Despite the protection of a contract, workers in fact had very little power to enforce its stipulations while on the job. For example, workers across the industry commonly faced "mandatory overtime" despite having in theory won the eight-hour workday decades earlier. Foremen could give "direct orders" and punish workers who disobeyed with a disciplinary layoff. Workers had the right to file a grievance, but a grievance might take months to arbitrate while a foreman could give orders and punish a worker without following any bureaucratic procedure. Some called this approach "guilty until proven innocent." Workers across the auto industry hated it. Managers used this bureaucratic channeling to speed up people on the line. One employee at Lordstown described what it looked like:

> Guy next to me, this boob Larry, he puts in alternators and they changed it to a one-man job. So he lets half the cars get away. Then he calls the committeeman and files a seventy-eight [a grievance claiming that the job cannot be done in the allotted time]. I walk up to him afterwards and say, "Look at you! Now you're smiling and you're doing the goddamn job. You can wipe your ass with that grievance." Two months later he's still doing the job just like GM wants him to. The union is saying, "Hang on fellah, we'll help you," and he's still on the line like a fucking machine.[52]

Automation at Lordstown was the same practice of mechanically abetted speedup that the auto industry had pursued for decades. But in one respect things were different in 1972. Now, as workers married their complaints to both the growing dissatisfaction with industrial society and the wave of militancy cresting across the country, the rest of the nation was forced to acknowledge what had been true all along. News organs now depicted Lordstown "automation" as speedup. Covering the strike, *Time* magazine put it neatly: "Speedup. Trouble began in mid-1971, about a year after the automated line was put into operation." The association of technological efficiency and speedup was prominent enough that the President of the United States felt compelled to address the issue, if only to deny it. "When you have the latest technology to help you do your job, it means you can do more with the same effort," said Nixon. "It sounds like the old 'speedup' or some new efficiency system that drives people harder. Productivity really means getting more out of your work." Remembering his 1957 essay "The Myth of the Happy Worker," writer and sometime auto worker Harvey Swados felt a "melancholy satisfaction" that finally the national discussion acknowledged the existence, as he had put it in the 1950s, of "millions of Americans who grind their lives away on an insane treadmill." He added, "Few people during the 1950s wished to learn of these people and their problems." By the early 1970s, their presence was undeniable; the upswing in labor militancy made the worker's laboring body visible.[53]

Nevertheless, many liberals remained unwilling to indict the affluent society for its failure to treat workers humanely. Instead, they claimed that the workers' rebellion wasn't actually a workers' rebellion at all. It was, they said, mere discontent among the nation's youth, more akin to teen angst than proletarian revolution. Once again Lordstown proved a useful symbol. Many of the workers there were under thirty, leading some to style the plant an "industrial Woodstock." This argument, what became known as the "generation gap" thesis, was especially popular among defenders of the status quo in government and the popular press.[54] Rebelling workers were young people first, this argument went. Only incidentally were they workers. The affluent society was not broken. If anything, it was too successful. Fulfilling its promises all too well, it had produced a generation of young people who were better educated and expected more from life than their parents, for whom the old methods of industrial discipline had been, supposedly, appropriate and not particularly burdensome. The young had grown up amidst plenty, this argument went, and had been raised with more freedom than any Americans who had come before them. Rebelling workers were spoiled children.

According to the generation gap thesis, humanization of work meant designing non-Taylorized jobs, not because Taylorized tasks outraged human sensibility but because they were wrong specifically for this new cohort of young people. "Increasingly, children from blue-collar families are being raised according to the values of autonomy, democracy, and meritocracy," said Michael Maccoby, director of Harvard University's Project on Technology, Work, and Character. "The values of the megamachine, compulsive order and obedience, no longer take root in children who are encouraged to be both more democratic and more self-indulgent." The manager of personnel for AT&T captured the sentiment best. Addressing a conference on the future of work, he complained: "We have run out of dumb people to handle those dumb jobs."[55]

This argument inverted what had been the postwar liberal verity that "automation" would eliminate unskilled manual labor in favor of professional middle-class employment. "The increased use of automation will be causing employers to seek a more educated and a more skilled work force," Walter Reuther had said in Senate hearings in 1963. Also testifying before the Senate, Donald Michael, coiner of the word "cybernation," had asked the committee chairman: "And what do you do with those low IQ people. . . . What do you do with them in this world?" The chairman had said in his opening address, "We have a paradox of 4 million unemployed on one hand and severe shortages of manpower needed to run our highly complex technology on the other."[56] According to the terms of the automation discourse, the average American had been intellectually unprepared either to be a middle-class professional or to enjoy the leisure befitting a gentleman. But now, in the early 1970s, the exact opposite argument came to the fore: The working class was too skilled and well-educated for its own good.

The generation gap thesis of the 1970s presumed that workers in the 1950s had never rebelled and never desired to do so. It also held that the workers demanding humanization in the 1970s were all young. Neither of these claims was true. In the same testimony before Congress in which he spoke of poor working conditions in Lordstown, twenty-five-year-old assembler Dan Clark rejected the argument that older workers were passive robots. "In the 1930's our fathers or forefathers, whatever you want to say, they revolted. They wanted the rights for a union. In 1970 we revolted and all we want to do is improve on things. That is all we want."[57] Those who had worked industrial jobs in the 1950s recalled unceasing resentment over working conditions. Lloyd Zimpel, in his edited volume *Man Against Work*, remembered laboring as a steelworker in the 1950s. His colleagues, he said, "were openly bitter and resented the pointlessness of their jobs and their lives." The difference, then, was not that workers had felt differently than those in 1972 but that the political horizon had been so effectively foreshortened that workers had been unable to launch an organized rebellion. "With a workers' apocalypse nowhere in sight," Zimpel said, "they swallowed their discontent or expressed it through conventional and not always serviceable union channels." If the generation gap thesis had any validity, it was that workers in the 1970s, unlike those in the 1950s, saw the New Deal state coming apart at the seams. The postwar order could no longer hold back and redirect the frustrations bred by the industrial workplace. This generation was of the same mood as workers in the 1950s, Zimpel said. If there was a difference, it was that the political ferment of the 1960s had given younger workers confidence that rebellion could succeed.[58]

Clearly, however, many older workers were coming around to that position as well. At the same time the young workers at Lordstown walked off the job in protest against the conditions that GMAD had introduced to the assembly line, so did workers at another GM factory in Ohio, and for the same reasons. The General Motors Assembly Division ran eighteen of GM's thirty-two assembly plants, including the Norwood, Ohio, plant that it took over in 1971. In reaction to GMAD's intensification of labor, including five hundred layoffs—about the same number as at Lordstown—along with a speedup on the line, four thousand workers at Norwood struck to demand the right to negotiate over working conditions. Unlike the Lordstown strike, however, which lasted six weeks, the Norwood strike went on for 174 days. The strike lasted so long that when workers returned to their jobs, the eleven hundred almost-finished Camaros, Novas, and Firebirds abandoned on the line were in violation of 1973 emissions and safety standards. The first task of returning workers was to destroy these cars. Nothing could have better symbolized the crisis of faith in American technological supremacy than the sight of GM sending all those brand-new automobiles through an industrial crusher in the hopes of salvaging them for scrap.[59]

The Norwood strikers could not be written off as truculent children. "There has been a lot written about the fact that young people will not tolerate the plant atmosphere anymore," said Irving Bluestone. "The strike at Lordstown, I guess, is symbolic of it, and it is a young people's plant. But we have a strike going into its 16th week this week at Norwood, one of the oldest plants in the General Motors Corp. While we have young people there, there is a large, large number proportionately of the older folk, who are saying exactly the same thing."[60] Before GMAD came to Norwood, thirty-six-year-old assembler Ernest Barnes installed two bolts on the bumper of each Camaro, Firebird, and Nova that came down the line. He had sixty-five seconds between each job. According to Barnes, GMAD "eliminated the man across from me." Now he installed four bolts, twice as much work.[61] The *AFL-CIO Federationist* took exception to the claim that "the new conventional wisdom holds that young workers will not be kept in line," while assuming that older workers were "of course, robots, mechanistic idiots, who will never talk back to their bosses."[62]

The revolt against GMAD went beyond Norwood and Lordstown. In response to line speed and working conditions, workers voted to strike at GMAD-controlled plants across the country: in St. Louis, in Doraville, Georgia, in Mansfield, Ohio, in Janesville, Wisconsin, and in Van Nuys, California. The *Christian Science Monitor* called this rash of strikes a contest over humanization.[63] Those closer to events on the side of management also dismissed the generation gap thesis. George Morris Jr., GM's chief labor negotiator, argued that in his experience this resistance from workers was "typical." The *Wall Street Journal* summarized Morris's opinion that the strikes resulted from the "inevitable resistance to manpower cuts and tighter work assignment," rather than "from assemblyline [sic] boredom or new attitudes about work among young workers."[64]

Nor were these strikes unique to GM. The fall in the rate of profit hit the entire U.S. auto industry hard. As companies doubled down on the old methods of speedup and labor intensification, workers increasingly demanded a say over the conditions of their jobs and a measure of control. The humanization campaign of 1964 had heralded an increase in rank-and-file militancy across the automobile industry, including the dramatic proliferation of wildcat strikes. Between 1960 and 1965 there were, on average, fifteen so-called unofficial actions at Chrysler every year. From 1965 to 1970 the company counted an increase of sixty-one per year, and from 1970 to the year worker militancy in the auto industry peaked, 1973, there were sixty-seven per year.[65]

With the intensification of speedup, workplace injuries become more common. Vera Edwards, president of a local of Industrial Nurses in a Warren, Michigan, auto plant, wrote to UAW vice president Douglas Fraser in the autumn of 1972 supporting the union's efforts toward humanizing the workplace. "We in the Medical Department," she wrote, "[have] most often seen the innumerable examples and the end results of the dehumanized air that pervades this industry." Nurses treated first- and second-degree burns caused by chemical solutions and wrapped hands blistered by hot vinyl. "We have numerous men in the Foundry plant who come in with floating or embedded foreign bodies in their eyes," Edwards reported. Worker fatigue from overtime and weekend production led to more accidents, as did speedup. Of one worker who came in for treatment, Edwards wrote, "He had started three different jobs and was ordered to start a fourth without completing the others, on order from the Superintendent."[66] At the Detroit Mack Avenue Plant in September 1972, a die setter died when an exploding bolster plate, the stationary base of a stamping machine, cut off the top of his head. In a leaflet, workers described factory conditions: "At least once or twice a month somebody loses a finger or a hand in a press. . . . Welders are always being burned and scarred by the sparks. . . . Whenever a worker refuses to place his hands under a die area or to operate an unsafe press, the foreman puts a probationary employee on the job who cannot refuse." In Chrysler's Detroit Forge Plant in 1973, for six months 60 percent of the employees worked seven days a week, including mandatory overtime. There were many gruesome accidents. In July a worker had his arm crushed; thirteen days later a worker lost half his middle finger. That same month there were ten simultaneous wildcat strikes occurring in auto factories across the country: at Dodge Main, GM Fleetwood Assembly, GMAD Norwood, a parts warehouse in Brownstown, Michigan, Ford Assembly in Mahwah, New Jersey, GM Linden, Ohio, two different strikes at Lordstown, Chevy Gear and Axle in Detroit, and the Mack Avenue plant.[67] Spoiled youth acting out would not explain this.

Rather, the strike wave was the result of an economy that was flagging in the midst of the disintegration of traditional institutions of authority. The postwar labor movement had in the wake of Taft-Hartley for the most part purged itself of its far-Left leaders. It had backed away from worker control in return for a welfare state provided by the employer. Maintaining this precarious position had always posed a difficult challenge for union leaders; the simultaneous onset of economic woes and a resurgent left wing upset the delicate balance. As companies responded to the drop in profitability with the tried-and-true practice of speedup, what managers and union leaders had effectively repressed for three decades broke out.

No longer able to dismiss workers as pliable robots, liberal authorities reeled to the opposing extreme and depicted rebelling workers as racist, backward, and unruly. Although by the late 1960s many unions, including the UAW, had come to oppose the war in Vietnam, many within the antiwar and student movements continued to see organized labor as a whole as lacking moral credibility and as counterrevolutionary. Never mind that the majority of American workers were by 1970 opposed to the war or that the most active wing of the labor movement consisted of women and people of color organizing both new unions and within old ones.[68] Speaking for liberals and a substantial portion of the Left, A. H. Raskin, labor reporter for the *New York Times*, summarized this attitude: "The typical worker—from construction craftsman to shoe clerk—has become probably the most reactionary political force in the country."[69] For decades the automation discourse had depicted the worker's body and its value as obsolete, allowing those who wished to do so to ignore the politics of work and the workplace. With the convenient argument that now, instead of a worker's body, it was the worker's politics standing between the United States and a wonderful future, those same actors hoped once again to avoid a potentially radical debate about the meaning of work and what part "progress" had played in its degradation.

Humanization and Workers' Control

"Industrialization can be compatible with a sense of self-worth for workers," declared Ted Kennedy during the 1972 Senate hearing on worker alienation that he chaired. But for millions of workers, that was a contestable point. Could industrial methods of production be made worthy of a human being? What exactly was the humanization of work? For rank-and-file workers and their immediate representatives, like Lordstown's Local 1112 president Gary Bryner, it meant workers gaining a significant share of power over their own lives through democratic control of the workplace. In a word, it meant freedom: "Can you imagine," Bryner asked Kennedy and his colleagues at the hearings, "that when you walk into the workplace, the due process of law that you enjoy as a citizen was gone, because they [management] determine if you are guilty, they determine the extent of your penalty, and they give it to you . . . and if you don't have a union, you do not have recourse. And this is fear." For Bryner, work had become incompatible with freedom not because it was the activity of meeting social necessity, as the automation discourse held, but because of unjust hierarchy. In his opinion, the only way to make work an inherently meaningful experience (a humanized activity) was to make it democratic. "[Workers] want to participate," he said, "and you cannot deny it to them in the workplace. They live too much of their lives there." Senator Jacob Javits answered him, and in doing so contradicted Kennedy's earlier assertion: "You cannot run a factory by plebiscite." In the senator's mind, industrial production and democracy inherently opposed one another.[70]

While across the country workers used the term "humanization" to argue for the democratization of the workplace and the redistribution of control over the labor process, managers and many of their liberal allies moved to seize and redefine the terms of the debate. Since Elton Mayo's Hawthorne experiments of the 1920s, managers had understood that by showing workers solicitude of almost any kind they could make employees more productive while also rechanneling their demands for democracy into less threatening conduits than collective bargaining. Managers in the late 1960s and early 1970s were quick to revive this insight, now appropriating the term "humanization" to describe "quality of life experiments" that sought to ease worker discontent without redistributing any real power away from management. Harvard Business School's

Fred Foulkes, writing for the American Management Association, noted that companies with "job enrichment programs" generally were free of a unionized workforce. He put it delicately: "One has to at least consider the possibility that such programs may represent a management effort to stay nonunion."[71] Managers and consultants suggested quelling the worker rebellion by means of profit sharing, nicer break rooms, and more company-organized morale-boosting events. Volvo's "team" building of automobiles, in which instead of laboring on an assembly line a group of workers built a car from beginning to end and watched it drive out of the factory, was a popular talking point. Some suggested, more modestly, allowing workers to change tasks regularly to fight boredom. A model humanized factory in Topeka, Kansas, the General Foods Pet Food factory, became a display plant where managers instituted the Volvo team system with some success. The rate of absenteeism was an enviable 2 percent. The General Foods Pet Food model did not catch on.[72]

Among many managers, the attempt to embrace humanization without endangering the managerial prerogative to control the labor process made little sense. The director of employee research and training in GM's Chevrolet Division complained that many well-meaning centrist and center-left gestures toward humanization had missed Byrner's point about democracy. Merely to invite humanization to the workplace in a limited way, he said, was full of danger. "In other words," he wrote in the pages of the *Harvard Business Review*, "management's present monopoly—on initiating participation, on the nomination of conferees, and on the limitation of legitimate areas for review—can in itself easily become a source of contention." He was even blunter: "What is really involved is politics, the conscious sharing of control and power. History does not offer many examples of oligarchies that have abdicated with grace and good will."[73] In the same congressional hearings where Lordstown workers equated humanization with democracy, General Motors issued a statement that acknowledged the incompatibility of workplace democracy and company profits. It wanted the best for its workers, management said. "We do not believe, however, that it is in the best interest of General Motors, its employe[e]s, its stockholders or the general public to disregard the traditional responsibilities of management to operate a successful, profitable business."[74] Once you brought the "human" into the factory and recognized the legitimacy of even a little self-determination, GM implied, you opened the door to a revolution.

Making that point explicit, William Gomberg, formerly a contract negotiator for the storied International Ladies' Garment Workers' Union and now a professor of industrial relations at the Wharton School, sought to break down what to him was an arbitrary distinction between political and economic democracy. "Democracy cannot exist where management is free to give and take without any countervailing force," he said. "Such 'democracy' makes as much sense as a U.S. government without any institutionalized checks and balances."[75] The UAW's Irving Bluestone agreed. Taking the stand after the Lordstown workers had spoken to address the Senate hearings, he defined "humanization" by making a distinction between "managing the enterprise" and "managing the job." Managing the enterprise meant workers would have representatives sitting on the board of GM, and they would share the management of day-to-day operations on the shop floor. He criticized managers and his fellow union leaders for failing to see the big picture, what he called "a revolution in terms of humanizing the workplace, of democratizing the workplace, both with regard to managing the job and the enterprise." If lawmakers, managers, and union leaders were serious about "job satisfaction," he said, they would be serious about democratizing the auto industry. Fraser agreed. To make work humane, he wrote to the head of the union's legal department in 1972, workers needed "control."[76]

In April 1973 the UAW held its first Production Workers' Conference, a meeting exclusively for the semiskilled workers at the bottom of the pay scale—those who had borne the brunt of postwar "automation." The conference produced three demands: better health and safety conditions, more time off, and "increased worker rights in the process of administering the plants." One rank-and-file participant, Kenneth Rainey, the co-chairman of the bargaining committee for Local 674 of the Norwood GM plant, said the national worker rebellion was about workers' gaining "a little more to say about their own destiny." Bernard Johnson, committeeman at Ford's plant in Mahwah, New Jersey, rejected the company's attempt to humanize the factory: "They proposed music in the plant and painting things psychedelic colors, but it's ridiculous. Those things aren't going to brighten up a person's spirit if he's got a foreman riding his back."[77]

According to executives in the auto industry, the material realities of the factory stood between production and the workers' definition of "humanization," or democratic control. "Ways of structuring the work are substantially the same as they were 10 years ago, when management considered them to be satisfactory," said the Ford Motor Company's Executive of Personnel in 1971. Now, despite the "unacceptable" behavior of workers—absenteeism, sabotage, wildcatting—the company could not humanize the labor process even if it wanted to. The demands of profit making by means of the detailed division of labor foreclosed that option. The layout of the factory presumed the presence of disempowered workers. "I don't know how much will be enough," he said, "or what the cost will be."[78] Ford, the company that first coined the word "automation," had invested hundreds of millions of dollars in its understanding of the term as the devaluation of human labor. It did so in the form of steel, concrete, rubber, glass, and brick. Valuing more today what yesterday had gone undervalued would mean rebuilding factories from the ground up.

A school of left-wing and centrist critics agreed with auto executives who argued that the basic organization of industrial production might stand in the way of humanization. The Nixon administration's 1973 report *Work in America* found a ready audience when it blamed the workers' rebellion on Taylorism—the detailed division of labor and the micromanagement of the movement of the laboring human body.[79] By the early 1970s it had become typical to see condemnations of modern-day Taylorism in print. In some jobs, these criticisms went, work under industrial conditions had always been unfit for people. In others, it had worsened.[80]

Foremost among Taylorism's critics was Harry Braverman, former pipefitter and metal worker and after 1967 the managing director of the socialist Monthly Review Press. His 1974 magnum opus, *Labor and Monopoly Capital*, became an instant classic among left-wing American intellectuals. As others did at the time, Braverman argued that labor remained critical to industrial production. Managers mechanized and broke up jobs, he wrote, not to abolish human labor but to make it cheaper.[81] At the same time, Braverman took the humanization argument to its logical extreme. Work, he wrote, was *the* defining characteristic of the human condition. Whereas animals acted by instinct, he asserted, humans combined "conception" with "execution." The distinctive human act was not the divorcing of the mind from the body, as the automation discourse held, but the unification of the two. This melding Braverman called "work," and it was "the force which created humankind and the force by which humankind created the world as we know it." The alienating character of industrial capitalism arose from the detailed division of labor, which was premised on the division of "conception from execution" and which "subdivides *humans*," he wrote. It was "a crime against the person and against humanity."[82]

Despite his intent to give his work a historical grounding, Braverman's definition placed the reader in a world of unchanging, ahistorical essences. His argument reduced the meaning of work from one born of historical political contest to a natural function as far beyond the realm of political negotiation as was that maintained in the automation discourse. According to this view, anything but workers' control violated not merely the conscience but the very biology of the human organism, of nature itself. The pitfalls of this approach would reveal themselves almost immediately, for in celebrating work as inherently and naturally valuable, Braverman's criticism ran the danger of being confused with the quite different politics of another champion of the meaning of work.

The Work Ethic

No longer able to invoke "automation" but also unwilling to concede that "humanization" meant democracy and worker control, defenders of the status quo took a different tack to defend the hierarchy of the workplace. On Labor Day, 1971, President Nixon addressed himself to the people of the United States live on nationwide radio: "The competitive spirit goes by many names," he said.

> Most simply and directly, it is called the work ethic. . . . The work ethic holds that labor is good in itself; that a man or woman at work not only makes a contribution to his fellow man but becomes a better person by virtue of the act of working. The work ethic is ingrained in the American character. That is why most of us consider it immoral to be lazy or slothful—even if a person is well off enough not to have to work or deliberately avoids work by going on welfare.[83]

Nixon's assertion that the meaning of work in the United States had remained singular and unchanged over the course of American history defied the record.[84] It certainly defied Nixon's personal record. In 1956 he had looked forward to the four-day workweek when "back-breaking toil and mind-wearying tension will be left to machines and electronic devices."[85] If the work ethic was so important to the American character, one wonders why the possibility of reducing the workweek had not only failed to trouble Nixon in the 1950s but, to the contrary, had at the time seemed to him a positive development. During the heyday of the automation discourse, Nixon had understood certain kinds of work as standing in the way of freedom; come 1971 and the explosion of worker militancy, he told the Republican Governors' Conference: "Scrubbing floors and emptying bedpans . . . [has] just as much dignity as there is in any work to be done in this country—including my own."[86]

It was a clever rhetorical move. As with many of Nixon's domestic policies, the "work ethic" speech co-opted as much of the center-Left position as possible to peel working-class voters away from the Democratic Party. The speech had two targets. First, left-wing and right-wing opponents of his welfare reform package, known as the Family Assistance Program, and second, rebellious industrial workers. Nixon's evocation of the work ethic represented an effort to enrich the meaning of work by infusing it with nationalism. In the same way that managerial "quality of life" improvements attempted to pacify dissatisfied workers by means of marginal improvements in the labor process and an upbeat attitude, Nixon's celebration of the work ethic did not intend to redistribute any real power over the labor process. Wanting to work for its own sake, he argued, regardless of whether a person directed his or her own activity, was an essential part of the "American character."

Consider the difference between Nixon's call in 1971 to recognize the "dignity of labor" and Martin Luther King Jr.'s insistence before Memphis sanitation workers in 1968 that "all labor has dignity." Nixon claimed that work was essentially meaningful so that he could portray those who either rebelled against the conditions of their employment or demanded an enlarged welfare state as morally deficient and un-American. "Lazy," he called them. King, speaking in defense of an ongoing union campaign, supported garbage collectors' demand for recognition of their contribution to the city of Memphis. Workers, he argued, should not accept the degraded conditions that transformed work into menial labor. They performed an essential service. Declaring that all labor had dignity was the first step for King in demanding that this essential work command better remuneration, safer conditions, and the measure of democracy that came with unionization. Nixon, on the other hand, spoke of dignity in order to circumvent attempts by workers to demand more. Work *already* had enough inherent value, Nixon told the nation. People should choose to find even oppressive working conditions meaningful, he argued, rather than make those conditions meaningful by their democratization.

Just as many liberals and conservatives hoped to dismiss the radicalism of the workers' rebellion by depicting it as a youth revolt, they also claimed that the "new" workers of the early 1970s lacked the traditional work ethic and that this was the fundamental cause of their discontent. Hot on the heels of the Lordstown strike, the *Economist* explained the event as the result of "a new 'anti-work ethic,' a new deep-seated rejection by the young of the traditional faith in hard work."[87] This defamation of workers took the form of a government information campaign when in 1973 the National Commission on Productivity launched an advertising blitz aimed at inspiring Americans to work harder. "What if we all had to sign the work we do?" asked one television spot. "Everyone would try to do his job better, just out of pride." The information campaign went so far in one print advertisement as to lay the blame for the economic crunch of the 1970s on the shoulders of working people and their ostensibly irresponsible attitude. "By taking more pride in our work," it said, "we'll more than likely see America regaining its strength in the competitive world trade arena. . . . If each of us cared just a smidge more about what we do for a living, we could actually turn that inflationary spiral around."[88]

The assumption of a traditional and consistent meaning of work in the United States appealed to Americans on both the Left and the Right. For some on the Left, the work ethic proved a ready-to-hand explanation for why workers did not behave as leftist theorists believed they should. Here the problem was the opposite of the one named by Nixon and the National Commission on Productivity. Far from having lost the traditional work ethic, these thinkers argued, workers were in thrall to it. Chicago workers did not desire an "automation" revolution, explained Todd Gitlin, because they were "afflicted with the Protestant ethic so egregiously."[89] In the academy, leftist scholars assumed, like Nixon, that such an ethic existed. Unlike the president, however, to them it appeared to haunt the working class like a ghost in need of exorcism. "In and of itself," wrote the historian Daniel Rodgers, "work involves only an element of burden. . . . Few cultures have presumed to call it anything more than a poor bargain in an imperfect world. It was the office ideas [sic] to turn the inescapable into an act of virtue, the burdensome into the vital center of living." Presuming the work ethic to be a self-sufficient agent of history, these thinkers granted it causal power.[90]

A few questioned where others presumed. "Who in America ever had the Protestant ethic and when?" the authors of *Work in America* asked. "Did we have it in the thirties? Did the poor people or even middle-class people ever have it?" Taking stock of the character of the workers' uprising, the report concluded that on the whole young people did not seem to have rejected "the concept of work." Union organizer and sociologist Stanley Aronowitz argued in the same vein. Rather than write off workers as mere automatons thinking thoughts others placed in their heads, Aronowitz saw them as complex, conflicted people. Ideologies promoted by elites certainly influenced them, but those ideas also had to compete with the messages workers received from their lived experiences of inequality and exploitation. The result of this dissonance culminated in the workers' rebellion: revolt, sabotage, and "dropping out." The solution, Aronowitz wrote, was for workers to "confront the nature of work itself," to fight over the material of the labor process and in so doing give it a new meaning in substance and thought—to define work for themselves.[91]

Conclusion

In December 2018 General Motors announced that it would shutter the Lordstown plant as part of a larger move to cut fourteen thousand jobs from its payroll in the United States and Canada. The move came less than a decade after the Great Recession and the U.S. government's bailout of the auto industry. In 2009 President Barack Obama had announced the bailout at Lordstown. "In the midst of a deep recession and financial crisis," he said, "for me to have just let the auto industry collapse, to vanish, would have caused unbelievable damage to our economy—not just here in Lordstown, but all across the country. So we intervened for one simple and compelling reason: Your survival and the success of our economy depended on making sure that we got the U.S. auto industry back on its feet." American taxpayers handed out $50 billion to General Motors, $11 billion of which was never repaid. Defending the decision to close Lordstown in 2018, Steven Rattner, former head of Obama's White House Auto Task Force and lead negotiator of the auto bailout, explained why in the name of profit GM had no choice but to abandon its workers. "Yes," he said, "automation played some role in lowering employment, but the bigger problem has been competition from countries like China that are now able to produce goods as well as we do or better using much cheaper labor. For carmakers, that has meant moving production to Mexico."[1] Although Rattner did not know it, what he said of "automation" in the early twenty-first century had been true of the word since its coining in the late 1940s. Yes, the introduction of machinery could reduce the amount of human labor necessary to produce goods, but it also obscured relationships among people. Under these conditions, social domination might appear the product of machine action rather than the decisions of managers, financiers, and lawmakers, all of whom are, of course, all too human.

All this had been many years in the making. Organized labor never recovered from the tumultuous 1970s. The workers' rebellion could not overcome the combined forces of business's renewed anti-unionism and the defection of Democrats from the house of labor in the second half of the 1970s. Rank-and-file militancy would persist throughout the decade, but as a sign of things to come, the activism of autoworkers fell apart with the onset of the 1973 oil shock and the recession that followed. By January 1975, half of all UAW members employed by the Big Three were on either indefinite or temporary layoff. The economic crunch of the late 1960s and early 1970s had encouraged workers to demand the humanization of their jobs, but when the bottom fell out of the auto industry, as it would soon enough for much of the rest of U.S. manufacturing, workers could no longer afford the radicalism of their demand to reconcile industrial production with a humane life. Abandoned by the New Democrats, divided among themselves, and facing the existential danger that was unemployment in the United States of America, the rebellion faltered, and with it, the demand for humanization. With the Reagan revolution of the 1980s and the loss of liberal allies in the halls of government, workers fought an ever-losing battle against the forces of neoliberalism and global capital.

The big dreams of the middle of the twentieth century were long over. Under conditions of tightening austerity and declining power, culture wars and a politics of division took up ever more of the political breathing space. The right wing offered white working Americans the meager consolations of patriotism and white supremacy, the liberal Left sold the bromides of globalization and the technocratic rule of experts, and the horizon of political possibility shrank from the full circumference of the Earth to a wall across the southern border. Also to suffer was any explicit national discussion of the meaning of work in the United States. Losing the power to organize among themselves, working people fought increasingly individual battles to keep body and soul together. Compared to the new regime of insecurity, what workers had once called inhuman industrial work was now considered a good job. Robots had not deprived these workers of their ability to provide for themselves. Managers chasing cheap labor around the globe had done that. In this moment of retreat, neither "automation" nor humanization described reality. Working people struggled instead for bare life, the most degraded meaning of work. Both "automation" and humanization had been instances of utopian thinking, but in the later years of the twentieth century, the nation seemed to have lost the ability to take utopia seriously. As some would insist in the last decade of the millennium, history appeared to have come to an end.

Irony once again proved itself the angel of history. In the decades immediately following World War II, critics had imagined with hope as much as dread a future in which "automation" would dispense with the need for industrial workers or perhaps any workers at all. Among those who expressed trepidation, Kurt Vonnegut had described a dystopian future when superfluous people wasted away in rundown cities, and James Boggs wrote of a hereafter in which an unemployed "scavenger" class had fallen out of society. Sure enough, by the turn of the twenty-first century once-booming American industrial cities stood in ruins while the under- and unemployed struggled to find well-paying jobs. But as had been true of industrial workers facing "automation" half a century earlier, these workers had not lost their jobs to the machine. Rather, for the most part, they lost them as they had in the postwar period—to other workers.[2]

Today, instead of going to their sped-up colleagues down the line, the jobs of the dispossessed go to sped-up and non-unionized workers in the right-to-work South, in the maquiladoras of Mexico, and in the transplanted factories of South and East Asia. Within the United States, hidden human labor likewise remains the secret of "automation" even in some of the most mechanized of American workplaces. This has led to an apparent paradox. On one hand, or so we are often told, "automation" is throwing people out of work. On the other, workers across the economy are undeniably working harder than before and for less. How can this be? How can the economy be wracked—simultaneously—by both chronic underemployment and ubiquitous overwork?[3] This same confusion confronted observers of "automation" in the middle of the twentieth century. As one auto worker put it in the late 1950s: "All Automation has meant to us is unemployment and overwork. *Both at the same time.*"[4] The explanation then was the same as it is now: Employers deploy technical innovations to speed up, degrade, and intensify human labor, allowing them to hire fewer workers and to sweat those who remain. Employers call this labor-saving; they call it "automation."

Take, for example, the notorious "fulfillment centers" of Amazon. The company has boasted that its robots autonomously move packages across the shop floor. "The bottom line is this," wrote one breathless journalist after taking a company tour: "We humans have to adapt to the machines as much as the machines have to adapt to us. . . . These days, industries that are short human labor *need* automation to survive." But as spectacular as these devices might appear, they have nevertheless made up a relatively minor element of Amazon's investment in "automation." Rather than robots, it has been the company's use of autonomous systems of worker surveillance that have saved on labor costs: wristbands that track the positions of the hands of workers and vibrate in warning when those hands appear idle, cameras that watch workers and alert managers when employees are in the wrong place or congregate in groups, and software designed to map potential union activity so it can be busted. Item scanners automatically tally the rate of packages processed per hour for each worker, measuring each employee's "time off task" and meting out punishments to the slow. None of these devices have performed any warehouse work. Rather, they have saved Amazon money by driving human laborers to work harder and faster. Machines inform workers when they are falling behind, but not when they exceed expectations; this keeps workers stowing, packing, and picking items at a consistently sped-up rate, all day long. And as with sped-up auto workers in postwar factories across the United States, the machine-accelerated pace of human labor takes a toll on the human frame. "It took my body two weeks to adjust to the agony of walking 15 miles a day and doing hundreds of squats," an Amazon employee explained. "But as the physical stress got more manageable, the mental stress of being held to the productivity standards of a robot became an even bigger problem." It was this combination of mental and physical injury that led the National Council for Occupation Safety and Health in 2018 to name Amazon one of the most dangerous places to work in the United States.[5]

Amazon's style of mechanization has been typical of twenty-first-century "automation." These machines do not do the work; they regiment, degrade, and harry human beings on the line so that they act as though they are machines. Workers operating telephones in the insurance industry are monitored by machines that discipline not only how long they spend on each call but also what they say and the tone in which they say it. The much-vaunted artificial intelligence at play in ride-hailing and delivery apps pushes workers to labor harder both by measuring how much time they take between tasks (punishing those who fall behind) and with secretive algorithms that garnish their wages according to undisclosed criteria. Sensors embedded in convenience stores and retail outlets calculate, in the words of their manufacturer, a "true productivity" score for each worker, ranking workers from least to most productive. Along those lines, employers in heavy manufacturing have made recourse to cameras that continuously film employees on the assembly line, allowing computers, in the words of an executive at Toyota, "to create continuous streams of data from video of manual actions" that managers may use in Taylorist fashion to further speed up workers.[6] Calling it "automation," employers do indeed use machines to degrade and eliminate jobs. But once again, as was the case in the postwar period, these machines themselves often do not replace human workers; other workers do.

The current celebration of speedup and labor degradation counts as the third wave of the automation discourse. After its retreat in the mid-1970s, the word "automation" enjoyed a renaissance between the late 1980s and the mid-1990s. Boosters of globalization spoke of "post-industrialism" and a new "information economy" as they sought to depict financial deregulation and international trade deals as epoch-making, irresistible developments in the story of civilization. But despite its popularity, "automation" at the end of the century did not hold the public imagination as it had in the postwar period.

The more recent debate surrounding "automation" arose in the aftermath of the Great Recession of 2008. Globalized production, the growing power of Silicon Valley, innovations in robotics and artificial intelligence, the ever-growing economic and political importance of the Internet, and the weakness of unions and nation-states alike to check neoliberal capital once again made "automation" an urgent concern. But while the automation discourse in the middle of the twentieth century fed as much on utopian enthusiasm as it did existential unease, its twenty-first-century incarnation has been fueled instead by fears of dystopia and a pervading sense of powerlessness. The new automation discourse returns to familiar debates from the postwar period, only now with an inverted significance. It indicates a technological determinism less breathless but just as tenacious: a belief that the destiny of the people has been taken out of their hands, either by elites or the technology itself. Whereas in the postwar period Americans believed that the technocratic management of the economy could solve the problems of capitalism and history both, the reemergence of "automation" has come at a time when many people believe they are not in control of their society. Established political and social institutions no longer answer the call of their putative masters—the people and their democratic will. Economic, social, and environmental emergencies go unaddressed. Corporations and the executives who run them act as though they are perfectly free to decide the fate of billions. In this environment, many ask, "What will the machines do to us?" rather than, "What do we want our machines to do?" While the postwar automation discourse was composed in a major key, the twenty-first-century arrangement is played in minor, although it has the same effect: It hides labor so that it will cost less, explaining a political phenomenon as the operation of dispassionate technics.

The many discursive assumptions that must prevail in order to maintain this story of technological determinism often go unaddressed and unnoticed, as does the automation discourse's implicit argument that the degradation of working conditions means industrial progress. When it appears in print, "automation" almost always seems to indicate a straightforward technological process.[7] Take, for example, the reaction to a widely circulated paper by two economists seeking to show how robots have the potential to replace human workers in manufacturing. The study addresses the possible changes that robots could bring about on shop floors, although at present, it states, "because there are relatively few robots in the US economy, the number of jobs lost due to robots has been limited so far." An op-ed in the *New York Times* reacted to this report by announcing, "The Robots Have Descended on Trump Country." Another article ran, "Automation Nation: Evidence That Robots Are Winning the Race for American Jobs."[8]

Yet while journalists pursue imaginary robots across the country, workers face degraded conditions, unemployment, and unremunerated labor, often in the very industries said to march in the vanguard of the automated future. Far from acting autonomously, artificial intelligence requires a vast amount of human labor if it is to create value. Human beings, hidden from public view and organized on a gig basis for extremely low pay, are absolutely necessary to assess content, verify decisions, and tailor results. This invisible labor of closing the gaps in artificial intelligence, what some have called "ghost work," powers the systems of such profitable concerns as Google, Facebook, Microsoft, and Twitter. Google relies on an enormous "shadow work force" to make money, with temp workers outnumbering by tens of thousands the giant company's full-time staff. New machines or applications, touted as breakthroughs in convenience, extend the reach of the workplace into hitherto inaccessible regions of an individual's life so that one is, in fact, never off the job. While many struggle to find regular employment, others find themselves working for their employer at all hours, at home, in bed at night just before falling asleep. "Surveillance capitalism" has found ways to commodify and trade in some of the most intimate aspects of daily life. By the harvesting of data, produced by an individual's often unremunerated interaction with a machine, private companies seek to trade in the labor of mere selfhood and, more remarkably, to shape it. Everywhere—everywhere—human labor remains of the utmost importance in the creation of value. Yet rarely is that labor recognized. And as long as labor remains invisible, those who profit from it need not pay for it.[9]

It is my hope that this book will help reorient the discussion away from speculation about the future and toward the facts of the past and present. The current use of the idea of "automation" allows critics to sidestep the question of how power should be distributed at the workplace today and to speak instead of the possible effects of one type of mechanism or another. The capabilities of our machines are, in fact, a separate point entirely. As Lewis Mumford wrote a half-century ago, it is not from machines that we learn the purpose of machines. Free people do not ask others, "What will happen to us?" They ask themselves, "What do we want?"

Notes

Introduction

1. Sugrue, *Origins of the Urban Crisis*, 130.

2. Steigerwald, "Walter Reuther," 429–53.

3. Diebold, *Beyond Automation*, 54.

4. Olerich, *Cityless and Countryless World*, 74. Paul Lafargue and Oscar Wilde aside, many socialist and protosocialist thinkers of the late nineteenth century, such as Edward Bellamy and Thorstein Veblen, believed that human labor could be made consistent with human dignity, as discussed in Chapter 3. "This is the age of work," wrote Bryon Brooks of technological utopia in *Earth Revisited* (1893), 45. See Segal, "Technological Utopians," 129.

5. For a similar use of the term "automation discourse," see Benanav, "Automation and the Future of Work—1."

6. *Automation and Technological Change*, 84th Congress, 1st sess., 4.

7. On the existence of feedback mechanisms decades before the coining of the word "automation" see Mindell, *Between Human and Machine*.

8. Appelbaum and Schettkat, "Employment and Productivity."

9. Noble, *Progress Without People*; Cowan, *More Work for Mother*; Strasser, *Never Done*; Warner, *Letters of the Republic*; Marx and Smith, *Does Technology Drive History?*

10. See, e.g., Bell, *Coming of Post-Industrial Society*; Cummings, "Of Sorcerers and Thought Leaders"; Brick, "Optimism of the Mind."

11. A few of the many examples of this line of argument from across the political spectrum are Livingston, *No More Work*; Frase, *Four Futures*; Yang, *War on Normal People*; Oppenheimer, *The Robots Are Coming!*; Carr, *Glass Cage*; Brynjolfsson and McAfee, *Second Machine Age*; Ford, *Rise of the Robots*; West, *Future of Work*; Kaplan, *Humans Need Not Apply*; Bastani, *Fully Automated Luxury Capitalism*.

12. See Hounshell, "Automation, Transfer Machinery, and Mass Production"; Noble,

Forces of Production; Shaiken, *Work Transformed*; Sugrue, "'Forget About Your Inalienable Right to Work.'" Deindustrialization and Its Discontents at Ford, 1950–1953."

13. For figures on the percentage of workers employed globally in manufacturing see Freeman, *Behemoth*, xiii. On the general miscalculation of labor productivity in the twenty-first century see the two-part series by Benanav, "Automation and the Future of Work—1"; Benanav, "Automation and the Future of Work—2."

14. See Cowie, *Capital Moves*.

15. Diebold, *Beyond Automation*, 207.

16. Harder, "Address Before the Quad-City Conference on Automation at the Davenport Masonic Temple, Davenport, Iowa, on August 27, 1954," file 12, box 45, UAW President's Office, Walter P. Reuther Collection, Accession no. 261, Walter P. Reuther Library (hereafter WPRL); Boggs, "American Revolution," 38; Bell, *Work and Its Discontents*, 49–53; Reuther quoted in Subcommittee on Economic Stabilization, *Automation and Technological Change*, 117; Norbert Wiener to Walter Reuther, August 13, 1949, https://libcom.org/history/father-cybernetics-norbert-wieners-letter-uaw-president -walter-reuther, accessed July 8, 2016. On Reuther's response and their meeting, see Masani, *Norbert Wiener*, 273–74. Arendt, *Human Condition*, 5; "President Will Name Panel for Study of Automation: Kennedy Asks Congress to Give Rail Dispute to ICC for Settlement," *Wall Street Journal*, July 23, 1963, p. 3; Solanas, *SCUM Manifesto*, 3.

17. Webster quoted in Mills, *White Collar*, 8–9. "The dignity of work and of personal achievement, and the contempt for aristocratic idleness," Judith Shklar has written, "were from colonial times onward at the very heart of American civic self-identification." Shklar, *American Citizenship*, 1; see also 63–66. Frazier quoted in Foner, *Reconstruction*, 70.

18. On the challenges of industrialization to traditional political theory and the meaning of work see Kasson, *Civilizing the Machine*; Nye, *American Technological Sublime*; Segal, *Technological Utopianism in American Culture*; Rodgers, *Work Ethic in Industrial America*; Pursell, *Machine in America*. See also Rabinbach, *Human Motor*; Rabinach, *Eclipse of the Utopias of Labor*. For a book that argues that the technical design of machines reflects political values, especially in what society considers "automatic," see Mayr, *Authority, Liberty, and Automatic Machinery*.

19. Lincoln quoted in Foner, *Story of American Freedom*, 67–68.

20. There is a rich literature concerning the "bare life" meaning of work under conditions of industrial capitalism, e.g., Polanyi, *Great Transformation*, in particular "Speenhamland, 1795"; Arendt, *Human Condition*; Mills, *White Collar*, chap. 10; Foucault, "Faire vivre et laisser mourir: La naissance du racism"; Foucault, *History of Sexuality*, vol.1, pt. 4; Gorz, *Farewell to the Working Class*; Agamben, *Homo Sacer*. For a further elaboration of my own understanding of the bare life meaning of work, see Resnikoff, "Problem with Post-Work."

21. Roediger and Foner, *Our Own Time*, ix, 209–19. See also Hunnicutt, *Work Without End*.

22. Giedion, *Mechanization Takes Command*, 41–42.

23. Fitzgerald, *Every Farm a Factory*, 3–9; Kirby, *Rural Worlds Lost*.

24. Taylor, *Principles of Scientific Management.*

25. Bix, *Inventing Ourselves out of Jobs?*

26. Keynes, "Economic Possibilities for Our Grandchildren," *Collected Writings*, 9:325. Democratic congressman Hatton W. Sumners proposed denying patents in early 1932. "In the first place, a patent is not a thing which anyone can claim as a matter of right. . . . With millions of people idle who are willing to work, as a matter of practical common sense it seems to me an absurd thing for the Government to continue to offer this inducement to persons who will devise methods for taking away jobs of persons now engaged." *Congressional Record: Proceedings and Debates*, 82:322–24.

27. Mumford, *Condition of Man*, 397–98.

28. Cohen, *Consumers' Republic.*

29. Lichtenstein, *Walter Reuther*, chap. 13.

30. See Noble, *America by Design*; Pursell, *Technology in Postwar America*, chap. 1.

31. Truman, "Statement by the President Announcing the Use of the A-Bomb at Hiroshima." Collapsing the two kinds of conquest into one another, in 1947 residents of Lee County, Florida, believed that an atomic bomb dropped on a hurricane could disperse the oncoming storm and, so, requested that the Army detonate one the next time nature threatened their homes. Kirby, *Mockingbird Song*, 8.

32. Galbraith, *Affluent Society*, 2–3; Brick, *Transcending Capitalism*; Horowitz, *Anxieties of Affluence*; Kerr, Dunlop, Harbison, and Myers, *Industrialism and Industrial Man*, 1, 12.

33. For a few examples, see Bagrit, *Age of Automation*; Bittorf, *Automation*; Savignat, *Automation*; Friedmann, *Où va le travail humain?*; Acquaviva, *Automazione*; Brodskii, *Automatizatsiia v mashinostroenii.*

34. Mills, *White Collar*, 229; Arendt, *Human Condition*, 105.

Chapter 1. "The Machine Tells the Body How to Work"

1. "'Wildcat' Strike Closes Ford's Buffalo Plant," *Sun* (Baltimore), March 19, 1950, 7.

2. Correspondence between Martin Greber, Director, UAW Region 9, and Carl Rachlin, Workers Defense League, August 20, 1958, file 26, box 33, UAW Region 9 Collection, Accession no. 283, WPRL.

3. "Agreement," September 1957, file 17, box 22, UAW Ford Department Collection, pt. 2, Accession #105, WPRL.

4. The number for workers emplyed: "Pushbutton Progress: Two Ford Plants Mark Big New Step Toward the Automatic Factory," *Wall Street Journal*, December 31, 1953, p. 1; "Ours is": "Ford's Cleveland Plant to Make V-8 Mercury Engines," *Wall Street Journal*, November 20, 1952, 7; "Tour Disappoints Soviet Engineers: 2 Automation Experts Say They Did Not See What They Hoped to Here," *New York Times*, November 30, 1955, 10. On the Cleveland Engine Plant, see Meyer, "'Economic Frankenstein.'"

5. "Disruption" has become a byword of Silicon Valley entrepreneurs. Strangely, the word's obvious negative implications—frustration, anxiety, and chaos—seem to be lost on its contemporary promoters.

6. Bright, *Automation and Management*, 4–5.

7. Hounshell, "Automation, Transfer Machinery, and Mass Production." Other accounts of "automation" in the postwar auto industry include Sugrue, *Origins of the Urban Crisis*; Sugrue, "'Forget About Your Inalienable Right to Work'"; Lichtenstein, *Walter Reuther*, 290–91. The first experiments with transfer machines in auto manufacturing occurred in the 1920s when the A. O. Smith Corporation used them to reduce labor costs in the manufacture of car frames for Ford's models T and N.

8. Hounshell, "Automation, Transfer Machinery, and Mass Production"; Asher and Edsforth, "The Speedup,"74.

9. Terborgh, *Automation Hysteria*.

10. D. S. Harder, "Address Before the Quad-City Conference on Automation at the Davenport Masonic Temple, Davenport, Iowa, on August 27, 1954," file 12, box 45, UAW President's Office, Walter P. Reuther Collection, Accession no. 261, WPRL.

11. Lichtenstein, *Labor's War at Home*.

12. Brown, "Retreat Is No Answer."

13. Bright, *Automation and Management*, 12.

14. Denby, *Indignant Heart*, 138–41.

15. Harder, "Address Before the Quad-City Conference."

16. R. H. Sullivan, "Before the Annual Meeting of the Cleveland Society of Professional Engineers," January 25, 1955, file 5, box 49, UAW Vice President's Office, Ken Bannon Collection, Accession no. 935, WPRL.

17. G. G. Murie, "Automation," presented at the meeting of the District of Columbia Society of Professional Engineers, Washington D.C., January 24, 1955, file 61, box 26, Ted F. Silvey Collection, Accession no.#625, WPRL.

18. "Notes—Cassidy Speech—March 9, 1962: Christian Principles in Modern Industry, A View of Management," file 10, box 49, UAW Vice President's Office, Ken Bannon Collection, Accession no. 935, WPRL, emphasis in original.

19. J. Oppenheimer, "Age of Science," 21; *Saturday Review, special issue, Atoms and Automation*, January 22, 1955. Caroll Pursell has referred to the postwar technological enthusiasm and breathlessness as "a fog of visionary rhetoric," that clouded most public debate. Pursell, *Technology in Postwar America*, 59.

20. Bell, *Work and Its Discontents*, 49–53.

21. Braverman, "Automation: Promise and Menace."

22. Sullivan, "Before the Annual Meeting of the Cleveland Society of Professional Engineers."

23. Montgomery, *Workers' Control in America*, especially chap. 1.

24. Ken Bannon and Nelson Samp, "The Impact of Automation on Wages and Working Conditions in Ford Motor Company–UAW Relationships," undated address [probably 1957], file 31, box 40, UAW Ford Department Collection, pt., accession no. 105, WPRL.

25. "Automation and the Second Industrial Revolution," resolution adopted by the UAW 16th Constitutional Convention, 1957, Atlantic City, NJ, file 47, box 26, Ted F. Silvey Collection, accession no. 625, WPRL.

26. Sylvia B. Gottlieb to J. A. Beirne, Subject: Automation Sub-Committee—AFL-CIO Economic Policy Committee, January 16, 1957, folder 8, box 100, Communications Workers of America Records, Wag. 124, TAM.

27. Asher, "1949 Ford Speedup Strike"; Lichtenstein, "From Corporatism to Collective Bargaining."

28. *Automation and Technological Change*, 84th Congress, 8–10.

29. *Nation's Manpower Revolution*, 88th Congress, 2, 311, 18–19, 192.

30. Minutes from National Negotiations, "Mon July," [probably July 31] 1967, page 7, file 23, box 23, UAW Vice President's Office Ken Bannon Collection, Accession no. 935, WPRL.

31. Charles J. Dillon, "Skilled Trades Conference—Report," *The Transmitter: Official Publication of Amalgamated Local 863, UAW-CIO*, vol. 5, no. 2, February, 1955, 3, file 3, box 21, UAW Ford Department Collection, pt. 2, Accession no. 105, WPRL.

32. Reuther quoted in *Nation's Manpower Revolution*, 88th Congress, 209; Minutes from National Negotiations and "Nat'l Negotiations, 7–12–67," both documents in file 23, box 23, UAW Vice President's Office, Ken Bannon Collection, Accession no. #935, WPRL; "Resolution: Article VIII, Submitted by Ford Sub-Council #4, U.A.W," file 26, box 35, UAW Vice President's Office, Ken Bannon Collection, Accession no. 935, WPRL.

33. *Automation and Technological Change*, 84th Congress, 65.

34. Kennedy quoted in Kenneth D. Cassidy, "Automation in Perspective," March 21, 1962, file 10, box 49, UAW Vice President's Office, Ken Bannon Collection, Accession no. 935, WPRL.

35. "Ford Motor Company Management Briefs, 'Automation—And Its Role in a Growing Economy,'" February 21, 1961, file 1, box 9, UAW Vice President's Office, Ken Bannon Collection, Accession no. 935, WPRL.

36. "Denise, Malcolm, Questions and Answers Relating to His April 17, 1961 Testimony Before Congress," April 28, 1961, file 9, box 49, UAW Vice President's Office, Ken Bannon Collection, Accession no 935, WPRL.

37. Henry Ford II, "Before the National Open Hearth Steel and Blast Furnace, Coke Oven and Raw Materials Conference at Detroit, Michigan," April 10, 1962, file 10, box 49, UAW Vice President's Office, Ken Bannon Collection, Accession no 935, WPRL.

38. I take this way of making this point from Braverman, *Labor and Monopoly Capital*.

39. Edsforth and Asher speak to the centrality of speedup as a grievance in the 1930s. Edsforth and Asher, *Autowork*, 70–71; Kraus, *Many and the Few*, 44.

40. Reuther quoted in Asher, "1949 Ford Speedup Strike," 140. Peterson quoted in Hounshell, "Planning and Executing 'Automation,'" 79. James Beniger has argued that managers sought control in order to keep up with a more rapidly moving society. I argue that managerial control was not a response to speedup but the means to effect it. Beniger, *Control Revolution*, vii–viii.

41. Keynes, "Economic Possibilities for Our Grandchildren," 358–73. For a history of the debate surrounding Keynesian "technological unemployment" in the 1930s, see Bix, *Inventing Ourselves Out of Jobs?*.

42. Edsforth, Asher, and Boryczka, "The Speedup," 74–75.

43. "Biog. Data Nat Ganley," 1952, file 16, box 4, Nat Ganley Collection, Accession no 320, WPRL. On the McCarthy show trial of Ganley and the Michigan Six see Kristin Chinery, "Trial of the Michigan Six," http://reuther.wayne.edu/node/10490, accessed February 10, 2016.

44. Boggs, "American Revolution," w26–27.

45. James C. Sanderson to Ken Bannon, November 20, 1961, file 20, box 21, UAW Ford Department Collection, pt. 2, Accession no. 105, WPRL.

46. Resolution No. 7, Concerning Predetermined Time for Establishment of Production Standards, UAW Borg-Warner Council Conference, January 28, 29, 1961, file 11, box 11, UAW Vice President's Office, Douglas A. Fraser Collection, Accession no. 827, WPRL; GM Worker, "Skilled and Unskilled'" "What's Next for Labor?," 8.

47. Mazey, "Labor and the Economy," 11; "Biog. Data Nat Ganley." For a discussion of the Reuther administration's retreat from the shorter-hours movement, see Cutler, *Labor's Time*, 15. Like auto manufacturers, executives in the steel industry also sought to increase profits in the postwar period with a policy of speedup. Whereas the UAW compromised on the issue of production standards, the United Steel Workers of America were somewhat better able to resist speedup, represented by Section 2-B of the national contract, which denied managers the right to alter work practices unless necessitated by major technical innovations in the labor process. In 1959 the steel industry sought to remove Section 2-B from the contract, leading to the 1959 steel strike, the largest work stoppage in U.S. history. Smemo, Sonti, and Winant, "Conflict and Consensus."

48. Walter E. Schilling, "Production Standards Report for Executive Board Production Standards Committee," April 3, 1961, file 10, box 11, UAW Vice President's Office, Douglas A. Fraser Collection, Accession no. 827, WPRL.

49. Ken Bannon, "Some Contract Experience Under Automation," February 22, 1957, file 32, box 40, UAW Ford Department Collection, pt. 2, Accession no. 105, WPRL.

50. "Automation and the Second Industrial Revolution," file 47, box 26, Ted F. Silvey Collection, Accession no. 625, WPRL.

51. "Resolution Dealing with Decentralization and Severance Pay," submitted by Local 600, 1958, file 15, box 7, UAW Vice President's Office, Ken Bannon Collection, Accession no. 935, WPRL.

52. Terrano, "Working Day," 3.

53. "Automation Brings Chaos," 1.

54. Bannon, "Some Contract Experience Under Automation."

55. Denby, *Workers Battle Automation*, 13.

56. Bannon and Samp, "Impact of Automation on Wages and Working Conditions."

57. Ibid.

58. Editorial, 4; Dunayevskaya, *Marxism and Freedom*, 268–69, italics original.

59. Butler, "Crisis in Auto."

60. Harder, "Before the Quad-City Conference."

61. R. E. Roberts, writing in *Advanced Management*, May 1954, quoted in Butler, "Crisis in Auto."

62. James R. Franklin, "Recommendations on Work Standards," February 24, 1961, file 11, box 11, UAW Vice President's Office, Douglas A. Fraser Collection, Accession no. 827, WPRL.

63. Ted F. Silvery, "The Technology of Automation," 1955, file 2, box 28, Ted F. Silvey Collection, Accession no. 625, WPRL.

64. "Black Workers Protest UAW Racism March on Cobo Hall," 1969, file 24, box 1, Detroit Revolutionary Movements, Accession no. 874, WPRL. On racism and autoworker employment in Detroit in the postwar period, see Lewis-Colman, *Race Against Liberalism*.

65. For a scholarly assessment of Owens's life and work, see Jones, *Dreadful Deceit*, chap. 6.

66. Denby [Owens], *Workers Battle Automation*, 54–55.

67. Ibid., 61, 16, 8–9.

68. Ibid., 10–11.

69. Ibid., 12–14.

70. Ibid., 51.

71. Ibid., 28.

72. Ibid., 21–22.

73. Ibid., 23.

74. "Readers' Views: Automation," 4.

75. Denby [Owens], *Workers Battle Automation*, 17–19.

76. Ibid., 22.

77. Ibid., 12.

78. Ibid., 51.

Chapter 2. The Electronic Brain's Tired Hands

1. Diebold quoted in Henderson, *Managerial Innovations*, 21; Willard D. Smith, "Personality: An Evangelist for Automation," *New York Times*, March 28, 1965, F3; Arendt, *Human Condition*, 129; *Automation and Technological Change*, 84th Congress, 7–8.

2. Henderson, *Managerial Innovations*, 1; Cross, *John Diebold*, 165.

3. Journal entry for July 11, 1965, folder 9, box 111, John Diebold Papers, ser. 2, Harvard Business School (hereafter HBS) (Note: The finding aid lists Diebold's journal as residing in box 109. At the time I consulted it, it was misfiled in 111.); Bing and Weindling, *Agent of Change*, 89–90, 92.

4. Bell, *Coming of Post-Industrial Society*, 20, 37 (emphasis original). For the view that the origins of the idea of a postindustrial society reside in the immediate postwar period, see Brick, "Optimism of the Mind," 348–80. Brick argues that the "formative, historical moment" for the "theory of postindustrial society" was 1958 to 1967. That may be. But the denigration of the act of laboring, as well as the elevation of "infor-

mation" to a commodity, two crucial elements of that theory, appeared in the late 1940s and early 1950s. For the view that "information" was central to this narrative, see Cummings, "Of Sorcerers and Thought Leaders."

5. Discussions of the historical importance of "information" often participate in its fetishization as a commodity rather than explaining how that commodification took place in the postwar period. For a critical interrogation of the information revolution see two pieces by Dan Schiller, "From Culture to Information and Back Again" and *How To Think About Information*. See also Kline, *Cybernetics Moment*, esp. 244. For the more typical accounts of "information" see Yates, *Control Through Communication*; Brock, *Second Information Revolution*; Cortada, *Digital Hand*; Cortada and Chandler, *Nation Transformed by Information*; Gleick, *Information*.

6. Frank Rose, "The Prince of Gurus," *Business Month Magazine*, 1989, quoted in Bing and Weindling, *Agent of Change*, 21; Drucker, "Foreword," vii–viii.

7. Memorandum, April 1953, folder 5, box 110, John Diebold Papers, ser. 2, HBS.

8. Diebold, *Automation*, ix.

9. On what Leo Marx calls a "semantic void" in the history of technology—specifically concerning "technology," which also became a household word in this period—see Marx, "Technology," 561–77.

10. "The Automatic Factory," 160. *Fortune*'s short editorial piece accompanied a now-famous article by Leaver and Brown, "Machines Without Men," 165, 192, 204. Leaver and Brown spoke of the coming of a "new industrial order." On Leaver's co-patent for a record playback system, see Noble, *Forces of Production*, 159.

11. Cohen, *Consumers' Republic*; Mills, *White Collar*, ix.

12. Diebold, Englert, Gage, Lazarus, Saslow, Siropolis, Yanowitz, and Wright, "Making the Automatic Factory a Reality," May 15, 1951, Georges F. Doriot Papers, Harvard Business School Teaching Records, 1925–1974, I. B. Manufacturing Course Student Reports, 1932–1966, HBS. Also available online: Harvard Business School, Baker Library Historical Collections, Georges F. Doriot, accessed March 17, 2019, https://www.library .hbs.edu/docs/MakingTheAutomaticFactoryAReality.pdf

13. Doriot, Manufacturing: Notes of lectures given at the Harvard Business School, 1951–1952, 88–89, 93; ser. I; V. 4, Mss: 784, Georges F. Doriot Papers, HBS.

14. On SAGE see Edwards, *Closed World*, chap. 3. For guest speakers in Doriot's class see "List of Guest speakers by year," Folder "Notes on Manufacturing Course, 1927–1974," box 1, Mss: 784, Georges F. Doriot Papers, 1921–1984, HBS.

15. Doriot, *Manufacturing*, 37, 106.

16. The literature concerning the cybernetics movement is extensive. The most lucid and accessible account, I find, is Kline, *Cybernetics Moment*.

17. Wiener, *Cybernetics*, 11.

18. Diebold, Journal entries, 1965, August 10.

19. Diebold et al., *Making the Automatic Factory a Reality*, 1.

20. Diebold, *Automation*, 2, 110.

21. See Susman, *Culture as History*, chap. 11; Kihlstedt, "Utopia Realized," 99–100. See also chap. 8 of Nye, *American Technological Sublime*.

22. Diebold, *Beyond Automation*, 117–18, 12–13 (emphasis in original).

23. Diebold, *Automation*, 67–68, 88–89.

24. Ibid., 33–34.

25. "Diebold Group Planning Paper—1962–1967—Working Paper No.1," undated (most likely 1962), folder 8, box 109, ser. 2, John Diebold Papers, HBS.

26. John Diebold, "The Revolution That Fails to Take Place," May 3, 1963, vol. 11, ser. 9, John Diebold Papers, HBS.

27. Diebold, *Beyond Automation*, 176, 178, chap. 10.

28. Kline, *Cybernetics Moment*, chap. 1; Shannon, "Mathematical Theory of Communication."

29. Diebold et al., "Making the Automatic Factory a Reality," 12–13.

30. Hayles, *How We Became Posthuman*, 2.

31. Diebold, *Automation*, 90–91, 110, 121, 94.

32. *Automation and Technological Change*, 8–9.

33. *Labor Looks at the White Collar Worker: Proceedings of the Conference on Problems of the White Collar Worker*, 1957, 12, 14, folder 5, box 66, Pamphlet Collection, Reference Center for Marxist Studies, TAM.

34. Shannan Wayne Clark has shown how in the 1930s many self-identified white-collar workers, especially in New York, saw themselves as a part of the working class. After the nationwide purges of the Left, many white-collar workers and the few unions they had organized lost much of their radicalism. Clark, "White-Collar Workers Organize."

35. Mills, *White Collar*, x. Statistics cited in Russakoff Hoos, *Automation in the Office*, 23–24. On the increasing number of women selling their labor on the labor market in the postwar period see Kessler-Harris, *Out to Work*, esp. chap. 11.

36. The manager is quoted in Newgarden, *Men, Machines, and Methods*, 5 (emphasis in original); Burr et al., *White-Collar Restiveness: A Growing Challenge*.

37. Louis Hyman relates how consultancies arose in the 1950s to advise companies on how to install digital computers to degrade clerical work, often by also bringing in temp workers to perform clerical tasks. Hyman, *Temp*, 135, 139–40, 212, 205.

38. Diebold quoted in Aulick and Cross, *Careers in the Age of Automation*, 8.

39. For the view that the computer industry relied on the commodification of "information" as a way to encourage private companies to purchase computers, see Cummings, "Of Sorcerers and Thought Leaders."

40. Levin, *Office Work and Automation*, 8. I take this point from Haigh, "Inventing Information Systems," 34.

41. Levin, *Office Work and Automation*, ix, 1, 16; "Howard S. Levin, 65; Founded 2 Companies," *New York Times*, July 29, 1989.

42. Haigh, "Inventing Information Systems," 39.

43. Russakoff Hoos, *Automation in the Office*, 2, 30–31. See Braverman, *Labor and Monopoly Capital*, chap. 15, "Clerical Workers."

44. "ADP—Technician's Lilliputian or Management's Gulliver," November 11, 1964, 5 (emphasis in original), vol. 14, ser. 9, John Diebold Papers, HBS; "Summary of

Research Activities, Second Quarter of 1967," 7–8, 5, vol. 65, ser. 2, John Diebold Papers, HBS.

45. *The Paperwork Explosion* (1967), accessed March 18, 2019, https://www.youtube.com/watch?v=_IZw2CoYztk

46. *The Information Machine*, 1958, accessed March 29, 2019, https://www.youtube.com/watch?v=oyA06KidoMA

47. Davies, *Woman's Place,* 4–6, 52–59.

48. Katherine Turk has written of the attempts by the National Secretaries Association to protect secretarial labor's craft associations from mechanization. Turk, "Labor's Pink-Collar Aristocracy"; Zuboff, "White-Collar Body in History,"; Zuboff, *In the Age of the Smart Machine.* On the mechanization of the American office in the late 1970s and 1980s by means of microcomputers, as opposed to mainframes and batch processing, see Resnikoff, "The Paradox of Automation: QWERTY and the Neuter Keyboard."

49. *Labor Looks at the White Collar Worker,* 22.

50. Reuther quoted in ibid., 8–9.

51. Ibid., 31–32.

52. Transcript #45, [name of interviewee redacted], file 11, box 2, MC 366, Jean Tepperman Papers, Harvard Business School, Schlesinger Library (hereafter SCH).

53. Humphrey, "IDP in the Pre-Computer Area," 7–8.

54. Freeman et al., *Impact of Office Automation,* 34.

55. Ibid., 5, 30, 28.

56. "Eleanor Coughlin," file 4, box 1, MC 365, Massachusetts History Workshop Records, 1980–1984, SCH.

57. Tepperman, *Not Servants,* 48.

58. "A Life Insurance Clerical Worker in Western Massachusetts, 1959–71, Mary Roberge," file 6, box 1, MC 365, Massachusetts History Workshop Records, 1980–1984, SCH.

59. Russakoff Hoos, *Automation in the Office,* 43.

60. Transcript #17, [name of interviewee redacted], file 4, box 1, MC 366, Jean Tepperman Papers, SCH.

61. Transcript #4, Laurie [name of interviewee], file 1, box 1, MC 366, Jean Tepperman Papers, SCH.

62. Transcript of Oral History—Shirley Haapanen, 4/10/82, Interviewer: Laurie Haapanen, file 4, box 1, MC 365, Massachusetts History Workshop Records, 1980–1984, SCH.

63. Transcript #15, [name of interviewee redacted], file 4, box 1, MC 366, Jean Tepperman Papers, SCH.

64. Ibid.

65. Transcript #12, [name of interviewee redacted], file 3, box 1, MC 366, Jean Tepperman Papers, SCH.

66. Transcript #17, Jean Tepperman Papers, SCH.

67. Transcript #4, Jean Tepperman Papers, SCH. On Frank Benson, see *U.S. News*

and World Report, September 18, 1978, quoted in, National Association of Office Workers, *Race Against Time*, 8.

68. Transcript #18, "Toni and Ramon," file 4, box 1, MC 366, Jean Tepperman Papers, SCH. On Perot's winning the Blue Cross Blue Shield contracts see Steven A. Holmes, "Billion-Dollar Enigma," *New York Times*, August 19, 1996; Gary Jacobson, "The Perot Era: EDS Grows From One-Man Operation to Industry Leader," *Dallas News*, December 8, 2012, accessed August 17, 2017, https://www.dallasnews.com/business/business/2012/12/08/the-perot-era-eds-grows-from-one-man-operation-to-industry-leader

69. Transcript #18, "Toni and Ramon."

70. National Association of Office Workers, *Race Against Time*, 26.

71. Marcia Blumenthal, "DDP," 1979, 9.

72. Wyatt and Hecker, "Occupational Changes," 47–48. On the "automation" of telephone switching as a speedup, see Green, *Race on the Line*, 128–29.

Chapter 3. The Liberation of the Leisure Class

1. J. R. Oppenheimer, "Age of Science," 21.

2. The newspaper is quoted in Arendt, *Human Condition*, 1; A. A. Kucher, speech at the final session of the 8th International Automobile Technical Congress, May 13, 1960, file 8, box 49, UAW Vice President's Office, Ken Bannon Collection, Accession no. 935, WPRL; "Rocket Takes off Today; Seeks Data 200 Miles Up," *Washington Post and Times Herald*, July 4, 1957, B10; John F. Kennedy, "Address Before a Joint Session of Congress."

3. Arendt, *Human Condition*, 2, 128–29.

4. Robert C. Cowen, "From the Bookshelf: When Machines Control Machines," *Christian Science Monitor*, April 15, 1953, 13.

5. Mills, *White Collar*, 235.

6. Hunnicut, *Work Without End*.

7. Foner and Roediger, *Our Own Time*, ix, 209–19.

8. Bellamy, *Looking Backward*.

9. "Predatory culture": Veblen, *Theory of the Leisure Class*, 36; "Labour acquires": Veblen, *Theory of the Leisure Class*, 17.

10. Department of Labor report cited in Philip Hampson, "Public Spends Vast Sums in Leisure Time: Shorter Work Week Spurs Recreation," *Chicago Daily Tribune*, May 4, 1952, A9.

11. Report cited in Shaffer, "Leisure in the Great Society."

12. William M. Blair, "Nixon Foresees 4-Day Work Week," *New York Times*, Sept. 23, 1956, 1.

13. "Automation: Man vs. Machine, Golden Age of Leisure or Nightmare of Lost Jobs?" *Hartford Courant*, May 17, 1955, 1.

14. "Labor Force Statistics from the Current Population," Survey Databases, Tables & Calculators; Bureau of Labor Statistics.

15. "Automation Is Upon Us," *Los Angeles Times*, October 25, 1953, B4; William M. Freeman, "Automation Stirs New Revolution," *New York Times*, January 4, 1954, 76.

16. *Automation and Technological Change*, 84th Congress, 1.

17. Ibid., 7–8.

18. Ibid., 117.

19. Ibid., 203; "Proceedings, Transcript," 3, folder 7, box 100, Communications Workers of America Records, WAG.124, TAM.

20. *Automation and Technological Change*, 120, 118.

21. *Ibid.*, 117.

22. *Ibid.*, 121.

23. Ibid., 4–5.

24. "Special Report to Readers On: Automation," *Business Week*, October 1, 1955.

25. *Automation and Technological Change*, 13–14.

26. Charlesworth, "Comprehensive Plan for the Wise Use of Leisure," 32, 36.

27. Mary Lou Loper, "Psychiatrist Cites Perils in Leisure," *Los Angeles Times*, April 21, 1960, A1.

28. Shaffer, "Leisure in the Great Society," n.p.

29. For an analysis of this postwar tendency that focuses mainly on literature see Greif, *Age of the Crisis of Man*. Even some of those concerned with the managing of factories felt it necessary to plumb these existential depths. Take, for example, some of John Diebold's colleagues at the Harvard Business School, who, in their final thesis, "Human Conditioning in the Factory," announced: "We have attempted to define the human." "Human Conditioning in the Factory," 1953 manufacturing course report, v. 28, Mss: 784, Georges F. Doriot Papers, 1921–1984, HBS.

30. "The Playboy Panel."

31. Potter, *People of Plenty*, xv, xx. For a discussion of Potter's conservatism and his love-hate relationship with aristocratic notions of the good life and an ideal society see Horowitz, *Anxieties of Affluence*, chap 3.

32. For Aristotle's understanding of natural slaves see *Politics*, bk. 1, chap. 5 of.

33. Richard, *Golden Age of the Classics in America*, 187–89. George Fitzhugh was pleasantly surprised to find that his arguments were identical to those Aristotle had made in defense of slave societies: "To our surprise, we found that our theory of the origin of society was identical with his, and that we had employed not only the same illustrations, but the very same words," *Cannibals All!*, xxii.

34. Pieper, *Leisure*, 94, 35 (emphasis in original).

35. Riesman, *Lonely Crowd*, 271, 268.

36. Bell, *Work and Its Discontents*, 36–38; Bell, "Bogey of Automation. On the history of the politics of working people's free time see Rosenzweig, *Eight Hours for What We Will*.

37. On the division between the early and late Marx on the place of labor in utopia see Rabinbach, *Eclipse of the Utopias of Labor*, chap. 7. On Marx's debt to Aristotelian philosophy see McCarthy, *Marx and the Ancients*; McCarthy, *Marx and Aristotle*.

38. Marcuse, *Eros and Civilization*, 85, 134 (emphasis in original).

39. Herbert Marcuse's preface to Dunayevskaya, *Marxism and Freedom*, 9–11.

40. Quotations from Anderson, "Marcuse's and Fromm's Correspondence."

41. De Grazia, *Of Time, Work, and Leisure*, 414; E. P. Thompson used de Grazia's book as a source in his classic essay "Time, Work-Discipline, and Industrial Capitalism," 56.

42. *Nation's Manpower Revolution*, 88th Congress, 163–64.

43. Charlesworth, "Comprehensive Plan," 35–36.

44. Theobald, *Free Men and Free Markets*, 24–25.

45. Quoted in Ward, *Ferrytale*, 91.

46. Alice Mary Hilton to James Boggs, August 31, 1963, File 17, Box 1, James and Grace Lee Boggs Collection, Acc #1342, WPRL.

47. James Boggs, "A paper presented to the Alliance for Jobs or Income Now," Dec. 5, 1964, file 13, box 3, James and Grace Lee Boggs Collection, Accession no. 1342, WPRL (emphasis in original).

48. Kirk, *Conservative Mind*, 228, 430; Weaver, *Ideas Have Consequences*.

49. Kirk, *Conservative Mind*, 427, 228, 430; Tate quoted in Pieper, *Leisure*, 148.

50. Weaver, *Ideas Have Consequences*, 71, 105–6.

51. Mills, *White Collar*, 233–35.

52. Ibid., 215 (emphasis added).

53. Ibid., 229, 236.

54. Swados, "Myth of the Happy Worker," 65–67.

55. Braverman, "Automation." In another ten years Braverman would in *Labor and Monopoly Capital* look back on the postwar changes to industrial production and abandon the automation discourse, coming instead to the conclusion that under conditions of capitalism the owners of capital degraded human labor to make it cheaper and that cheap labor remained the backbone of industrial capitalism.

56. Braverman, "World of Work."

57. Arendt, *Human Condition*, 6, 1–3.

58. Ibid., 5, 346.

59. Ibid., 43–44, 5.

60. Arendt, *Eichmann in Jerusalem*, 250.

61. "Remarks by UAW President Walter P. Reuther," January 24, 1958, file 15, box 7, UAW Vice President's Office, Ken Bannon Collection, Accession no. 935, WPRL.

62. "Recommended UAW 1958 Collective Bargaining Program," January 1958, file 12, box 7, UAW Vice President's Office, Ken Bannon Collection, Accession no. 935, WPRL.

63. Arendt, *Human Condition*, 1–3.

64. Clarke, *Childhood's End*.

65. Clynes and Kline, "Cyborgs and Space," 26–27, 74–76.

66. Halacy, *Cyborg*, 8.

67. *Nation's Manpower Revolution*, 88th Congress, 19–20.

68. Speaking of the rise of "modern man," Lewis Mumford wrote in 1952: "In the very act of giving authority to the automaton, he released the id and recognized the

forces of life only in their most raw and brutal manifestations." Mumford, *Art and Technics*, 57. For a discussion of *The Tempest* see L. Marx, *Machine in the Garden*, chap. 2; Vonnegut, *Player Piano*. The idea for the novel came to Vonnegut while working for General Electric, where he learned of the company's early experiments in record playback technology, a means of making skilled machining an automatic process. Noble, *Forces of Production*, 166, 359–60.

69. Arendt, *Human Condition*, 6–7.

70. Ibid., 103–5; King, *Arendt in America*, 161.

71. Albert Sejlstedt Jr., "Astronaut Recovered After 4,500 M.P.H. Flight," *Sun* (Baltimore), May 6, 1961, 1; Reinhold G. Ensz, "Moscow Will Greet Gagarin on Friday: Soviet Hero Reveals Historic Flight Details," *Austin Statesman*, April 13, 1961, A1.

Chapter 4. Anticipating Oblivion

1. "Proceedings, Transcript," 3, folder 7, box 100, Communications Workers of America Records, WAG.124, TAM.

2. The idea of a guaranteed annual income was not unheard-of in the 1950s, however. John Kenneth Galbraith included it in combination with full employment policies in *The Affluent Society*, chap. 21. See also Steensland, *Failed Welfare Revolution*.

3. *Automation and Technological Change*, 84th Congress, 4–5.

4. Galbraith, *Affluent Society*, 345–46, 355. Italics original.

5. Silverman and Yanowitch, *Worker in "Post-Industrial" Capitalism*, 8, 10.

6. Quoted in Shaffer, "Leisure in the Great Society."

7. Clark and Wirtz quoted in *Nation's Manpower Revolution*, 88th Congress, 2, 18–19.

8. Stuart Gerry Brown, "The Recession in Automobiles and Farm Implements, and the Problem of Automation," June 1, 1956, File: "Labor: Automation," box 93, Adlai Stevenson II, W. Willard Wirtz, Papers, JFKPL.

9. John F. Kennedy, 1968 Democratic National Convention, 15 July, 1960, http://www.jfklibrary.org/Asset-Viewer/AS08q50Yz0SFUZg9uOi4iw.aspx, accessed August 9, 2016.

10. White, *Making of the President*, 99.

11. Hudis, "Workers as Reason," 271. See also Phillips and Dunayevskaya, *Coal Miners' General Strike*.

12. "Editorial: Who Is in Control of Production?" *News and Letters*, November 11, 1955.

13. "No Way Out: Miners Often Trapped Behind Tons of Coal," *News and Letters*, March 5, 1957, 2.

14. Lewis quoted in Nyden, "Rank-and-File Movements," 176–81; White, *Making of the President*, 99.

15. *Nation's Manpower Revolution*, 6.

16. Journal Entry, April 28, 1965, folder 9, box 111 (finding aid listed journals in box 109, but I found them in box 111), ser. 2, John Diebold Papers, HBS.

17. Ibid., entry for July 31, 1965.

18. "President Will Name Panel for Study of Automation: Kennedy Asks Congress to Give Rail Dispute to ICC for Settlement," *Wall Street Journal*, July 23, 1963, 3.

19. Brotherhood of Railroad Trainmen, "Facts and Issues," July 15, 1963, File: "Automation," box 28, ser. 5, Theodore C. Sorenson Personal Papers, JFKPL.

20. Brotherhood of Railroad Trainmen, "Position of the Employees," July 15, 1963, File: "Automation," box 28, ser. 5, Theodore C. Sorenson Personal Papers, JFKPL.

21. John D. Pomfret, "Arbiters Order Gradual Cutback in Rail Firemen: Panel Rules 90% of Such Jobs in Freight and Yard Service Unnecessary," *New York Times*, November 27, 1963, 1; "Issues Involved in the Railroad Dispute," *Wall Street Journal*, July 11, 1963, 3; Brotherhood of Railroad Trainmen, "Facts and Issues."

22. Pomfret, "Arbiters Order Gradual Cutback."

23. Jones, *March on Washington*.

24. Kersten and Lang, *Reframing Randolph*, 21.

25. Ibid., 144.

26. Ibid., 237; "March on Washington for Jobs and Freedom, Transcript, pt. 6 of 17, accessed April 7, 2019, http://openvault.wgbh.org/catalog/A_CB387942466C46 F6BAE6528BAFD53055. Randolph and Rustin, along with Martin Luther King Jr., would maintain the demand for full employment and the right to a job in their 1966 *Freedom Budget*.

27. Since the early twentieth century, job training had appeared as a middle way for liberals. The MDTA was different from earlier initiatives in its commitment to support programs anywhere in the nation, its promise to provide 100 percent federal funding for the first two years, and its declared desire to see trainees move immediately into full-time jobs. Seymour L. Wolfbein to K. John Domar, March 4, 1963, File: Branch Chron (1), box 1, Accession no. 68A-2834, RG 369, Albert Shostack's Subject Files, 1962–1967, Records of the Employment and Training Administration, Office of Manpower, Automation, and Training, NARA; Stein, "Conflict, Change, and Economic Policy," 84. On education as a liberal answer to the degradation of labor, see Silverman and Yanowitch, *Worker in "Post-Industrial" Capitalism*, 8.

28. Matusow, *Unraveling of America*, 32–35, 104; Attewell, *People Must Live by Work*, 191–93; Kremen, "MDTA: The Origins of the Manpower Development and Training Act of 1962."

29. Manpower Administration, "On the Job Training Under the Manpower Development and Training Act," File: "OJT programs—MDTA," box 2, Accession no. 68A-2834, RG 369, Albert Shostack's Subject Files, 1962–1967, Records of the Employment and Training Administration, Office of Manpower, Automation, and Training, NARA; Stein, *Pivotal Decade*, 335; Weir, *Politics and Jobs*, 9, 69; O'Connor, *Poverty Knowledge*.

30. Memorandum from Merwin Hans to Sam Morganstein, August 11, 1965, File: "Adult Work Experience Program Planning, FY 1966," box 1, Accession no. 68A-2834, RG 369, Albert Shostack's Subject Files, 1962–1967, Records of the Employment and Training Administration, Office of Manpower, Automation, and Training, NARA.

31. "Manpower" (master copy), 1964–1965, "Manpower" (master copy) [not dated or signed, probably from 1965], folder 5, box 22, TAM 050, J. B. S. Hardman Papers, TAM.

32. Elmer L. Baab to Charles A. Gilmore, March 29, 1965; "Program of Evaluation and Counseling for the Retraining of Displaced Factory Workers as Practical Psychiatric Nurses"; "Meeting Held at Shapero School of Nursing, Detroit, Michigan, April 2, 1963, Summary'" all located in File: "Sinai Hospital, Detroit, Michigan," box 9, A29, RG 369, Field Services Division Subject Files and Special Case Files, 1963–1965/Frank Purcell and Reading File, Records of the Employment and Training Administration, Office of Manpower, Automation, and Training, NARA.

33. Mangum, *MDTA*, 2; "Employment and Training Legislation—1968," Committee on Labor and Public Welfare, Senate Hearings (1968), 389, quoted in Matusow, *Unraveling of America*, 105. See also Kremen, "MDTA."

34. Earl D. Main, "A Nationwide Evaluation of M.D.T.A. Institutional Job Training Programs," September, 1966, file N/A, box 2, A1/28, RG 369, Records of the Employment and Training Administration, Office of Manpower, Automation, and Training, NARA.

35. "70 Persons in Job Training," *Self-Determination*, The Woodlawn Organization Newsletter, Aug. 26, 1964, 1, File: "Region VIII–Chicago, Illinois, The Woodlawn Organization, Chicago, News Clippings, box 9, A1 25, RG 369, Field Project Case Files 1963–1965, Records of the Employment and Training Administration, Office of Manpower, Automation, and Training, NARA.

36. Boggs, "American Revolution"; M. T. Puryear, "Automation and the Retraining of Negro Workers," September, 1962, File: "National Urban League," box 1, A1.23, RG 369, National Organizations Subject Files, 1963–1965, Records of the Employment and Training Administration, Office of Manpower, Automation, and Training, NARA.

37. Matusow, *Unraveling of America*, 237–240.

38. National Association of Manufacturers quoted in Maclean, *Freedom Is Not Enough*, 68.

39. "Speech by Secretary of Labor Wirtz," May 28, 1964, File: "President's Advisory Committee on Labor Management Policy," Box 136, W. Willard Wirtz Speech Files, JFKPL.

40. Robinson, *Marching with Dr. King*, 36, 80–82.

41. "Fort Worth Project of the Armour Automation Committee," 53–57.

42. "Longshoring and Meatpacking Automation Settlements," 1108–10; "Progress Report of Armour's Tripartite Automation Committee," 851–57; "Fort Worth Project of the Armour Automation Committee," 53–57. See also Halpern, *Down on the Killing Floor*.

43. Robinson, *Marching with Dr. King*, 139.

44. Quoted in Horowitz, "*Negro and White, Unite and Fight!*" 255.

45. Ibid., 248.

46. Ibid., chap. 10; Slichter quotation, 24; Horowitz quotation, 278–79. See also Genoways, *Chain*; Pachirat, *Every Twelve Seconds*; Striffler, *Chicken*.

47. Cotton quoted in Robinson, *Marching with Dr. King*, 131–33.

48. Ibid.

49. Ibid.

50. "Longshoring and Meatpacking Automation Settlements," 1108–10.

51. "Progress Report of Armour's Tripartite Automation Committee," 851–57. Helstein quoted in Horowitz, *"Negro and White, Unite and Fight!"* 256.

52. "Fort Worth Project," 56–57.

53. Helstein quoted in Horowitz, *"Negro and White, Unite and Fight!"* 256; Armour's concessions: Halpern, *Down on the Killing* Floor, 247–50.

54. Levinson, *Box*, 116–17; Lim, "Automation and San Francisco Class 'B' Longshoremen."

55. Hilo worker quoted in Weir, *Singlejack Solidarity*, 98. Harry Bridges quoted in Moody, "Understanding the Rank-and-File Rebellion," 115.

56. Levinson, *Box*, 116–17, 251, 122–33; Weir, *Singlejack Solidarity*, 48–49.

57. "While these changes": Weir, *Singlejack Solidarity*, 48; "Production almost doubled": ibid., 49; Bridges quoted in Levinson, *Box*, 156.

58. "Automation Held Deep Administration Concern: Kennedy Commission Plan Viewed as Showing the Gravity of Outlook," *New York Times*, July 24, 1963, 32.

59. Kremen, "MDTA."

60. *Nation's Manpower Revolution*, pt. 2. The three bills were: H.R. 8429, 88th Congress, 1st sess., Sept. 12, 1963; H.R. 9980, 88th Congress, 2nd sess., Feb. 13, 1964; and H.R. 10310, 88th Congress, 2nd sess., Mar. 10, 1964.

61. Pomfret, "Arbiters Order Gradual Cutback in Rail Firemen," 1.

62. *Nation's Manpower Revolution*, 7; *National Commission on Technology, Automation, and Economic Progress*.

63. "President Names 14 to Automation Unit," *New York Times*, November 15, 1964, 64.

64. Public Law 88–444, quoted in *Technology and the American Economy*, xiv.

65. Bell, "Government by Commission," 3–4.

66. All quoted in "Commission Splits over Automation: Three Union Leaders Said to Be Irked by Report," *Sun* (Baltimore), December 24, 1965, A1.

67. Bell, "Government by Commission," 3–4, 5.

68. Bell, "The Bogey of Automation," *New York Review of Books*, Aug. 26, 1965; Bell, *Work and Its Discontents*, 49–53.

69. *Technology and the American Economy*, 6. Some of the commission's business representatives felt obligated, in response, to include their own General Comment, claiming that "this report fails to give adequate emphasis to the positive contributions of technology." Ibid., 7.

70. Ibid., 109–13.

71. Ibid.

72. Bell, "Government by Commission," 3–6. Bell concluded that the use of commissions was beneficial to government. Congress was not a "forum," he said.

Chapter 5. Machines of Loving Grace

1. Ad Hoc Committee on the Triple Revolution, *Triple Revolution*. Pursell, *Technology in Postwar America*, 148–49; Elrod, "Fully Automated Luxury Socialism." Many at the time were quick to note that the idea of a guaranteed annual income had precedents: Bertrand Russell's 1932 "In Praise of Idleness" had suggested a similar idea. Steensland, *Failed Welfare Revolution*.

2. "Wirtz Criticizes Proposal to Guarantee Pay for All," *Louisville (KY) Times*, March 24, 1964, 3.

3. "Goldwater," *Los Angeles Times*, April 1, 1964, pt. 1, 2.

4. Kristol, "Jobs and the Man," 6–7.

5. W. H. Ferry to Todd Gitlin, September 10, [1963], TGPC.

6. *Nation's Manpower Revolution*, 88th Congress, 114.

7. Author interview with Todd Gitlin, December 3, 2015; Memorandum, W. H. Ferry to all members of the October Group, all other signers of *The Triple Revolution*, March 4, 1964: "Please note, pursuant to our agreement with Dr. Oppenheimer, that no mention of the Institute for Advanced Studies or of him is to be made in connection with the preparation of the Statement," TGPC. Oppenheimer "looked ethereal," Gitlin remembered; he had a "spectral quality."

8. Ward, *Ferrytale*, 93.

9. "A Proposal from Ralph Helstein, Robert Theobald, and W. H. Ferry," July 15, 1963, TGPC. "I can't dispute the general observations made by Helstein, Theobald, and Ferry," Harry Braverman responded. "I wonder, however, if the changes in our social and economic being are as imminent as they envisage." Harry Braverman to an unknown correspondent, undated, written from Los Angeles, TGPC. On the unemployment rate see Bureau of Labor Statistics, Databases, Tables, and Calculators by Subject, "Unemployment Rate," accessed March 8, 2018, https://data.bls.gov/timeseries/LNU04000000?periods=Annual+Data&periods_option=specific_periods&years_option=all_years. Not everyone invited to the meeting accepted the predictions of an immediate collapse.

10. *Nation's Manpower Revolution*, 151.

11. Michael, *Cybernation*, 6.

12. Ferry, *Caught on the Horn of Plenty*, 2, 3.

13. Theobald, *Free Men and Free Markets*, 16–17, 24–25 (emphasis in original).

14. Todd Gitlin to W. H. Ferry, October 14, 1963, TGPC.

15. John D. Pomfret, "Guaranteed Income Asked for All, Employed or Not," *New York Times*, March 23, 1964, 1.

16. Whether Marx himself believed that freedom meant freedom from work is not clear. The early Marx seemed to think that work and freedom could be reconciled. The late Marx disagreed. Compare point 8 of the *Communist Manifesto*, where Marx calls for the creation of an industrial army, with the third volume of *Capital*, in which he argues that freedom is the realm beyond necessity.

17. Grace Lee Boggs, *Living for Change*, 134, 94–97; Ward, *In Love and Struggle*.

18. James Boggs, "American Revolution," 58, 57.

19. Marx, in the *Manifesto of the Communist Party*: "The proletariat will use its political supremacy to wrest, by degrees, all capital from the bourgeoisie, to centralise all instruments of production in the hands of the State i.e., of the proletariat organised as the ruling class; and to increase the total productive forces as rapidly as possible." Tucker, *Marx-Engels Reader*, 490.

20. Grace Lee Boggs, *Living for Change*, 108–9.

21. James Boggs, "American Revolution," 23–24.

22. Ibid., 52; Cruse, *Rebellion or Revolution*, 74–96; James Boggs, *Racism and the Class Struggle*, 13, 157; Kelley, *Freedom Dreams*, chap. 3; Johnson, *Revolutionaries to Race Leaders*, chap. 1.

23. James Boggs, *Racism and the Class* Struggle, 16–17; James Boggs, "American Revolution," 85–86.

24. James Boggs, "American Revolution," 48, 46, 38, 52; James Boggs, "A paper presented to the Alliance for Jobs or Income Now," 1964, file 13, box 3, James and Grace Lee Boggs Collection, Accession no. 1342, WPRL.

25. Boggs, "American Revolution," 26–27, 23–24; "Black Workers Protest UAW Racism March on Cobo Hall," 1969, file 24, box 1, Detroit Revolutionary Movements, Accession no. 874, WPRL.

26. In 1974, after he had been retired from Chrysler for six years, James Boggs said, "I was one of the first blacks to become a material handler in the Chrysler plant." Previously, the vast majority of Black workers in the automobile industry in Detroit had worked in "foundry, paint, sanding, grinding—all very unhealthy jobs; or they were janitors, the most menial job." Boggs, "Beyond Militancy," January 10, 1974, file 16, box 3, James and Grace Lee Boggs Collection, Accession no. 1342, WPRL. For background information on the Jefferson Avenue Chrysler plant, I would like to thank Professor Charles Hyde. Correspondence with the author, November 29, 2015.

27. James Boggs to Mary Gibson, August 24, 1964, underlining original; Boggs, "The Triple Revolution," draft of speech for Detroit ADA, July 10, 1964, file 21, box 1, James and Grace Lee Boggs Collection, Accession no. 1342, WPRL.

28. Grace Lee Boggs, *Living for Change*, 149.

29. James Boggs, "Jobs and Politics: The Revolution for Self-Governing Man," 1964, file 13, box 3, James and Grace Lee Boggs Collection, Accession no. 1342, WPRL.

30. Grace Lee Boggs, *Living for Change*, 151–53; James Boggs, "American Revolution," 87.

31. James Boggs, "Practical Applications of Automation," March 23, 1965, file 13, box 3, James and Grace Lee Boggs Collection, Accession no. 1342, WPRL.

32. "Ford Motor Company Management Briefs, 'Automation—And Its Role in a Growing Economy,'" February 21, 1961, vol. 4, no. 3, file 1, box 9, UAW Vice President's Office, Ken Bannon Collection, Accession no. 935, WPRL.

33. Mills, "Letter to the New Left," accessed April 18, 2019, https://www.marxists .org/subject/humanism/mills-c-wright/letter-new-left.htm.

34. Marcuse, *Eros and Civilization*; Marcuse, *One-Dimensional Man*, 27–28, 6 (emphasis in original).

35. Dunayevskaya, *Marxism and Freedom*, 275–76.

36. Ibid.

37. Van Der Linden, "Prehistory of *Post-Scarcity Anarchism*."

38. Bookchin, *Post-Scarcity Anarchism*, 19–40, viii. "The notion that man must dominate nature emerges directly from the domination of man by man," ibid., 24. On Bookchin's contribution to the revival of anarchism see Marshall, *Demanding the Impossible*, chap. 39.

39. Bookchin, *Post-Scarcity Anarchism*, 2, 48, iv.

40. Ibid., 2–3.

41. Ibid., 54–55.

42. Ibid., 65, 76. On subsistence labor as meaningful activity beyond toil, see Cronon, "Modes of Prophecy and Production"; White, *Organic Machine*, 6–7; 44–47, 80.

43. Bookchin, *Post-Scarcity Anarchism*, xiv.

44. Sale, *SDS*, 99; author interview with Todd Gitlin. On Aronowitz and Rustin, see "Biography," accessed March 19, 2018, https://web.archive.org/web/20160303214143/ http://www.stanleyaronowitz.org/new/biography.

45. Students for a Democratic Society, *Port Huron Statement*, 8.

46. Mills, *White Collar*, 215.

47. Goodman, *Growing up Absurd*, 35–37, 21, 35; Blake, "Paul Goodman," 196.

48. Ibid., 24, 141–42.

49. Ibid., 35–37, 211.

50. Todd Gitlin to W. H. Ferry, October 14, 1963, TGPC.

51. Gitlin, "Toward a Democracy of Participation," October 19, 1963, TGPC.

52. David Strauss quoted in Frost, *Interracial Movement*, 2; Tom Hayden and Carl Wittman, "An Interracial Movement of the Poor?" distributed by Students for a Democratic Society, Room 302, 119 Fifth Avenue, New York, NY, and its Economic and Research Action Project, 1100 E. Washington, Ann Arbor, MI, accessed March 20, 2018: http://www.sds-1960s.org/Interracial-Movement-Poor.pdf.

53. Frost, *Interracial Movement*, 54; author interview with Todd Gitlin.

54. Todd Gitlin to Robert Theobald, October 2, 1964, TGPC.

55. Ibid; Todd Gitlin to James Boggs, September 22, 1964, TGPC.

56. On the JOIN-GROIN debate within ERAP, see Frost, *Interracial Movement*, 96–101.

57. Ed Jahn, "Automation," *New Left Notes*, December 30, 1966.

58. David Gilbert, Robert Gottlieb, and Gerry Tenney, "The Port Authority Statement," (1967), 113, accessed April 19, 2019, https://archive.org/details/PortAuthority Statement; Ed Jahn, "Automation—III," *New Left Notes*, March 13, 1967.

59. Jahn, "Automation," *New Left Notes*.

60. Todd Gitlin, "New Chances: The Reality and Dynamic of the New Left," November 1969, quoted in Sale, *SDS*, 505.

61. Gilbert, Gottlieb, and Tenney, "Port Authority Statement," 89–90.

62. Honey, *To the Promised Land*, 103, 193, 64, 124.

63. West, *Radical King*, 245–52.

Chapter 6. Slaves in Tomorrowland

1. Stimson, "A House to Make Life Easy." *Popular Mechanics*, June 1952.

2. Wright, *Building the Dream*, 252.

3. Stimson, "A House to Make Life Easy," 65–69, 228, 230.

4. Harder, "Before the Quad-City Conference on Automation," 1954, file 12, box 45, UAW President's Office, Walter P. Reuther Collection, Accession no. 261, WPRL; Cross, *John Diebold*, 218–19, 211.

5. Cross, *John Diebold*, 168–69. Chapter 17 of that book is titled "Robot Housekeepers."

6. Giedion, *Mechanization Takes Command*, 710, 622.

7. "A Word to the Wives," 1955, *Woman's Home Companion*, posted courtesy of the Library of Congress Prelinger Archive, https://www.youtube.com/watch?v=uoN1lusxsoA, accessed September 25, 2015. On postwar freedom as the freedom to consume, see Foner, *Story of American Freedom*, chap. 11, esp. 264.

8. *Live Better Electrically*, accessed April 25, 2019, https://www.youtube.com/watch?v=u5Lz1C53RwI

9. Pursell, *Technology in Postwar America*, 21; Kessler-Harris, *Out to Work*, 300–302, 319.

10. Hayden, *Grand Domestic Revolution*; Hayden, *Redesigning the American Dream*.

11. Strasser, *Never Done*, 74–78, 121–24, 179, 264, 267; Cowan, *More Work for Mother*, 99–101, and esp. chaps. 6 and 7. See also Hayden, *Redesigning the American Dream*, 75–76: "What is astonishing is that these inventions eroded the autonomy of women at least as much as they contributed to saving women's labor. Eventually the haven strategy produced not a skilled housewife happy at home, supported by her husband's 'family' wage, but a harried woman constantly struggling to keep up standards."

12. Stevenson, undated statement quoted in Cross, *John Diebold*, 81–82.

13. Bradbury, *Illustrated* Man, 13.

14. Theobald, *Free Men and Free Markets,* 19; Bell, "Study of the Future," 127–28. On the metaphor of the robot in American history see Abnet, *American Robot*, in particular chap. 5.

15. Higbie, "Why Do Robots Rebel?"

16. Čapek, *R.U.R.*

17. Asimov, *I, Robot*, 25, 11.

18. On the connection between Taylorist notions of organizing work and modernist architecture see Guillén, *Taylorized Beauty of the Mechanical*.

19. Giedion, *Mechanization Takes Command*, 624–25.

20. Ibid.

21. Friedan, *Feminine Mystique*, 245–46.

22. A decade later, the President's Commission on the Status of Women came to a similar conclusion. Although once the home had been "largely self-sufficient" and a housewife's work highly skilled, "today's image of young married women is very different," the commission's report said. "It shows suburban mothers reading directions on packages or cans as they cook frozen or otherwise preprocessed food by gas or electricity." *American Women,* 60–61.

23. Jackson, "Westward-Moving House"; Keats, *Crack in the Picture Window*; Yates, *Revolutionary Road*.

24. On Friedan's radicalism and her liberalism see Horowitz, *Betty Friedan and the Making of* The Feminine Mystique.

25. Friedan, *Feminine Mystique*, 236, 242–43, 252.

26. *American Women*, 16.

27. Friedan, *Feminine Mystique*, 254–55, 240–41; Michael, *Cybernation*, 31.

28. Friedan, *Feminine Mystique*, 255.

29. Ibid., 252, 239.

30. Ibid., 248.

31. Jones, "Dynamics of Marriage and Motherhood," 56.

32. Nadasen, *Welfare Warriors*.

33. Echols, *Daring to Be Bad*, 78–79.

34. Firestone, *Dialectic of Sex*.

35. *Push Buttons and People*, 1959, accessed January 31, 2018, https://www.youtube.com/watch?v=c2GNIYhi8Dw

36. Firestone, *Dialectic of Sex*, 175. For several different views of Firestone's biological determinism see Wacjman, "From Women and Technology to Gendered Technoscience"; Merck and Sandford, *Further Adventures of* The Dialectic of Sex; Halbert, "Shulamith Firestone"; Halberstam, "Automating Gender."

37. Echols, *Daring to Be Bad*, 141; Firestone, *Dialectic of Sex*, 180.

38. Firestone, *Dialectic of Sex*, 94.

39. Solanas, *SCUM Manifesto*, 3; David Behrens and Jack Mann, "Andy Warhol Is Shot by Actress: Figures in Warhol Drama," *Newsday*, June 4, 1968, 1.

40. Solanas, *SCUM Manifesto*, 29–30.

41. Echols, *Daring to Be Bad*, 104–5. Ti-Grace Atkinson and The Feminists argued that all sex, whether straight or lesbian, reproduced male oppression. Ibid., 172–73.

42. Firestone, *Dialectic of Sex*, 210.

43. Fuller, *Education Automation*, 9–10.

44. Firestone, *Dialectic of Sex*, 210–14.

45. Nadasen, *Welfare Warriors*, 12. On the consolidation of farms by industrialization and bankruptcy, see Fitzgerald, *Every Farm a Factory*.

46. Steensland, *Failed Welfare Revolution*, 97–98.

47. Ibid., 111–12.

48. Nadasen, *Welfare Warriors*, 189; Steensland, *Failed Welfare Revolution*, 107.

49. Richard Nixon, "Labor Day Message," September 3, 1972, The American Presidency Project, University of California, Santa Barbara. Accessed August 14, 2018, www.presidency.ucsb.edu/ws/index.php?pid=3557

50. Nixon Tapes, May 13, 1971, Time: 10:32 A.M.–12:20 P.M., Location: Oval Office Conversation No. 498–5, timestamp: 1:25:00. Accessed November 8. 2017, nixontape-audio.org/chron1/rmn_e498a.mp3

51. Tillmon, "Welfare Is a Women's Issue," n.p. The welfare rights movement in this period went the farthest in legally challenging the industrial, bare life meaning of work. The radicalism of its demand went straight to the heart of the dissonance between democracy and the commodification of labor. Activists argued that the equal protection clause of the Fourteenth Amendment meant that the U.S. government was legally obligated to grant all citizens access to the means of subsistence. Two Supreme Court decisions, *Rosado V. Wyman* (1970) and *Dandridge v. Williams* (1970), dismissed this argument. Nadasen, *Welfare Warriors*, 160–61. (On Tillmon's biography see 19–20.) The importance of these decisions deserves emphasis. With them, it was decided that the United States government had no legal obligation to prevent its citizens from starving to death.

52. Goodwin, *Do the Poor Want to Work?*, 117.

53. Nadasen, *Welfare Warriors*, 140, 165, 166.

54. Tillmon, "Welfare Is a Women's Issue."

55. Jordan, "Economics of Women's Liberation." On Jordan's biography see Baxandall, "Re-Visioning the Women's Liberation Movement's Narrative," 232.

56. Federici, "Wages Against Housework" (1975), in Federici, *Revolution at Point Zero*, 18–19; Tillmon, "Welfare Is a Women's Issue." For Federici's biography see Vishmidt, "Permanent Reproductive Crisis."

57. Welfare recipients' defense of the sentimental value of reproductive labor should not be confused with the criticism of the wages-for-housework movement that came from the Left. Reacting to the radical individualism espoused by thinkers like Shulamith Firestone, some argued that a society of individuals who felt no sense of communal responsibility seemed more the logical conclusion of capitalist alienation than of socialist revolution. These thinkers did not see how a sentimental defense of the family, divorced from a discussion of appropriate remuneration for labor, could slip into a sexist defense of exploitation. See Braverman, *Labor and Monopoly Capital*, 193; Lasch, *Haven in a Heartless World*, xvii; Gorz, *Farewell to the Working Class*, 82–85.

Chapter 7. Where Have All the Robots Gone?

1. Goodman, *New Reformation*, 31.

2. Mills, *Sociological Imagination*, 172.

3. Cowie, *Stayin' Alive*,2; Lawrence Swaim, "The Postal Strike of 1970: Relevance to Today," *Talking Union*, October 25, 2018, accessed October 25, 2018, http://portside.org/2018–10–25/postal-strike-1970-relevance-today; Weir, *Singlejack Solidarity*, 78–79.

4. Brenner, Brenner, and Winslow, *Rebel Rank and File*; Windham, *Knocking on Labor's Door*, 31; MacLean, *Freedom Is Not Enough*.

5. Alice and Staughton Lynd, *Rank and File*, 1.

6. Price, *New Directions in the World of Work*.

7. *First Annual Report of the National Commission on Productivity*, vii; Philip Shabecoff, "Half-Hearted Search for Peace," *New York Times*, March 3, 1974, 148.

8. Sheppard and Herrick, *Where Have All the Robots Gone?*

9. John Haynes quoted in Zimpel, *Man Against Work*, 141–53; Aronowitz, *False Promises*, 393–94, 418–19.

10. *Worker Alienation, 1972*, 126; Schrank, *Ten Thousand Working Days*, 174–210.

11. *Work in America*, 20.

12. *Second Annual Report, the National Commission on Productivity March 1973*, x.

13. Belasco, *Appetite for Change*, 18.

14. Quoted in Commoner, *Closing Circle*, 294.

15. Mumford, *Pentagon of Power*, 191, 91, 179.

16. Fenton quoted in Zimpel, *Man Against Work*.

17. Brooks, "Job Satisfaction I."

18. Garson, *All the Livelong Day*, xi, 97–98; Foulkes, *Creating More Meaningful Work*; Reich, *Greening of America*, 198; *Work in America*, vii; Rosow, "Problem of the Blue-Collar Worker."

19. The bill proposed allocating funds to experimental programs that would discover means to lessen "worker alienation."

20. *Worker Alienation, 1972*, 2–4, 8, 10–12.

21. *Work in America*, 4 (italics added), 1, 3, 10.

22. In this case, the "banner" was a bumper stick campaign. Weir, *Singlejack Solidarity*, 78–79, 295.

23. Savio quoted in Turner, *From Counterculture to Cyberculture*, 11.

24. Galbraith, *New Industrial State*.

25. Ellul, *Technological Society*, xxv, 3–4.

26. The "idea of abolishing work," wrote Mumford, was only ever "a slave's dream, and it revealed a desperate but unimaginative slave's hope. . . . No one who has ever found his life-work and tasted its reward would entertain such a fantasy, for it would mean suicide." Mumford, *Myth of the Machine*, 3–4, 237, 242.

27. Roszak, *Making of a Counter Culture*, 5, 149–50, 294; Reich, *Greening of America*, 88. For the contemporary criticism of progress in the academy see Sahlins, *Stone Age Economics*.

28. Quoted in Gibson, *Perfect War*, 15.

29. Edwards, *Closed World*, 3–5, 142–43.

30. Gibson, *Perfect War*, 193–96. Also Scales, "Gun Trouble"; Fallows, "M-16: A Bureaucratic Horror Story."

31. McDermott, "Technology: The Opiate of the Intellectuals." Also Cowan, "Looking Back in Order to Move Forward."

32. Moberg, "Rattling the Golden Chains," 350.

33. Berry, *Continuous Harmony*, 174.

34. Kirk, *Counterculture Green*; Commoner, *Closing Circle*, 5, 298, 177.

35. J. R. Oppenheimer, "Age of Science," 21.

36. Mumford, *Pentagon of Power*, 379.

37. *Earthrise*. (2018).

38. *Worker Alienation, 1972*, 36–37.

39. Moberg, "Rattling the Golden Chains," 253.

40. Quoted in Levy, *New Left and Labor in the 1960s*, 157.

41. *Worker Alienation 1972*, 10–12.

42. "Spreading Lordstown Syndrome," 69. "Lordstown syndrome" is also used in Clayton Fritchey, "The 'Big' Grind of the Assembly Line," *Chicago Tribune*, April 9, 1972, A5; Dennis Duggan, "Big 3 Developing Foreign Accent," *Newsday*, March 31, 1972, 80A; "Revolt of the Robots," *New York Times*, March 7, 1972, 38.

43. Cowie, *Stayin' Alive*, 117.

44. *Work in America*, 19.

45. Brenner, Brenner, and Winslow, *Rebel Rank and File*, 62.

46. Moberg, "Rattling the Golden Chains," 209; Rothschild, *Paradise Lost*, 107.

47. Rothschild, *Paradise Lost*, 97–101, 104–5, 111–12.

48. Ibid., 105.

49. Levy, *New Left and Labor in the 1960s*, 157.

50. Rothschild, *Paradise Lost*, 108; Moberg, "Rattling the Golden Chains," 167, 225–26; *Worker Alienation, 1972*, 13.

51. Rothschild, *Paradise Lost*, 106–11; Agis Salpukas, "G.M.'s Toughest Division 'Binbuster?'" *New York Times* April 16, 1972, 1; Moberg; "Rattling the Golden Chains," 136.

52. Garson, *All the Livelong Day*, 92.

53. "Labor: Sabotage at Lordstown?"; Nixon, "Address to the Nation on Labor Day"; Swados, "Foreword"; Lichtenstein, *Contest of Ideas*, chap. 16.

54. Levy, *New Left and Labor in the 1960s*, 118–19.

55. Gooding, "Blue-Collar Blues"; Sheppard and Herrick, *Where Have All the Robots Gone?*, xxxi; Price, *New Directions in the World of Work*, 4–6; AT&T executive also quoted in Brooks, "Job Satisfaction I."

56. *Nation's Manpower Revolution*, 194, 163–64, 2.

57. *Worker Alienation, 1972*, 13.

58. Zimpel, *Man Against Work*, 8.

59. "GM's Stranded Cars Will Be Marketed by Bits and Pieces," *Wall Street Journal*, October 13, 1972, 7.

60. *Worker Alienation, 1972*, 123.

61. Laurence G. O'Donnell, "A Day's Work: General Motors' Plan to Increase Efficiency Draws Ire of Unions," *Wall Street Journal*, December 6, 1972, 1; "UAW Strikes GM at Norwood, Ohio, Over Job Standards," *Wall Street Journal*, April 10, 1972, 4.

62. Brooks, "Job Satisfaction I."

63. Ed Townsend, "UAW, GM Collide on Assembly-Line 'Humanization,'" *Christian Science Monitor*, October 10, 1972, 1.

64. O'Donnell, "Day's Work"; Rothschild, *Paradise Lost*, 120–21.

65. Jones, "Rank-and-File Opposition," 285–87.

66. Vera Edwards to Douglas Fraser, September 6, 1972, file 15, box 8, UAW Vice President's Office, Douglas A. Fraser Collection, Accession no. 827, WPRL.

67. Jones, "Rank-and-File Opposition."

68. Levy, *New Left and Labor in the 1960s*, chap. 3.

69. Arnold Beichman, "The Making of a Monster: The 'Hard Hat' That Never Was," *Christian Science Monitor*, August 7, 1972, 9.

70. *Worker Alienation, 1972*, 9, 15, 17–18, 27.

71. Foulkes, *Creating More Meaningful Work*, 28–29, 203.

72. Gomberg, "Job Satisfaction II."

73. T. Fitzgerald, "Why Motivation Theory Doesn't Work."

74. *Worker Alienation, 1972*, 189.

75. Gomberg, "Job Satisfaction II.

76. *Worker Alienation, 1972*, 112, 116; Doug Fraser to John Fillion, September 22, 1972, file 15, box 8, UAW Vice President's Office, Douglas A. Fraser Collection, Accession no. 827, WPRL.

77. Walter Mossberg, "Factory Boredom: How Vital an Issue?" *Wall Street Journal*, March 23, 1973, 10.

78. Price, *New Directions in the World of Work*.

79. *Work in America*, 18. The report asserted against the evidence that Taylorism had been accepted by earlier generations of workers in "an era when people were willing to be motivated by the stick." Ibid., 49. Nonetheless, the idea of a person willing to be motivated by coercion seems like a contradiction in terms.

80. For example, see Zimpel, *Man Against Work*, 11. Newspapers covering the 1972 release of the *Work in America* report described to readers what Taylorism was: Agis Salpukass, "Conflicting Theories on Efficient Work: Repetition vs. Satisfaction," *New York Times*, December 22, 1972, 14; Herbert Brucker, "Getting America Back to Work," *Hartford Courant*, December 28, 1972, 16; Peter Milius, "Workers Bored with Jobs," *Washington Post*, December 22, 1972, A1.

81. Braverman, *Labor and Monopoly Capital*, 11. Among those also showing a renewed interest in work and the workplace were Marxist autonomist thinkers who in New York in the mid-1970s organized themselves under the banner of Zerowork. *Zerowork, Political Materials #1*, editorial collective George Caffentzis et al., December 1975. See Harry Cleaver, "General Introduction to Zerowork," n.d. Accessed December 12, 2018, http://zerowork.org/o.GenIntro.html

82. Braverman, *Labor and Monopoly Capital*, 31, 32, 34, 49, 50–51, 78 (emphasis in original).

83. Nixon, "Address to the Nation on Labor Day."

84. On the problems that attend presuming the historical agency of the "work ethic," see Resnikoff, "Problem with Post-Work."

85. William M. Blair, "Nixon Foresees 4-Day Work Week," *New York Times*, September 23, 1956, 1.

86. Quoted in Sheppard and Herrick, *Where Have All the Robots Gone?*, xii–xiii.

87. The *Economist* is quoted in *Work in America*, 35.

88. For the televised ad see "Sign Your Work National Commission on Productivity PSA 1973," Youtube, published August 24, 2013, accessed November 1, 2018, https://m .youtube.com/watch?v=iSOOFNWzv4o. For the print ads see *Second Annual Report*, xxiii, 25. All the ads adopted the tagline "America. It only works as well as we do." Robert Brenner argues that union wages did not undermine the U.S. economy in the late 1960s and early 1970s. See R. Brenner, "Political Economy of the Rank-and-File Rebellion."

89. Todd Gitlin to Robert Theobald, October 2, 1964, TGPC.

90. Rodgers, *Work Ethic in Industrial America*, xi, xiii. On ideology as a historical agent, see Fields, "Slavery, Race, and Ideology."

91. Aronowitz, *False Promises*, 130–31.

Conclusion

1. Barack Obama, "Remarks of President Barack Obama at GM's Lordstown Assembly Plant."; Steven Rattner, "Trump Is Wrong About the General Motors Bailout," *New York Times*, November 28, 2018, accessed December 7, 2018. https://www.nytimes .com/2018/11/28/opinion/trump-gm-layoffs.html

2. Vonnegut, *Player Piano*; Boggs, *Racism and the Class Struggle*, 157.

3. On the increase in long working hours in the United States since the middle of the twentieth century see Pencavel, *Diminishing Returns at Work*, 6–7. Regarding this increase alongside the stagnation in the rise in wages see DeSilver, "For Most Workers, Real Wages Have Barely Budged for Decades." In addition, the number of people engaged in "alternative" or "contingent" employment rose between 2005 and 2015 from 10 percent to 15 percent of all workers in the United States: Katz and Krueger, "Rise and Nature of Alternative Work Arrangements." Gig workers, in particular, "are not always being paid to work, but they are always working," writes Alexandra J. Ravenelle, *Hustle and Gig*, 6.

4. Dunayevskaya, *Marxism and Freedom*, 268–69, italics original.

5. Quoted in Simon, "Inside the Amazon Warehouse," n.p.; Del Rey and Ghaffery, "Leaked," n.p.; Daniel A. Hanley and Sally Hubbard, "Eyes Everywhere: Amazon's Surveillance Infrastructure and Revitalizing Worker Power," Open Markets Institute, September 2020, 10–11, accessed October 1, 2020, https://static1.squarespace.com/ static/5e449c8c3ef68d752f3e70dc/t/5f4cffea23958d79eae1ab23/1598881772432/Amazon _Report_Final.pdf. After a tour of an Amazon fulfillment center, Nelson Lichtenstein reported: "Amazon's approach to discipline also points to its greatest vulnerability: its need for speed." Lichtenstein, "Making History at Amazon," n.p.

6. Faiz Siddiqui, "Uber and Lyft Drivers Strike for Pay Transparence—After Algorithms Made It Harder to Understand," *Washington Post*, May 8, 2019; Kevin Roose, "A Machine May Not Take Your Job, but One Could Become Your Boss," *New York Times*, June 23, 2019; "Voices from Industry," drishti.com, accessed October 1, 2020, https://drishti.com/resources/industry-voices/.

7. Some thinkers on the Left likewise assume that "automation" is a discrete and inevitable technological phenomenon. In the mid-century style, they premise their visions of utopia on "automation" and the abolition of work. In the process they subscribe to a degraded notion of work, especially physical labor. See, e.g., Livingston, *No More Work*; Frase, *Four Futures*; and Aaron Bastani, "The World Is a Mess. We Need Fully Automated Luxury Communism," *New York Times*, June 11, 2019. Bastani writes: "For many, work is drudgery. And automation could set us free from it," as though work itself, rather than hierarchy, exploitation, and politics led to lives of drudgery. For other contributors to this discussion, see Carr, *Glass Cage*; Sennett, *Craftsman*.

8. Acemoglu and Restrepo, "Robots and Jobs." I am not quite persuaded by the authors' claim that they have isolated the effect of machines on employment. Thomas B. Edsall, "The Robots Have Descended on Trump Country," *New York Times*, December 13, 2018; Claire Cain Miller, "Automation Nation: Evidence That Robots Are Winning the Race for American Jobs," *New York Times*, March 28, 2017.

9. Gray and Suri, *Ghost Work*; Daisuke Wakabayashi, "Google's Shadow Work Force: Temps Who Outnumber Full-Time Employees," *New York Times*, May 28, 2019; Burns, "Please Let's Never Call Uber 'The Future of Work' Ever Again"; Henwood, "Uber Is a Scam"; Klein, "Screen New Deal"; Zuboff, *Age of Surveillance Capitalism*.

Bibliography

Archival Collections

Harvard Business School, Baker Library (HBS)
    Georges F. Doriot Papers
    John Diebold Papers
Harvard University, Radcliffe Institute for Advanced Study, Schlesinger Library (SCH)
    Jean Tepperman Papers
    Massachusetts History Workshop Records
John F. Kennedy Presidential Library (JFKPL)
    Theodore C. Sorenson Personal Papers
    W. Willard Wirtz Papers
    W. Willard Wirtz Speech Files
National Archives and Records Administration, College Park (NARA)
    Records of the Employment and Training Administration, Office of Manpower, Automation, and Training
New York University, Tamiment Library and Robert F. Wagner Labor Archive (TAM)
    Communications Workers of America Records
    J. B. S. Hardman Papers
    Pamphlet Collection, Reference Center for Marxist Studies
Todd Gitlin Personal Collection (TGPC)
Wayne State University, Walter P. Reuther Library (WPRL)
    Detroit Revolutionary Movements
    James and Grace Lee Boggs Collection
    Nat Ganley Collection
    Ted F. Silvey Collection
    UAW Ford Department Collection
    UAW President's Office, Walter P. Reuther Collection

UAW Vice President's Office, Douglas A. Fraser Collection
UAW Vice President's Office, Ken Bannon Collection
UAW Region 9 Collection

Interviews

Davies, Margery. Personal interview by Jason Resnikoff. Cambridge, Massachusetts, June 14, 2017.
Gitlin, Todd. Personal interview by Jason Resnikoff. New York, New York, December 3, 2015.
Nussbaum, Karen. Telephone interview by Jason Resnikoff. June 12, 2017.

Government Reports

American Women: Report of the President's Commission on the Status of Women. Washington, DC: U.S. Government Printing Office, 1963.
Automation and Technological Change: Hearings Before the Subcommittee on Economic Stabilization of the Joint Committee on the Economic Report, 84th Congress, 1st sess. Washington, DC: U.S. Government Printing Office, 1955.
Congressional Record: Proceedings and Debates. Vol. 82, pt. 1, November–December 1937. Washington, DC: U.S. Government Printing Office, 1938.
First Annual Report of the National Commission on Productivity. Washington, DC: U.S. Government Printing Office, March 1972.
"The Fort Worth Project of the Armour Automation Committee," *Monthly Labor Review* 87, no. 1. Published by the Bureau of Labor Statistics, U.S. Department of Labor, January 1964.
Freeman, Audrey, et al. *Impact of Office Automation in the Insurance Industry.* United States Department of Labor, Bureau of Labor Statistics, Bulletin no. 1468. Washington, DC: U.S. Government Printing Office, 1966.
Hecker, Daniel E., and Ian D. Wyatt. "Occupational Changes During the 20th Century." *Monthly Labor Review*, 129, no. 3. Washington, DC: Bureau of Labor Statistics, March 2006.
"Labor Force Statistics from the Current Population." Survey Databases, Tables, and Calculators. Bureau of Labor Statistics, United States Department of Labor. Accessed March 17, 2019, https://data.bls.gov/timeseries/LNU04000000?periods=Annual
"Longshoring and Meatpacking Automation Settlements." *Monthly Labor Review* 82, no. 10. Washinton, DC: Bureau of Labor Statistics, October 1959.
Moynihan, Daniel Patrick. *The Negro Family: The Case for National Action.* U.S. Department of Labor, Office of Policy Planning and Research. Washington, DC: U.S. Government Printing Office, 1965.
National Commission on Technology, Automation, and Economic Progress: Hearings Before the Subcommittee on Labor of the Committee on Education and Labor, 88th Congress, 2nd sess., on H.R. 10310 and Related Bills, To Establish a National Com-

mission on Automation and Technological Progress, Hearings Held in Washington, DC, April 14, 15, and 27, 1964. Washington, DC: U.S. Government Printing Office, 1964.

Nation's Manpower Revolution: Hearings Before the Subcommittee on Employment and Manpower of the Committee on Labor and Public Welfare, Relating to the Training and Utilization of the Manpower Resources of the Nation, 88th Congress, 1st sess. Washington, DC: U.S. Government Printing Office, 1963.

Office of Technology Assessment, U.S. Congress. *Automation of America's Offices.* Washington, DC: U.S. Government Printing Office, OTA-CIT-287, December 1985.

"Progress Report of Armour's Tripartite Automation Committee," *Monthly Labor Review* 84, no. 8. Washington, DC: Bureau of Labor Statistics, August 1961.

Rosow, Jerome M. "The Problem of the Blue-Collar Worker." Memorandum, Department of Labor, April 16, 1970. Accessed December 4, 2018, https://files.eric.ed.gov/fulltext/ED045810.pdf.

Second Annual Report: The National Commission on Productivity. Washington, DC: U.S. Government Printing Office, March 1973.

Technology and the American Economy: Report of the National Commission on Technology, Automation, and Economic Progress, Vol. 1. Washington, DC: U.S. Government Printing Office, 1966.

Work in America: Report of a Special Task Force to the Secretary of Health, Education, and Welfare. Cambridge, MA: MIT Press, 1973.

Worker Alienation, 1972. Hearings Before the Subcommittee on Employment, Manpower, and Poverty, of the Committee on Labor and Public Welfare, 92nd Congress, 2nd sess. Washington, DC: U.S. Government Printing Office, 1972.

Public Papers of Presidents

Kennedy, John F. "Acceptance of Democratic Nomination for President." July 15, 1960. Accessed August 9, 2016, http://www.jfklibrary.org/Asset-Viewer/AS08q50YzoSFUZg9uOi4iw.aspx.

———. "Address Before a Joint Session of Congress." May 25, 1961. Accessed April 14, 2019, https://www.jfklibrary.org/Asset-Viewer/xzw1gaeeTES6khED14P1Iw.aspx.

Nixon, Richard. "Address to the Nation on Labor Day." September 6, 1971. The American Presidency Project, University of California, Santa Barbara. Accessed August 14, 2018, www.presidency.ucsb.edu/ws/index.php?pid=3138.

———. "Labor Day Message." September 3, 1972. The American Presidency Project, University of California, Santa Barbara. Accessed August 14, 2018, www.presidency.ucsb.edu/ws/index.php?pid=3557.

Nixon Tapes, May 13, 1971; time: 10:32 A.M.–12:20 P.M.; Location: Oval Office Conversation No. 498–5; time stamp: 1:25:00. Accessed November 2017, nixontapeaudio.org/chron1/rmn_e498a.mp3.

Obama, Barack. "Remarks of President Barack Obama at GM's Lordstown Assembly Plant." September 15, 2009. Accessed June 5, 2019, https://obamawhitehouse.archives

.gov/the-press-office/remarks-president-gm-lordstown-assembly-plant-employees-ohio-9152009.

Truman, Harry S. "Statement by the President Announcing the Use of the A-Bomb at Hiroshima." August 6, 1945. Accessed April 23, 2019, https://millercenter.org/the-presidency/presidential-speeches/august-6–1945-statement-president-announcing-use-bomb.

Print Sources

Abnet, Dustin A. *The American Robot: A Cultural History*. Chicago: Chicago University Press, 2020.

Acemoglu, Daron, and Pascual Restrepo. "Robots and Jobs: Evidence from US Labor Markets." New Working Paper Series, Working Paper 23285, National Bureau of Economic Research, March 2017. Accessed April 23, 2019, https://www.nber.org/papers/w23285.pdf.

Acquaviva, Sabiano S. *Automazione e nuove classe: problem di sociologia industriale*. Bologna: Il Mulino, 1958.

Ad Hoc Committee on the Triple Revolution. *The Triple Revolution*. Santa Barbara, CA: Students for a Democratic Society, 1964.

Adams, John. *Discourses on Davila: A Series of Papers on Political History*. 1790. Reprint, Boston: Russell and Cutler, 1805.

Adas, Michael. *Dominance by Design: Technological Imperatives and America's Civilizing Mission*. Cambridge, MA: Belknap Press of Harvard University Press, 2006.

Agamben, Giorgio. *Homo Sacer: Sovereign Power and Bare Life*. Translated by Daniel Heller-Roazen. 1995. Reprint, Stanford: Stanford University Press, 1998.

Anderson, Kevin B. "Marcuse's and Fromm's Correspondence with the Socialist Feminist Raya Dunayevskaya: A New Window on Critical Theory." *Logos* 11, no. 1 (2012): n.p. Accessed March 6, 2018, http://logosjournal.com/2012/winter_anderson/

Applebaum, Eileen, and Ronald Schettkat. "Employment and Productivity in Industrialized Economies." *International Labor Review* 134, nos. 4–5 (1995): 603–23.

Arendt, Hannah. *Eichmann in Jerusalem: A Report on the Banality of Evil*. New York: Viking, 1963.

———. *The Human Condition: A Study of the Central Dilemmas Facing Modern Man*. 1958. Reprint, New York: Doubleday Anchor, 1959.

Aronowitz, Stanley. *False Promises: The Shaping of American Working Class Consciousness*. New York: McGraw Hill, 1973.

Asher, Robert. "The 1949 Ford Speedup Strike and the Post War Social Compact, 1946–1961." In *Autowork*, edited by Robert Asher and Ronald Edsforth with the assistance of Stephen Merlino, 127–54. Albany: State University of New York Press, 1995.

Asher, Robert, and Ronald Edsforth. "The Speedup." In *Autowork*, ed. Robert Asher and Ronald Edsforth with the assistance of Stephen Merlino, 64–98. Albany: State University of New York Press, 1995.

Asher, Robert, and Ronald Edsforth with the assistance of Stephen Merlino, eds. *Autowork*. Albany: State University of New York Press, 1995.

Asimov, Isaac. *I, Robot*. Garden City, NY: Doubleday, 1950.

Attewell, Steven. *People Must Live by Work: Direct Job Creation in America, from FDR to Reagan*. Philadelphia: University of Pennsylvania Press, 2018.

Aulick, Jane L., and Wilbur Cross. *Careers in the Age of Automation*. New York: Hawthorn, 1968.

"The Automatic Factory." *Fortune*, November 1, 1946, 160.

Baldwin, Richard. *The Globotics Upheaval: Globalization, Robotics, and the Future of Work*. New York: Oxford University Press, 2019.

Barrat, James. *Our Final Invention: Artificial Intelligence and the End of the Human Era*. New York: Thomas Dunne Books, St. Martin's Press, 2013.

Bastani, Aaron. *Fully Automated Luxury Capitalism: A Manifesto*. London: Verso, 2019.

Baxandall, Rosalyn. "Re-Visioning the Women's Liberation Movement's Narrative: Early Second Wave African American Feminists." *Feminist Studies* 27, no. 1 (Spring 2001): 225–245.

Belasco, Warren J. *Appetite for Change: How the Counterculture Took on the Food Industry, 1966–1988*. New York: Pantheon, 1993.

Bell, Daniel. "The Bogey of Automation." *New York Review of Books*, August 26, 1965.

———. *The Coming of Post-Industrial Society: A Venture in Social Forecasting*. New York: Basic Books, 1973.

———. "Government by Commission." *Public Interest*, Spring 1966.

———. "The Study of the Future." *Public Interest*, Fall 1965.

———. *Work and Its Discontents: The Cult of Efficiency in America*. Boston: Beacon, 1956.

Bellamy, Edward. *Looking Backward: 2000–1887*. 1888. Reprint, Chicago: Packard, 1946.

Benanav, Aaron. "Automation and the Future of Work—1." *New Left Review*, September–October 2019.

———. "Automation and the Future of Work—2." *New Left Review*, November–December 2019.

Bendix, Reinhard. *Work and Authority in Industry: Ideologies of Management in the Course of Industrialization*. New York: Wiley, 1956.

Beniger, James R. *The Control Revolution: Technological and Economic Origins of the Information Society*. Cambridge, MA: Harvard University Press, 1986.

Bernstein, Irving. *The Lean Years: A History of the American Worker, 1920–1933*. 1969. Reprint, Chicago: Haymarket, 2010.

Berry, Wendell. "Mayhem in the Industrial Paradise." In *A Continuous Harmony: Essays Cultural and Agricultural*. New York: Harcourt Brace Jovanovich, 1972.

Bing, Liesa, and Ralph E. Weindling, eds. *Agent of Change: Forty Years of the Diebold Group*. Bedford Hills, NY: The Diebold Institute, 2001.

Bittorf, Wilhelm. *Automation: Die zweite industrielle Revolution*. Darmstadt: Leske, 1956.

Bix, Amy Sue. *Inventing Ourselves Out of Jobs? America's Debate over Technological Unemployment, 1929–1981*. Baltimore: Johns Hopkins University Press, 2000.

Blake, Casey Nelson. "Paul Goodman: Anarchist and Patriot." *Raritan*, Summer 2012.

Boggs, Grace Lee. *Living for Change: An Autobiography*. Minneapolis: University of Minneapolis Press, 1998.

Boggs, James. "The American Revolution: Pages from a Negro Worker's Notebook." *Monthly Review*, July–August, 1963.

———. *Racism and the Class Struggle: Further Pages from a Black Worker's Notebook.* New York: Monthly Review Press, 1970.

Bookchin, Murray. *Post-Scarcity Anarchism.* 1971. Reprint, Edinburgh: AK Press, 2004.

Bradbury, Ray. *The Illustrated Man.* 1951. New York: Simon and Schuster, 2012.

———. *The Martian Chronicles.* Garden City, NY: Doubleday, 1952.

Brand, Stewart. "'Whole earth' origin." 1976. Accessed October 2, 2018, sb.longnow.org/SB_homepage/WholeEarth_button.html.

Braverman, Harry. "Automation: Promise and Menace." *American Socialist*, October 1955.

———. *Labor and Monopoly Capital: The Degradation of Work in the Twentieth Century.* 1974. Reprint, New York: Monthly Review Press, 1998.

———. "The World of Work." *American Socialist*, June 1959.

Bright, James R. *Automation and Management.* Boston: Division of Research, Graduate School of Business Administration, Harvard University, 1958.

Bregman, Rutger. *Utopia for Realists: How We Can Build the Ideal World.* Translated by Elizabeth Manton. New York: Little, Brown, 2017.

Brenner, Aaron, Robert Brenner, and Cal Winslow. *Rebel Rank and File: Labor Militancy and Revolt from Below During the Long 1970s.* New York: Verso, 2010.

Brenner, Robert. "The Political Economy of the Rank-and-File Rebellion." In *Rebel Rank and File: Labor Militancy and Revolt from Below During the Long 1970s*, ed. Aaron Brenner, Robert Brenner, and Cal Winslow, 37–76. New York: Verso, 2010.

Brick, Howard. "Optimism of the Mind: Imagining Postindustrial Society in the 1960s and 1970s." *American Quarterly* 44, no. 3 (September 1992): 348–80.

———. *Transcending Capitalism: Visions of a New Society in Modern American Thought.* Ithaca: Cornell University Press, 2006.

Brock, Gerald W. *The Second Information Revolution.* Cambridge, MA: Harvard University Press, 2003.

Brodskii, M. G., ed. *Automatizatsiia v maschinostroenii.* Moscow: Mashgiz, 1957.

Brooks, Bryon A. *Earth Revisited.* Boston: Arena, 1893.

Brooks, Thomas R. "Job Satisfaction I: An Elusive Goal," *AFL-CIO American Federationist*, October 1972.

Brown, Douglas. "Retreat Is No Answer." *American Socialist*, October 1954.

Brynjolfsson, Erik, and Andrew McAfee. *The Second Machine Age: Work, Progress, and Prosperity in a Time of Brilliant Technologies.* New York: Norton, 2014.

Buckingham, Walter. *Automation: Its Impact on Business and People.* New York: Harper and Row, 1961.

Bunch, Will. "In 1970s, Workers at This GM Plant Tried to Reinvent the American Dream. Instead, They Watched It Fade Away." *Post Bulletin*, December 6, 2018. Accessed on Portside, December 7, 2018. https://portside.org/2018–12–06/1970s-workers-gm-plant-tried-reinvent-american-dream-instead-they-watched-it-fade-away.

Burns, Rebecca. "Please Let's Never Call Uber 'The Future of Work' Ever Again." *In These Times*, May 8, 2019.

Butler, H. "Crisis in Auto." *American Socialist*, September 1954.

Čapek, Karel. *R.U.R.: A Play in Three Acts and an Epilogue*. Translated by P. Selver. London: H. Milford, 1923.

Carpignano, Paolo. "U.S. Class Composition in the Sixties: Capital's 'New Dimensions': The Kennedy Initiative." *Zerowork, Political Materials #1*, December 1975.

Carr, Nicholas. *The Glass Cage: Automation and Us*. New York: Norton, 2014.

Chandler, Alfred D., and James W. Cortada, eds. *A Nation Transformed by Information: How Information Has Shaped the United States from Colonial Times to the Present*. Oxford: Oxford University Press, 2000.

Charlesworth, James C., ed. *Leisure in America: Blessing or Curse?* Philadelphia: American Academy of Political and Social Science, 1964.

Chaulieu, Pierre, Grace C. Lee, and J. R. Johnson. *Facing Reality*. Detroit: Correspondence Publishing, 1958.

Chinoy, Ely. *Automobile Workers and the American Dream*. Garden City, NY: Doubleday, 1955.

Clarke, Arthur C. *Childhood's End*. New York: Harcourt, Brace and World, 1953.

Cleaver, Harry. "General Introduction to Zerowork." N.d. Accessed December 12, 2018. http://zerowork.org/0.GenIntro.html

Clynes, Manfred, and Nathan S. Kline. "Cyborgs and Space." *Astronautics*, September 1960.

Cohen, Lizabeth. *A Consumers' Republic: The Politics of Mass Consumption in Postwar America*. New York: Vintage, 2003.

Commoner, Barry. *The Closing Circle: Nature, Man, and Technology*. New York: Knopf, 1972.

Corn, Joseph J. *Imagining Tomorrow: History, Technology, and the American Future*. Cambridge, MA: MIT Press, 1986.

Cortada, James W. *The Digital Hand: How Computers Changed the Work of American Manufacturing, Transportation, and Retail Industries*. Oxford: Oxford University Press, 2004.

———. ed. *The Rise of the Knowledge Worker*. Boston: Butterworth-Heinemann, 1998.

Cowan, Ruth Schwartz. "Looking Back in Order to Move Forward: John McDermott, 'Technology: The Opiate of the Intellectuals.'" *Technology and Culture*, 51, no. 1 (January 2010): 199–215.

———. *More Work for Mother: The Ironies of Household Technology from the Open Hearth to the Microwave*. New York: Basic Books, 1983.

Cowie, Jefferson. *Capital Moves: RCA's Seventy Year Quest for Cheap Labor*. 1999. Reprint, New York: New Press, 2001.

———. *Stayin' Alive: The 1970s and the Last Days of the Working Class*. New York: New Press, 2010.

Cross, Wilbur. *John Diebold: Breaking the Confines of the Possible*. New York: Heineman, 1965.

Cummings, Alex Sayf. "Of Sorcerers and Thought Leaders: Marketing the Information Revolution in the 1960s." *The Sixties* 9, no. 1 (2016): 1–25. Proofs kindly shared by the author.

Cutler, Jonathan. *Labor's Time: Shorter Hours, the UAW, and the Struggle for American Unionism.* Philadelphia: Temple University Press, 2004.

Davies, Margery W. *A Woman's Place Is at the Typewriter: Office Work and Office Workers, 1870–1930.* Philadelphia: Temple University Press, 1982.

De Grazia, Sebastian. *Of Time, Work, and Leisure.* New York: Twentieth Century Fund, 1962.

Del Rey, Jason, and Shirin Ghaffery, "Leaked: Confidential Amazon Memo Reveals New Software to Track Unions," *Vox*, October 6, 2010. Accessed October 9, 2020. https://portside.org/2020–10–06/leaked-confidential-amazon-memo-reveals-new -software-track-unions

Denby, Charles [Simon Owens]. *Indignant Heart: A Black Worker's Journal.* 1962. Montreal: Black Rose, 1979.

———. "Workers Battle Automation." *News and Letters*, November 1960.

DeSilver, Drew. "For Most Workers, Real Wages Have Barely Budged for Decades." Pew Research Institute Fact Tank. August 7, 2018. Accessed October 2, 2020. https://www .pewresearch.org/fact-tank/2018/08/07/for-most-us-workers-real-wages-have -barely-budged-for-decades/

Diebold, John. *Automation: The Advent of the Automatic Factory.* New York: Van Nostrand, 1952.

———. *Beyond Automation: Managerial Problems of an Exploding Technology.* 1964. Reprint, New York: Praeger, 1970.

Drucker, Peter. Foreword to *Beyond Automation: Managerial Problems of an Exploding Technology*, by John Diebold. 1964. Reprint, New York: Praeger, 1970.

Dunayevskaya, Raya. *Marxism and Freedom: From 1776 Until Today.* New York: Bookman, 1958.

Dunayevskaya, Raya, and Andy Phillips. *The Coal Miners' General Strike of 1949–50 and the Birth of Marxist-Humanism in the US.* Chicago: News and Letters, 1984.

Echols, Alice. *Daring to Be Bad: Radical Feminism in American, 1967–1975.* Minneapolis: University of Minnesota Press, 1989.

Edwards, Paul. *The Closed World: Computers and the Politics of Discourse in Cold War America.* Cambridge, MA: MIT Press, 1996.

Ellsberg, Daniel. *The Doomsday Machine: Confessions of a Nuclear War Planner.* New York: Bloomsburg, 2017.

Ellul, Jacques. *The Technological Society.* Translated by John Wilkinson. 1954. New York: Knopf, 1967.

Elrod, Andrew. "Fully Automated Luxury Socialism: The Case for a New Public Sector." *Dissent*, Winter 2018.

Fallows, James. "M-16: A Bureaucratic Horror Story." *Atlantic*, June 1981.

Federici, Silvia. *Revolution at Point Zero: Housework, Reproduction, and Feminist Struggle.* Oakland, CA: PM Press, 2012.

———. "Wages Against Housework." In *Revolution at Point Zero: Housework, Reproduction, and Feminist Struggle*, 15–22. Oakland, CA: PM Press, 2012.

Fields, Barbara J. "Slavery, Race, and Ideology in the United States of America." *New Left Review* 1/181 (May–June 1990): 95–118.

Firestone, Shulamith. *The Dialectic of Sex: The Case for Feminist Revolution*. 1970. Reprint, New York: Farrar, Straus and Giroux, 2003.

Fitzgerald, Deborah. *Every Farm a Factory: The Industrial Ideal in American Agriculture*. New Haven: Yale University Press, 2003.

Fitzgerald, Thomas H. "Why Motivation Theory Doesn't Work." *Harvard Business Review*, July–August, 1971.

Fitzhugh, George. *Cannibals All! or, Slaves Without Masters*. Richmond, VA: A. Morris, 1857.

Foner, Eric. *Reconstruction: America's Unfinished Revolution, 1863–1877*. New York: Harper and Row, 1988.

———. *The Story of American Freedom*. New York: Norton, 1998.

Foner, Philip S., and David R. Roediger. *Our Own Time: A History of American Labor and the Working Day*. New York: Greenwood, 1989.

Ford, Martin. *Rise of the Robots: Technology and the Threat of a Jobless Future*. New York: Basic Books, 2015.

Foucault, Michel. "Faire vivre et laisser mourir: La naissance du racism." *Temps modernes* 46, no. 535 (February 1991): 37–61.

———. *The History of Sexuality*. Vol. 1, *An Introduction*. 1976. Reprint, New York: Vintage, 1978, c.1976.

Foulkes, Fred K. *Creating More Meaningful Work*. N.p.: American Management Association, 1969.

Frase, Peter. *Four Futures: Visions of the World After Capitalism*. London: Verso, 2016.

Fraser, Steve, and Gary Gerstle, eds. *The Rise and Fall of the New Deal Order, 1930–1980*. Princeton: Princeton University Press, 1989.

Freeman, Joshua B. *Behemoth: A History of the Factory and the Making of the Modern World*. New York: Norton, 2018.

Frey, Carl Benedikt. *The Technology Trap: Capital, Labor, and Power in the Age of Automation*. Princeton: Princeton University Press, 2019.

Friedan, Betty. *The Feminine Mystique*. 1963. Reprint, New York: Norton, 2013.

Friedmann, Georges. *Où va la travail humain?* Paris: Gallimard, 1960.

Frost, Jennifer. *An Interracial Movement of the Poor: Community Organizing and the New Left in the 1960s*. New York: New York University Press, 2001.

Fuller, R. Buckminster. *Education Automation: Freeing the Scholar to Return to His Studies*. 1962. Reprint, Garden City, NY: Anchor, 1971.

Galbraith, John Kenneth. *The Affluent Society*. Boston: Houghton Mifflin, 1958.

———. *The New Industrial State*. New York: New American Library, 1967.

Garson, Barbara. *All the Livelong Day: The Meaning and Demeaning of Routine Work*. New York: Penguin, 1975.

Genoways, Ted. *The Chain: Farm, Factory, and the Fate of Our Food*. New York: Harper, 2014.

Gibson, William James. *The Perfect War: Technowar in Vietnam*. Boston: Atlantic Monthly Press, 1986.

Giedion, Siegfried. *Mechanization Takes Command: A Contribution to Anonymous History*. New York: Oxford University Press, 1948.

Gleick, James. *The Information: A History, a Theory, a Flood.* New York: Pantheon, 2011.

GM Worker. "Skilled and Unskilled." *American Socialist,* June 1955.

Gomberg, William. "Job Satisfaction II: Sorting out the Nonsense." *AFL-CIO American Federationist,* June 1973.

Gooding, Judson. "Blue-Collar Blues on the Assembly Line." *Fortune,* July 1970.

Goodman, Paul. *Growing Up Absurd: Problems of Youth in the Organized Society.* 1960. Reprint, New York: New York Review of Books, 2012. .

———. *New Reformation: Notes of a Neolithic Conservative.* 1970. Reprint, Oakland, CA: PM Press, 2010.

Goodwin, Leonard. *Do the Poor Want to Work? A Social-Psychological Study of Work Orientations.* Washington, DC: Brookings Institution, 1972.

Gorz, André. *Farewell to the Working Class: An Essay on Post-Industrial Socialism.* Translated by Michael Sonenscher. London: Pluto, 1982.

Gray, Mary L., and Siddharth Suri. *Ghost Work: How to Stop Silicon Valley from Building a New Global Underclass.* New York: Houghton Mifflin Harcourt, 2019.

Green, Venus. *Race on the Line: Gender, Labor, and Technology in the Bell System, 1880–1980.* Durham, NC: Duke University Press, 2001.

Greif, Mark. *The Age of the Crisis of Man: Thought and Fiction in America, 1933–1973.* Princeton: Princeton University Press, 2015.

Guillén, Mauro F. *The Taylorized Beauty of the Mechanical.* Princeton: Princeton University Press, 2006.

Hagood, Charlotte Amanda. "Rethinking the Nuclear Family: Judith Merril's *Shadow on the Hearth* and Domestic Science Fiction." *Women's Studies* 40, no. 8 (December 2011): 1006–1029.

Haigh, Thomas. "Inventing Information Systems: The Systems Men and the Computer, 1950–1968." *Business History Review* 75, no. 1 (Spring 2001): 15–61.

Halberstam, Judith. "Automating Gender: Postmodern Feminism in the Age of the Intelligent Machine." *Feminist Studies* 17, no. 3 (Autumn 1991): 439–61.

Halpern, Rick. *Down on the Killing Floor: Black and White Workers in Chicago's Packinghouses, 1904–1954.* Urbana: University of Illinois Press, 1997.

Harrington, Michael. *The Other America: Poverty in the United States.* New York: MacMillan, 1962.

Hayden, Dolores. *The Grand Domestic Revolution: A History of Feminist Designs for American Homes, Neighborhoods, and Cities.* Cambridge, MA: MIT Press, 1981.

———. *Redesigning the American Dream: The Future of Housing, Work, and Family Life.* New York: Norton, 1984.

Hayden, Tom, and Carl Wittman. "An Interracial Movement of the Poor?" New York: Students for a Democratic Society. Accessed March 20, 2018, http://www.sds-1960s .org/Interracial-Movement-Poor.pdf.

Hayles, N. Katherine. *How We Became Posthuman: Virtual Bodies in Cybernetics, Literature, and Informatics.* Chicago: University of Chicago Press, 1999.

Henderson, Mary Stephens-Caldwell. *Managerial Innovations of John Diebold: An Analysis of Their Content and Dissemination.* Washington, DC: LeBaron Foundation, 1965.

Henwood, Doug. "Uber Is a Scam." *Jacobin*, May 6, 2019.

Herrick, Neal Q., and Harold L. Sheppard. *Where Have All the Robots Gone? Worker Dissatisfaction in the '70s.* New York: Free Press, 1972.

Higbie, Tobias. "Why Do Robots Rebel? The Labor History of a Cultural Icon." *Labor* 10, no. 1 (Spring 2013): 99–121.

Honey, Michael K. *To the Promised Land: Martin Luther King and the Fight for Economic Justice.* New York: Norton, 2018.

Horowitz, Daniel. *The Anxieties of Affluence: Critiques of American Consumer Culture, 1939–1979.* Amherst: University of Massachusetts Press, 2004.

———. *Betty Friedan and the Making of* The Feminine Mystique: *The American Left, the Cold War, and Modern Feminism.* Amherst: University of Massachusetts Press, 1998.

Horowitz, Roger. *"Negro and White, Unite and Fight!" A Social History of Industrial Unionism in Meatpacking, 1930–90.* Urbana: University of Illinois Press, 1997.

Hounshell, David A. "Automation, Transfer Machinery, and Mass Production in the U.S. Automobile Industry in the Post–World War II Era." *Enterprise & Society* 1 (March 2000): 100–138

Hudis, Peter. "Workers as Reason: The Development of a New Relation of Worker and Intellectual in American Marxist Humanism." *Historical Materialism* 11, no. 4 (2003) 267–93.

Hunnicutt, Benjamin Kline. *Work Without End: Abandoning Shorter Hours for the Right to Work.* Philadelphia: Temple University Press, 1988.

Hyman, Louis. *Temp: How American Work, American Business, and the American Dream Became Temporary.* New York: Viking, 2018.

Jackson, J. B. "The Westward-Moving House: Three American Houses and the People Who Lived in Them." *Landscape*, Spring 1953.

Johnson, Cedric. *Revolutionaries to Race Leaders: Black Power and the Making of African American Politics.* Minneapolis: University of Minnesota Press, 2007.

Jones, A. C. "Rank-and-File Opposition in the UAW During the Long 1970s." In *Rebel Rank and File: Labor Militancy and Revolt from Below During the Long 1970s*, ed. Aaron Brenner, Robert Brenner, and Cal Winslow, 281–310. New York: Verso, 2010.

Jones, Beverly. "The Dynamics of Marriage and Motherhood." In *Sisterhood Is Powerful: An Anthology of Writings from the Women's Liberation Movement*, ed. Robin Morgan, 46–61. New York: Vintage, 1970.

Jones, William P. *The March on Washington: Jobs, Freedom, and the Forgotten History of Civil Rights.* New York: Norton, 2013.

Jordan, Joan. "The Economics of Women's Liberation." In *Man Against Work*, ed. Lloyd Zimpel, 97–107. Grand Rapids, MI: Eerdmans, 1974.

Kahn, Herman. *On Thermonuclear War.* Princeton: Princeton University Press, 1960.

Kaplan, Jerry. *Humans Need Not Apply: A Guide to Wealth and Work in the Age of Artificial Intelligence.* New Haven: Yale University Press, 2015.

Kasson, John F. *Civilizing the Machine: Technology and Republican Values in America, 1776–1900.* New York: Grossman, 1976.

Katz, Lawrence F., and Alan B. Krueger. "The Rise and Nature of Alternative Work Arrangements in the United States, 1995–2015." National Bureau of Economic Research,

NBER Working Paper No. 22667. Cambridge, MA: National Bureau of Economic Research, 2016.

Keats, John. *The Crack in the Picture Window*. Boston: Houghton Mifflin, 1956.

Kelley, Robin D. G. *Freedom Dreams: The Black Radical Imagination*. Boston: Beacon, 2002.

Kerr, Clark, et al. *Industrialism and Industrial Man: The Problems of Labor and Management in Economic Growth*. Cambridge, MA: Harvard University Press, 1960.

Kersten, Andrew E., and Clarence Lang, eds. *Reframing Randolph: Labor, Freedom, and the Legacies of A. Philip Randolph*. New York: New York University Press, 2015.

Kessler-Harris, Alice. *In Pursuit of Equity: Women, Men, and the Quest for Economic Citizenship in 20th-Century America*. New York: Oxford University Press, 2001.

———. *Out to Work: A History of Wage-Earning Women in the United States*. 1982. Reprint, New York: Oxford University Press, 2003.

Keynes, John Maynard. *The Collected Writings of John Maynard Keynes*. Vol. 9, *Essays in Persuasion*. Cambridge: Cambridge University Press for the Royal Economic Society, 2013.

Kihlstedt, Folke. "Utopia Realized: The World's Fairs of the 1930s." In *Imagining Tomorrow: History, Technology, and the American Future*, ed. Joseph J. Corn, 97–118. Cambridge, MA: MIT Press, 1986.

King Jr., Martin Luther. *The Radical King*. Edited by Cornel West. Boston: Beacon, 2015.

Kirby, Jack Templeton. *Mockingbird Song: Ecological Landscapes of the South*. Chapel Hill: University of North Carolina Press, 2006.

———. *Rural Worlds Lost: The American South, 1920–1960*. Baton Rouge: Louisiana State University Press, 1987.

Kirk, Andrew G. *Counterculture Green: The Whole Earth Catalog and American Environmentalism*. Lawrence: University Press of Kansas, 2007.

Kirk, Russell. *The Conservative Mind: From Burke to Santayana*. Chicago: Regnery, 1953.

Klein, Naomi. "Screen New Deal." *The Intercept*, May 8, 2020, accessed May 18, 2020, https://theintercept.com/2020/05/08/andrew-cuomo-eric-schmidt-coronavirus-tech-shock-doctrine/

Kline, Ronald R. *The Cybernetics Moment: Or Why We Call Our Age the Information Age*. Baltimore: Johns Hopkins University Press, 2015.

Koselleck, Reinhart. *The Practice of Conceptual History: Timing History, Spacing Concepts*. Translated by Todd Samuel Presner. Stanford: Stanford University Press, 2002.

Kraus, Henry. *The Many and the Few: A Chronicle of the Dynamic Auto Workers*. 2nd ed. 1947. Reprint, Urbana: University of Illinois Press, 1985.

Kremen, Gladys Roth. "MDTA: The Origins of the Manpower Development and Training Act of 1962." United States Department of Labor monograph, 1974. Accessed August 9, 2016, https://www.dol.gov/general/aboutdol/history/mono-mdtatext

Kristol, Irving. "Jobs and the Man." *New Leader*, January 6, 1964.

"Labor: Sabotage at Lordstown?" *Time*, February 7, 1972.

Lasch, Christoper. *Haven in a Heartless World: The Family Besieged*. New York: Norton, 1977.

Leavitt, Harold J., and Thomas L. Whisler. "Management in the 1980's." *Harvard Business Review*, November–December 1958.

Levin, Howard S. *Office Work and Automation*. New York: John Wiley, 1956.

Levinson, Marc. *The Box: How the Shipping Container Made the World Smaller and the World Economy Bigger*. Princeton: Princeton University Press, 2006.

Levy, Paul. *The New Left and Labor in the 1960s*. Urbana: University of Illinois Press, 1994.

Lewis, James G. "Gallery: James G. Lewis on Smokey Bear in Vietnam." *Environmental History* 11 (July 2006): 598–603.

Lewis-Colman, David M. *Race Against Liberalism: Black Workers and the UAW in Detroit*. Urbana: University of Illinois Press, 2008.

Lichtenstein, Nelson. *A Contest of Ideas: Capital, Politics, and Labor*. Urbana: University of Illinois Press, 2013.

———. *Labor's War at Home: The CIO in World War II*. Cambridge: Cambridge University Press, 1982.

———. "Making History at Amazon." *Dissent*, February 12, 2020. Accessed October 1, 2020. https://www.dissentmagazine.org/online_articles/making-history-at-amazon

———. *Walter Reuther: The Most Dangerous Man in Detroit*. New York: Basic Books, 1995.

Lifton, Robert Jay. *Home from the War: Learning from Vietnam Veterans*. New York: Simon and Schuster, 1973.

Livingston, James. *No More Work: Why Full Employment Is a Bad Idea*. Chapel Hill: University of North Carolina Press, 2016.

Lynd, Alice, and Staughton Lynd. *Rank and File: Personal Histories by Working-Class Organizers*. Boston: Beacon, 1973.

Maclean, Nancy. *Freedom Is Not Enough: The Opening of the American Workplace*. Cambridge, MA: Harvard University Press, 2006.

Mangum, Garth. *MDTA: Foundation of Federal Manpower Policy*. Baltimore: Johns Hopkins University Press, 1968.

Marcuse, Herbert. *Eros and Civilization: A Philosophical Inquiry into Freud*. 1955. Reprint, Boston: Beacon, 1966.

———. *One-Dimensional Man: Studies in the Ideology of Advanced Industrial Society*. 1964. Reprint, London: Routledge Classics, 2002.

Marshall, Peter. *Demanding the Impossible: A History of Anarchism*. 1992. Reprint, Oakland, CA: PM Press, 2010.

Marx, Karl. *Grundrisse: Foundations of the Critique of Political Economy*. Translated by Martin Nicolaus. London: Penguin, 1973.

Marx, Leo. *The Machine in the Garden: Technology and the Pastoral Ideal in America*. New York: Oxford University Press, 1964.

———. "Technology: The Emergence of a Hazardous Concept." *Technology and Culture* 51, no. 3 (July 2010): 561–77.

Marx, Leo, and Merritt Roe Smith, eds. *Does Technology Drive History? The Dilemma of Technological Determinism*. Cambridge, MA: MIT Press, 1994.

Masani, P. R. *Norbert Wiener, 1894–1964*. Basel: Birkhäuser, 1990.

Matusow, Allen J. *The Unraveling of America: A History of Liberalism in the 1960s*. New York: Harper Torchbooks, 1986.

May, Elaine Tyler. *Homeward Bound: American Families in the Cold War*. New York: Basic Books, 1988.

Mayr, Otto. *Authority, Liberty, and Automatic Machinery in Early Modern Europe*. Baltimore: Johns Hopkins University Press, 1986.

McCarthy, George E., ed. *Marx and Aristotle: Nineteenth-Century German Social Theory and Classical Antiquity*. Savage, MD: Rowman and Littlefield, 1992.

———. *Marx and the Ancients: Classical Ethics, Social Justice, and Nineteenth-Century Political Economy*. Savage, MD: Rowman and Littlefield, 1990.

McDermott, John. "Technology: The Opiate of the Intellectuals," *New York Review of Books*, July 31, 1969.

Merck, Mandy, and Stella Sandford, eds. *Further Adventures of* The Dialectic of Sex. New York: Palgrave Macmillan, 2010.

Merril, Judith. *Shadow on the Hearth*. Garden City, NY: Doubleday, 1950.

Meyer, Stephen. "'An Economic Frankenstein': UAW Workers' Response to Automation at the Ford Brook Park Plant in the 1950s." *Michigan Historical Review* 28 (2002): 63–90.

Meyer, Stephen, and Nelson Lichtenstein, eds. *On the Line: Essays in the History of Auto Work*. Urbana: University of Illinois Press, 1989.

Michael, Donald N. *Cybernation: The Silent Conquest*. Santa Barbara, CA: Center for the Study of Democratic Institutions, 1962.

Mills, C. Wright. "Letter to the New Left." *New Left Review*, no. 5, September–October, 1960.

———. *The Sociological Imagination*. New York: Oxford University Press, 1959.

———. *White Collar: The American Middle Classes*. 1951. Reprint, New York: Oxford University Press, 1969.

Mindell, David A. *Between Human and Machine: Feedback, Control, and Computing Before Cybernetics*. Baltimore: Johns Hopkins University Press, 2002.

Montgomery, David. *Workers' Control in America: Studies in the History of Work, Technology, and Labor Struggles*. New York: Cambridge University Press, 1979.

Moody, Kim. "Understanding the Rank-and-File Rebellion in the Long 1970s." In *Rebel Rank and File: Labor Militancy and Revolt from Below During the Long 1970s*, ed. Aaron Brenner, Robert Brenner, and Cal Winslow, 105–48. New York: Verso, 2010.

Morgan, Robin, ed. *Sisterhood Is Powerful: An Anthology of Writings from the Women's Liberation Movement*. New York: Vintage, 1970.

Morris, William. *News from Nowhere*. 1890. Reprint, New York: Penguin, 1986.

Mumford, Lewis. *Art and Technics*. New York: Columbia University Press, 1952.

———. *The Condition of Man*. New York: Harcourt, Brace, 1944.

———. *The Myth of the Machine: Technics and Human Development*. New York: Harcourt, Brace, & World, 1966.

———. *The Pentagon of Power: Myth of the Machine*. Vol. 2. New York: Harcourt Brace Jovanovich, 1970.

———. *Technics and Civilization*. New York: Harcourt, Brace, 1934.

Nadasen, Premilla. *Rethinking the Welfare Rights Movement*. New York: Routledge, 2012.

———. *Welfare Warriors: The Welfare Rights Movement in the United States*. New York: Routledge, 2005.

National Association of Office Workers. *Race Against Time: Automation of the Office; An Analysis of the Trends in Office Automation and the Impact on the Office*. Cleveland, OH: National Association of Office Workers, April 1980.

Newell, Diana. "Home Truths: Women Writing Science in the Nuclear Dawn." *European Journal of American Culture* 22, no. 3 (2003): 193–203.

Newgarden, Albert. *Men, Machines, and Methods in the Modern Office*. AMA Management Report no.6. New York: American Management Association, 1958.

9to5 National Association of Working Women. *Hidden Victims: Clerical Workers, Automation, and the Changing Economy*. Cleveland, Ohio: 9to5 National Association of Working Women, 1985.

Noble, David F. *Forces of Production: A Social History of Industrial Automation*. 1984. Reprint, New York: Oxford University Press, 1986.

———. *Progress Without People: New Technology, Unemployment, and the Message of Resistance*. Toronto: Between the Lines, 1995.

Nyden, Paul J. "Rank-and-File Movements in the United Mine Workers of America." In *Rebel Rank and File: Labor Militancy and Revolt from Below During the Long 1970s*, ed. Aaron Brenner, Robert Brenner, and Cal Winslow, 173–98. New York: Verso, 2010.

Nye, David E. *American Technological Sublime*. Cambridge, MA: MIT Press, 1994.

O'Connor, Alice. *Poverty Knowledge: Social Science, Social Policy, and the Poor in Twentieth-Century U.S. History*. Princeton: Princeton University Press, 2001.

Olerich, Henry. *A Cityless and Countryless World: An Outline of Practical Co-Operative Individualism*. Holstein, IA: Gilmore and Olerich, 1893.

Oppenheimer, Andres. *The Robots Are Coming! The Future of Jobs in the Age of Automation*. New York: Vintage, 2019.

Oppenheimer, J. Robert. "The Age of Science, 1900–1950." *Scientific American*, September 1950.

Pachirat, Timothy. *Every Twelve Seconds: Industrialized Slaughter and the Politics of Sight*. New Haven: Yale University Press, 2013.

Pencavel, John H. *Diminishing Returns at Work: The Consequences of Long Working Hours*. New York: Oxford University Press, 2018.

Pieper, Josef. *Leisure: The Basis of Culture*. Translated by Gerald Malsbary. 1948. Reprint, South Bend, IN: St. Augustine's, 1998.

"The Playboy Panel: Uses and Abuses of the New Leisure." *Playboy*, March 1965.

Polanyi, Karl. *The Great Transformation: The Political and Economic Origins of Our Time*. 1944. Reprint, Boston: Beacon, 1957.

Poole, Robert K. *Earthrise: How Man First Saw the Earth*. New Haven: Yale University Press, 2008.

Potter, David M. *People of Plenty: Economic Abundance and American Character*. Chicago: University of Chicago Press, 1954.

Price, Charlton R. *New Directions in the World of Work: A Conference Report*. Washington, DC: W. E. Upjohn Institute for Employment Research, March 1972.

Pursell, Carroll. *The Machine in America: A Social History of Technology*. 2nd ed.Baltimore: Johns Hopkins University Press, 2007.

———. *Technology in Postwar America: A History*. New York: Columbia University Press, 2007.

Rabinbach, Anson. *The Eclipse of the Utopias of Labor*. New York: Fordham University Press, 2018.

———. *The Human Motor: Energy, Fatigue, and the Origins of Modernity*. Berkeley: University of California Press, 1990.

Randolph, A. Philip, and Bayard Rustin. *A Freedom Budget for All Americans*. New York: A. Philip Randolph Institute, January 1967.

Ravenelle, Alexandra J. *Hustle and Gig: Struggling and Surviving in the Sharing Economy*. Oakland: University of California Press, 2019.

"Readers' Views: Automation." *News and Letters*, December 11, 1956.

Reich, Charles. *The Greening of America: How the Youth Revolution Is Trying to Make America Livable*. New York: Random House, 1970.

Resnikoff, Jason. "The Problem with Post-Work: Work and the Work Ethic as Units of Historical Analysis." *International Labor and Working Class History* no. 94 (Fall 2018): 207–218.

Richard, Carl J. *The Golden Age of the Classics in America: Greece, Rome, and the Antebellum United States*. Cambridge: Harvard University Press, 2009.

Riesman, David, et al. *The Lonely Crowd: A Study of the Changing American Character*. 1950. Reprint, New Haven: Yale University Press, 2001

Robinson, Cyril. *Marching with Dr. King: Ralph Helstein and the United Packinghouse Workers of America*. Santa Barbara: Praeger, 2011.

Rodgers, Daniel T. *The Work Ethic in Industrial America, 1850–1920*. Chicago: University of Chicago Press, 1974.

Rose, Kenneth D. *One Nation Underground: The Fallout Shelter in American Culture*. New York: New York University Press, 2001.

Rosenzweig, Roy. *Eight Hours for What We Will: Workers and Leisure in an Industrial City, 1870–1921*. Cambridge: Cambridge University Press, 1983.

Roszak, Theodore. *The Making of a Counter Culture: Reflections on the Technocratic Society and Its Youthful Opposition*. Garden City, NY: Doubleday, 1969.

Rothschild, Emma. *Paradise Lost: The Decline of the Auto-Industrial Age*. New York: Random House, 1973.

Russakoff Hoos, Ida. *Automation in the Office*. Washington DC: Public Affairs Press, 1961.

Sahlins, Marshall. *Stone Age Economics*. Chicago: Aldine-Atherton, 1972.

Sale, Kirkpatrick. *SDS*. New York: Random House, 1973.

Savignat, Alan, ed. *Automation: Positions et Propositions*. Fribourg: Editions Universitaires, 1957.

Scales, Robert H. "Gun Trouble." *Atlantic*, January–February, 2015.

Schiller, Dan. "From Culture to Information and Back Again: Commoditization as a Route to Knowledge." *Critical Studies in Mass Communication* 11 (1994): 93–115.

———. *How to Think About Information*. Urbana: University of Illinois Press, 2007.

Schrank, Robert. *Ten Thousand Working Days*. Cambridge, MA: MIT Press, 1978.

Scott, James C. *Against the Grain: A Deep History of the Earliest States*. New Haven: Yale University Press, 2017.

Seed, David. *American Science Fiction and the Cold War: Literature and Film*. Edinburgh: Edinburgh University Press, 1999.

Segal, Howard P. *Technological Utopianism in American Culture*. 1985. Reprint, Syracuse, NY: Syracuse University Press, 2005.

———. "The Technological Utopians." In Corn, Joseph J. *Imagining Tomorrow: History, Technology, and the American Future.*, ed. Joseph J. Corn, 119–36. Cambridge, MA: MIT Press, 1986.

Sennett, Richard. *The Craftsman*. New Haven: Yale University Press, 2008.

Seligman, Benjamin. *Most Notorious Victory: Man in an Age of Automation*. New York: Free Press, 1966.

Shaffer, H. B. "Leisure in the Great Society." *Editorial Research Reports 1964*. Vol. 2. Washington, DC: CQ Press. Accessed February 17, 2019. http://library.cqpress.com/cqresearcher/cqresrre1964120900

Shaiken, Harley. *Work Transformed: Automation and Labor in the Computer Age*. Lexington, MA: Lexington Books, 1984.

Shannon, Claude. "A Mathematical Theory of Communication." *Bell Technical Journal*, July 1948.

Shiomi, Haruhito, and Kazuo Wada, es. *Fordism Transformed: The Development of Production Methods in the Automobile Industry*. Oxford: Oxford University Press, 1995.

Shklar, Judith. *American Citizenship: The Quest for Inclusion*. Cambridge, MA: Harvard University Press, 1991.

Silverman, Bertram, and Murray Yanowitch. *The Worker in 'Post-Industrial' Capitalism: Liberal and Radical Responses*. New York: Free Press, 1974.

Simon, Matt. "Inside the Amazon Warehouse Where Humans and Machines Become One." *Wired*, June 5, 2019. Accessed October 2, 2020. https://www.wired.com/story/amazon-warehouse-robots/

Smemo, Kristoffer, Samir Sonti, and Gabriel Winant. "Conflict and Consensus: The Steel Strike of 1959 and the Anatomy of the New Deal Order." *Critical History Studies* 4, no. 1 (Spring 2017): 39–73.

Solanas, Valerie. *SCUM Manifesto*. 1968. Reprint, London: Phoenix, 1991.

"The Spreading Lordstown Syndrome." *Business Week*, March 4, 1972.

Srnicek, Nick, and Alex Williams. *Inventing the Future: Postcapitalism and a World Without Work*. London: Verso, 2015.

Steensland, Brian. *The Failed Welfare Revolution: America's Struggle over Guaranteed Income Policy*. Princeton: Princeton University Press, 2008.

Steigerwald, David. "Walter Reuther, the UAW, and the Dilemmas of Automation." *Labor History* 51, no. 3 (August 2010): 429–53.

Stein, Judith. "Conflict, Change, and Economic Policy in the Long 1970s." In *Rebel Rank and File: Labor Militancy and Revolt from Below During the Long 1970s*, ed. Aaron Brenner, Robert Brenner, and Cal Winslow, 77–104. New York: Verso, 2010.

———. *Pivotal Decade: How the United States Traded Factories for Finance in the Seventies*. New Haven: Yale University Press, 2011.

Stimson, Thomas E., Jr. "A House to Make Life Easy." *Popular Mechanics*, June 1952.

Strasser, Susan. *Never Done: A History of American Housework*. New York: Pantheon, 1982.

Striffler, Steve. *Chicken: The Dangerous Transformation of America's Favorite Food*. New Haven: Yale University Press, 2005.

Students for a Democratic Society. *The Port Huron Statement*. New York: Students for a Democratic Society, 1964.

Sugrue, Thomas J. "'Forget About Your Inalienable Right to Work': Deindustrialization and Its Discontents at Ford, 1950–1953." *International Labor and Working-Class History* 48 (October 1995): 112–30.

———. *The Origins of the Urban Crisis: Race and Inequality in Postwar Detroit*. Princeton: Princeton University Press, 1996.

Susman, Warren I. *Culture as History: The Transformation of American Society in the Twentieth Century*. New York: Pantheon, 1984.

Swados, Harvey. Foreword to *Worker Dissatisfaction in the '70s*. New York: Free Press, 1972.

———. "The Myth of the Happy Worker." *Nation*, August 17, 1957.

Swaim, Lawrence. "The Postal Strike of 1970: Relevance to Today." *Talking Union*, October 25, 2018. Accessed on October 25, 2018. http://portside.org/2018-10-25/postal-strike-1970-relevance-today

Taylor, Frederick Winslow. *The Principles of Scientific Management*. 1911. Reprint, New York: Harper and Brothers, 1916.

Tepperman, Jean. *Not Servants, Not Machines: Office Workers Speak Out!* Boston: Beacon, 1976.

Terborgh, George Willard. *The Automation Hysteria*. Washington, D.C.: Machinery and Allied Products Institute, 1965.

Theobald, Robert. *Free Men and Free Markets*. New York: Clarkson N. Potter, 1963.

Thomas, Keith. "Work and Leisure in Industrial Society," *Past and Present*, April 1965.

———. "Work and Leisure in Pre-Industrial Society." *Past and Present*, December 1964.

Thompson, E. P. "Time, Work-Discipline, and Industrial Capitalism." *Past & Present*, December 1967.

Tillmon, Johnnie. "Welfare Is a Women's Issue," *Ms.*, 1972. Accessed December 11, 2018. http://www.msmagazine.com/spring2002/tillmon.asp

Tucker, Robert C., ed. *The Marx-Engels Reader*. New York: Norton, 1972.

Turk, Katherine. "Labor's Pink-Collar Aristocracy: The National Secretaries Association's Encounters with Feminism in the Age of Automation." *Labor* 11, no. 2 (Summer 2014): 85–109.

Turner, Fred. *From Counterculture to Cyberculture: Steward Brand, the Whole Earth Network, and the Rise of Digital Utopianism.* Chicago: University of Chicago Press, 2006.

Van Der Linden, Marcel. "The Prehistory of *Post-Scarcity Anarchism*: Josef Weber and the Movement for a Democracy of Content (1947–1964)." Translated by Lee Mitzman. Accessed January 16, 2016. http://www.bopsecrets.org/images/weber.pdf.

Veblen, Thorstein. *The Theory of the Leisure Class: An Economic Study in the Evolution of Institutions.* London: MacMillan, 1899.

Vishmidt, Marina. "Permanent Reproductive Crisis: An Interview with Silvia Federici." *Mute*, March 7, 2013. Accessed December 11, 2018, http://www.metamute.org/editorial/articles/permanent-reproductive-crisis-interview-silvia-federici

Vonnegut, Kurt. *Player Piano.* New York: Scribner, 1952.

Wacjman, Judy. "From Women and Technology to Gendered Technoscience." *Information, Communication & Society* 10, no. 3 (June 2007): 287–98.

Ward, James A. *Ferrytale: The Career of W. H. "Ping" Ferry.* Stanford: Stanford University Press, 2001.

Ward, Stephan M. *In Love and Struggle: The Revolutionary Lives of James and Grace Lee Boggs.* Chapel Hill: University of North Carolina Press, 2016.

Warner, Michael. *Letters of the Republic: Publication and the Public Sphere in Eighteenth-Century America.* Cambridge, MA: Harvard University Press, 1990.

Weaver, Richard. *Ideas Have Consequences.* 1948. Reprint, Chicago: University of Chicago Press, 2013.

Weir, Margaret. *Politics and Jobs: The Boundaries of Employment Policy in the United States.* Princeton: Princeton University Press, 1993.

Weir, Stan. *Singlejack Solidarity.* Minneapolis: University of Minnesota Press, 2004.

West, Darrell M. *The Future of Work: Robots, AI, and Automation.* Washington, DC: Brookings Institution Press, 2018.

"What's Next for Labor?" *News and Letters*, April 30, 1957, 8.

White, Theodore H. *The Making of the President: 1960.* 1961. Reprint, New York: Harper Perennial, 2009.

Wiener, Norbert. *Cybernetics, or Control and Communication in the Animal and the Machine.* New York: Wiley, 1948.

Windham, Lane. *Knocking on Labor's Door: Union Organizing in the 1970s and the Roots of a New Economic Divide.* Chapel Hill: University of North Carolina Press, 2017.

Working Women. *An Analysis of the Trends in Office Automation and the Impact on the Office Workforce,* April 1980.

Wright, Gwendolyn. *Building the Dream: A Social History of Housing in America.* New York: Pantheon, 1981.

Yang, Andrew. *The War on Normal People: The Truth About America's Disappearing Jobs and Why Universal Basic Income Is Our Future.* New York: Hachette, 2018.

Yates, JoAnne. *Control Through Communication: The Rise of System in American Management*. Baltimore: Johns Hopkins University Press, 1989.

Yates, Richard. *Revolutionary Road*. Boston: Little, Brown, 1961.

Zarlengo, Kristina. "Civilian Threat, the Suburban Citadel, and Atomic Age American Women." *Signs* 24, no. 4 (Summer 1999): 925–58.

Zimpel, Lloyd, ed. *Man Against Work*. Grand Rapids, MI: Eerdmans, 1974.

Zuboff, Shoshana. *The Age of Surveillance Capitalism: The Fight for a Human Future at the New Frontier of Power*. New York: Public Affairs, 2019.

———. *In the Age of the Smart Machine: The Future of Work and Power*. New York: Basic Books, 1988.

Film and Photographs

Eames, Charles, and Ray Eames, dirs. The Information Machine. Eames Office, 1957.

General Electric. Live Better Electrically. Feat. Ronald Reagan and Nancy Reagan. Accessed April 25, 2019, https://www.youtube.com/watch?v=u5Lz1C53RwI

Henson, Jim, dir. The Paperwork Explosion. The Jim Henson Company, 1967.

Lloyd, Norman, dir. A Word to the Wives. Woman's Home Companion, 1955.

Push Buttons and People. UAW Education and Citizenship Departments, 1959. Accessed January 31, 2018, https://www.youtube.com/watch?v=c2GNIYhi8Dw

Sanna, Gavino, Eileen Rodgers, and Orrie Frutkin. "Sign Your Work National Commission on Productivity PSA 1973." National Commission on Productivity, Washington, D.C. Accessed November 1, 2018, https://m.youtube.com/watch?v=iSOOFNWzv4o

Vaughan-Lee, Emmanuel, dir. *Earthrise*. Global Oneness Project, 2018.

Unpublished Dissertations

Clark, Shannan Wayne. "White-Collar Workers Organize: Class-Consciousness and the Transformation of the Culture Industries in the United States, 1925–1955." PhD diss., Columbia University, 2006.

Lim, Seonghee. "Automation and San Francisco Class 'B' Longshoremen: Power, Race, and Workplace Democracy, 1958–1981." PhD diss., University of California, Santa Barbara, 2015.

Moberg, David F. "Rattling the Golden Chains: Conflict and Consciousness of Auto Workers." PhD diss., University of Chicago, 1978.

Index

automation discourse: adaptation to the Black liberation movement, 120–24; in the automobile industry, 4, 15–38, 46, 175, 178–79 (*see also* automobile industry); in clerical / office work, 4, 49–63 (*see also* digital computers); in coal mining, 4, 91–93; collective bargaining and, 101–9; conservative / traditionalist views of freedom and, 71–75, 78–80; in the containerization of dock work, 4, 106–9; domestic labor and, 7, 136–53 (*see also* domestic labor); feedback mechanisms vs., 3, 43; humanization of labor vs. (*see* humanization of labor); information revolution and, 40–41, 47–48, 50, 54 (*see also* digital computers); labor movement and, 6–7, 101–9 (*see also* collective bargaining); leisure and political freedom in (*see* freedom; leisure); liberal / leftist views of freedom and, 75–78, 80–82; in meatpacking, 4, 101–6, 131; mechanization and, 2–3, 8–9, 69, 122, 162; post-scarcity and, 125–27, 130, 133–34, 135; railroads and, 4, 93, 94–96, 110, 112, 113; Senate hearings on automation and technological change (1955), 3, 24, 25–26, 68–71, 90, 134, 150; Senate hearings on automation and technological change (1963), 24, 86, 93, 109–10, 175; Senate hearings on worker alienation (1972), 165, 179, 181; space exploration and escape from earth, 64–66, 74, 85–88; speedup and denigration of work in, 11–12 (*see also* speedup and labor degradation); Students for a Democratic Society (SDS) and, 116, 127–35; as term, 2–3; as vision of management's freedom from workers, 20–21, 45–47; work in the human condition and, 182–83

automobile industry, 15–38; automation as speedup and mechanized disruption in, 4–7, 13, 15–17, 27–38, 41–42, 122–23, 170–78; automation discourse and, 4, 15–38, 46, 175, 178–79; decentralized production in, 16, 18, 20, 31, 122–23; humanization in the General Motors Vega plant (Lordstown, Ohio), 169–79, 184; semiskilled worker downsizing and, 19–27, 121, 122–23, 181; transfer machines and, 16–17, 26, 46; Volvo team system and, 180. See also Chrysler; Ford Motor Company; General Motors

banking, digital computers and clerical workers in, 59–60, 61

Bank of America, 59–60, 61
Bannon, Ken, 22
Barnes, Ernest, 176–77
Beirne, Joseph, 69–70, 89, 111
Bell, Daniel, 6, 21, 121–22; information revolution and, 40; and the National Commission on Technology, Automation, and Economic Progress, 110–13; on the post-industrial society, 40; robots and, 142; *Work and Its Discontents,* 74–75, 76
Bellamy, Edward, *Looking Backward,* 66
Benanav, Aaron, 5
Benson, Frank, 61
Berkeley Free Speech Movement, 166–67
Berry, Wendell, 168
Bigelow, Julian, 43
biological determinism, 150–53
bit (binary digit), 47
Black liberation theorists: automation discourse and, 120–24; James Boggs (*see* Boggs, James); Martin Luther King, Jr., 96, 102, 134–35, 184; League of Revolutionary Black Workers and, 34, 122, 161; Simon Owens, 34–38; A. Phillip Randolph, 96–97, 100
Blue Cross Blue Shield of Texas, 62
Blue Shield of California, 62
Bluestone, Irving, 172–73, 176, 181
Boggs, Grace Lee, 119, 120, 121, 125
Boggs, James, 6, 118–24; and the Ad Hoc Committee on the Triple Revolution (October Group, 1963), 116–18, 119, 130, 131; *The American Revolution,* 119–22; as Chrysler autoworker, 29, 118–19, 122–23; on "scavenger" jobs, 121, 189; slavery and, 77–78
Bookchin, Murray, 125–27; *Post-Scarcity Anarchism,* 126, 133–34
Booz, Allen, Hamilton, 63
Borman, Frank, 169
Bradbury, Ray, 87, 141–42
Brautigan, Richard, 114
Braverman, Harry, 21, 81–82; *Labor and Monopoly Capital,* 182–83
Bridges, Harry, 107–9
Bright, James, 19
Brookings Institution, *Do the Poor Want to Work?,* 156
Brotherhood of Railroad Trainmen, 95
Brotherhood of Sleeping Car Porters, 96–97
Brown, Ray, 128
Bryner, Gary, 170, 179, 180
Bush, Vannevar, 69
Butler, H., 33, 34

Čapek, Karel, *Rossum's Universal Robots* (*R.U.R.*), 142
capitalism: alienation and, 125, 126; as anti-ecological, 125–26; automation and, 76, 124; feminism and, 149–50; industrial, 9–10, 22–23, 127; labor-management antagonisms of, 22; profitability as goal in, 6, 9–10 (*see also* profitability); surveillance, 189–90, 192; technological determinism in solving problems of, 4, 191
Carey, James, 116
Carmichael, Stokeley, 128
Cassidy, Kenneth D., 20–21
Center for the Study of Democratic Institutions, 116, 117
Chaplin, Charlie, 3
Charlesworth, James C., 71–72
China: global competition and, 6, 187; industrial employment in, 6
Chrysler: James Boggs as autoworker and, 29, 118–19, 122–23; opposition to democracy in factories, 18; semiskilled worker downsizing and, 19–20, 121, 122–23; speedup and mechanized disruption and, 29, 31–35, 37–38, 178; transfer machines, 46; unofficial actions (1960–65), 177
civil rights movement, 96, 100, 114–17, 119, 128, 149, 169
Clark, Dan, 172, 175
Clark, Joseph S., 24, 76–77, 86, 91
Clarke, Arthur C., *Childhood's End*, 85
clerical workers: collective bargaining and, 54–56, 61–62; feminization of clerical work and, 49, 52–62, 63; speedup of clerical work and, 49–50, 59–63. *See also* digital computers
Clynes, Manfred, 85–86
coal mining, 4, 91–93, 168
collective bargaining: and the automation discourse, 101–9; clerical work and, 54–56, 61–62; National Labor Relations Act (1935) and, 9, 18; railroad workers and, 94–96; technological determinism and, 10. *See also* strikes *and names of specific unions*
Commoner, Barry, 168
Commonwealth Edison, 61
Communications Workers of America, 23, 69–70, 89, 111
Communism, 120
computers. *See* digital computers
Congress of Industrial Organizations (CIO), 21, 23, 34, 121

containerization and shipping workers, 4, 106–9
Correspondence Group, 35, 120, 125
Cotton, Eugene, 103–4
Council of Economic Advisors, 98, 101, 111
counterculture, humanization of labor and, 166–67
Cowan, Ruth Schwartz, 141
Cruse, Harold, 120
cultural feminism, 150
"culture of poverty" thesis, 99
"cybernation," as synonym for automation, 115, 117, 126, 134, 147, 151, 152, 175
cybernetics movement, 22, 111, 131; automatic office and, 47–48; founders of, 43–44; radical feminism and, 151–52; as the second industrial revolution, 7, 44
cyborg (cybernetic organism), 85–86

Davis, D. J., 25
de Grazia, Sebastian, *Of Time, Work, and Leisure,* 76
democracy: automation discourse and, 76; humanization of labor and, 183, 184 (*see also* humanization of labor); shop-floor, 18, 23, 25, 97, 166, 179–81; slavery and, 72–73, 77
Diebold, John: *Automation,* 39, 41, 43, 44, 48–49, 66, 68, 83; "automation," as term and, 1, 39–40, 41–49, 56, 68–71, 134; consulting businesses, 39–40, 68–69; digital computers and clerical work, 43, 47–49, 50, 56; at the Harvard Business School, 39, 43–44, 47–48; as "high priest of automation," 1, 6, 39–40, 68–71, 93–94, 109; home "automation" and, 138–39; human limitations in the workplace and, 45, 48–49, 69; on leisure, 73; the "second industrial revolution" and, 44–45; Senate hearings on automation and technological change, 68–71, 93–94, 109–10, 134; workerless factory and, 44–46
Diggers (guerrilla theater group), 163
digital computers, 47–63; artificial intelligence and, 191–92; automation discourse and, 4, 49–63; cybernetics movement and, 43–44; data processing and, 51–54, 58–59, 61; J. Diebold and, 43, 47–49, 50, 56; in the early postwar period, 40–41; electronic data processing and, 54, 56–63; ENIAC, 43–44; feminization of clerical work and, 49, 52–62, 63; human labor and, 54, 56–63; IBM and, 51–54; "information" as commodity and, 40–41, 47–48, 50, 54; in the insurance

and banking industries, 56–62, 190; Management Information Systems (MIS) and, 50–51; Operation Igloo White (Vietnam War), 167–68; speedup of clerical work and, 49–50, 59–63, 190; surveillance capitalism and, 189–90, 192; typewriters vs., 4, 49, 54. *See also* robots and robotics

domestic labor, 136–59; automation discourse and, 7, 136–53; double shift of wage work and housework, 148–49; home design and, 136–40, 143–44; liberal feminism and, 144, 145–49, 153, 157, 159; material feminism and socialization of, 140–41, 153–58; mechanical innovations and, 136–45, 158–59; patriarchal family and, 141–42, 147–51; radical feminism and, 149–53, 157, 159; reproductive labor and, 137–38, 150–53; robots and, 139, 142–43, 148, 159; social reproduction ideal and, 138–42, 145, 153, 156–57; as unpaid labor, 138, 140–41, 144, 156–57

Doriot, Georges, 43, 47

Do the Poor Want to Work? (Brookings Institution), 156

Douglas, Paul H., 68

Downer, Cassie, 156–57

Drucker, Peter, 41

Du Bois, W. E. B., 121

Dunayevskaya, Raya, 35, 76, 125

Dunbar, Roxanne, 152

Dunlop, John T., 24

Eames, Charles and Ray, 52, 53

eco-anarchism, 125–27

Economic Research and Action Project (ERAP), 128–32

Edwards, Vera, 177–78

Eichmann, Adolf, 84

Eisenhower, Dwight, 117

Electronic Data Systems (EDS), 62

electronic digital computers. *See* digital computers

Ellul, Jacques, *The Technological Society*, 167

Employment Act (1946), 71, 112

environmental movement, 125–27, 162, 163, 168–69

Facebook, 192

Fair Employment Practices Act, 97

Fair Labor Standards Act (1938), 96

Family Assistance Program (FAP, proposed), 154–55, 156, 183

Fanon, Frantz, 121

Federici, Sylvia, 157–59

feedback mechanisms, automation vs., 3, 43

feminism: cultural feminism, 150; liberal feminism, 144, 145–49, 153, 154, 157, 159; material feminism and the socialization of domestic labor, 140–41, 153–58; radical feminism, 149–53, 157, 159

Fenton, Patrick, 164

Ferry, W. H. "Ping," 77; and the Ad Hoc Committee on the Triple Revolution (October Group, 1963), 116–18, 128, 130, 167; *Caught on the Horns of Plenty*, 118

Firestone, Shulamith, *The Dialectic of Sex*, 149–53, 154, 157, 159

Forbidden Planet (1956 movie), 87, 143

Ford, Henry, II, 26–27

Fordism, 10

Ford Motor Company: Automation Department, 16–17, 20, 28, 41–42, 121–22, 126; Buffalo Stamping plant "wildcat" strike (1950), 15–16; collective bargaining and, 10, 23–26, 28, 166; contract of 1949, 10, 23, 28, 166; flying car and, 64; opposition to democracy in factories, 18; origins of "automation," as term and, 1–2, 6, 15–17, 20, 26–27, 41–42, 138, 181–82; "people problem" and, 161, 181–82; postwar speedup and mechanized disruption and, 15–17, 28, 29, 32–34; semiskilled worker downsizing and, 20–22; strikes (1973), 178; transfer machines, 16–17, 26

Fordyce, Raymond, 144

Forrester, Jay W., 43

Foulkes, Fred, 179–80

Fraser, Douglas, 177, 181

Frazier, George, 7

freedom: as aristocratic ideal, 71–75, 84; Aristotle and, 72, 74; in classical American liberalism, 7, 8; conservative / traditionalist views of, 71–75, 78–80; desire to leave earth and, 64–66, 74, 85–88; from drudgery of domestic labor, 139–40, 141–42, 146–49; as freedom from labor, 66, 69–78, 90–91, 117–18, 119–25, 127–34; incompatibility of wage labor and, 2, 7, 8, 10–12; liberal / leftist views of, 75–78, 80–82; as "play," 74–76; reconciliation with the natural world and, 163; reconciliation with work, 78–85. *See also* leisure

French, John, 169

Freud, Sigmund, 75

Friedan, Betty, *The Feminine Mystique*, 141, 144, 145–49, 153, 157, 159

Friedman, Milton, 153–54
Fuller, R. Buckminster, 111, 139, 152

Gagarin, Yuri, 88
Galbraith, John Kenneth: *The Affluent Society*, 11, 90–91, 164; "techno-structure" and, 167
Gallup, George, 72
Ganley, Nat, 29
Garson, Barbara, *The Meaning and Demeaning of Work*, 164
gender: domestic labor and (*see* domestic labor); in the feminization of clerical work, 49, 52–62, 63 (*see also* digital computers); in Manpower retraining programs, 99–100; reproductive labor and, 137–38, 150–53. *See also* feminism
General Electric, 140, 161
General Foods Pet Food factory, 180
General Motors: General Motors Assembly Division (GMAD), 171–73, 176–78; humanization of labor and, 169–79, 181; Lordstown (Ohio) plant closing (2018), 187–88; Lordstown (Ohio) Vega plant strike (1972), 169–79, 184; Norwood (Ohio) plant strike (1972), 176–77; opposition to democracy in factories, 18; speedup and mechanized disruption and, 29, 30; strikes (1973), 178; transfer machines, 17
Gerstenberg, Richard, 171
ghost work, 192
Giedion, Siegfried, 8, 139, 144
Gitlin, Todd, 116, 118, 127–28, 130, 131, 133, 185
Gleason, Teddy, 108
Godfrey, Joseph, 172
Goldwater, Barry, 115
Gomberg, William, 180–81
Goodman, Paul, 160; *Growing Up Absurd*, 129
Google, 192
Gorz, André, *Strategy for Labor*, 134
Great Depression: full employment and, 18, 67, 89; speedup during, 29; unemployment during, 9, 71, 116, 117; unionization during, 27
Great Recession, 187, 191
Great Society, 113
Greenspan, Alan, 40
GROIN (Garbage Removal or Income Now), 132
Groves, Leslie, 43
guaranteed annual income, 89; Ad Hoc Committee on the Triple Revolution (October Group, 1963) and, 106, 115; auto workers

and, 24–25; Family Assistance Program (FAP, proposed), 154–55, 156, 183; government policy recommendation for, 112; Martin Luther King, Jr. and, 134; longshoremen and, 107, 108–9; for mothers, 132, 153–58; National Welfare Rights Organization (NWRO) and, 153–58

Haapanen, Shirley, 60
Halacy, D. S., Jr., *Cyborg*, 86
Harder, D. S., 16–17, 20, 26, 33, 41, 138
Hardman, J. B. S., 99
Harrington, Michael, 114
Harvard University: John Diebold at the Harvard Business School, 39, 43–44, 47–48; Project on Technology, Work, and Character, 175
Hawkins, Augustus, 98
Hawthorne experiments, 179
Hayden, Dolores, 140–41
Hayden, Tom, 116, 128, 130
Hayes, A. J., 111
Heinlein, Robert, 136–40, 143–44
Heinlein, Virginia "Ginny," 136–40, 144
Helstein, Ralph, 101–6, 116–17, 131
Henson, Jim, 51–52
Herrick, Neal Q., *Where Have All the Robots Gone?* (with H. Sheppard), 161
Hester, Hugh B., 114
Hilton, Alice Mary, 77
Hochheimer, Theo, 168
Holland, Elmer J., 110
Horowitz, Roger, 103
House Un-American Activities Committee, 116
housework. *See* domestic labor
Howe, Irving, 114
Hughes, H. Stuart, 114
humanization of labor, 76, 112–13, 163–85; alienation of workers vs., 3, 9, 80–82, 121, 125–27, 163–65, 179; defining, 169; General Foods Pet Food factory and, 180; at the General Motors Vega plant (Lordstown, Ohio), 168, 169–79, 181, 184; meaning of work and, 7–12, 79–84, 127–34, 142–44, 164–66, 170; nature of, 163–64; origins of "humanization," 166–69; "quality of life" experiments vs., 179–80, 183–84; speedup and labor degradation vs. (*see* speedup and labor degradation); strikes and (*see* strikes); twenty-first century style of, 189–90; Volvo team system, 180; worker demands for, 166,

169; workers' control and, 169, 173, 178, 179–83; work ethic in, 81, 131–32, 155, 156, 183–85; work in the human condition, 182–83
Humphrey, Hubert, 91

IBM, 51–54, 58–59, 61, 62
industrialization: automation vs., 3; centralization of productive property in, 7–8; in the postwar period, 11; work and property ownership vs., 7–8
Industrial Revolution, 21, 78, 140; second phase of, 7, 22, 44, 70
information: as a commodity, 40–41, 47–48, 50, 54; data vs., 50–51; freeing from the body of the worker, 51–53
Information Machine, The (film), 52, 53
information theory, 47–48, 51
insurance industry: digital computers and clerical workers in, 56–62; speedup and labor degradation in, 190
International Association of Machinists, 111
International Ladies' Garment Workers' Union (ILGWU), 180–81
International Longshoremen's and Warehousemen's Union (ILWU), 106–9
International Longshoremen's Association, 108
International Union of Electrical, Radio, and Machine Workers, 116, 162
International Wages for Housework Campaign, 158

Jackson, J. B., 145
James, C. L. R., 35, 120, 125
Javits, Jacob, 179
Jefferson, Thomas, 76, 81
Jetsons, The (animated sitcom), 143
Job Corps, 100–101
job training / retraining programs, 36, 97–101, 104–6, 154
Johnson, Bernard, 181
Johnson, Lyndon B., 97–101; Great Society, 113; Job Corps, 100–101; Manpower Development and Training Act (MDTA), 97–101, 104–6, 109–10; National Commission on Technology, Automation, and Economic Progress, 109–13; War on Poverty, 12, 98–100
Johnson-Forest Tendency, 35
JOIN (Jobs or Income Now), 132
Jones, Beverly, 148
Jordan, Joan, 157

Keats, John, 145
Keller, K. T., 43
Kennedy, John F., 112; "automation" and, 7, 26, 93–94, 109–10; Manpower Development and Training Act (MDTA) and, 97–101, 104–6, 109–10; New Frontier, 91–98; President's Commission on the Status of Women, 146; space exploration and, 64–65
Kennedy, Ted, 165, 179
Kerr, Clark: *Industrialism and Industrial Man,* 11; University of California system and, 11, 102
Keynes, John Maynard: full employment as goal and, 23–26, 67, 71, 85, 89–91; on technological unemployment, 9, 28–29, 93, 115–16, 117, 130–31
King, Martin Luther, Jr., 96, 102, 134–35, 184
Kirk, Russell, *The Conservative Mind,* 78, 79
Kissinger, Henry, 167
Kline, Nathan S., 85–86
Koedt, Anne, 149
Kraus, Henry, 27
Kristol, Irving, 115–16

labor movement. *See* collective bargaining
Landrum, Phillip, 155
League of Revolutionary Black Workers, 34, 122, 161
leisure: affluent society and, 164; aristocratic views of, 71–75, 79, 84, 87; conservative / traditionalist views of work and, 71–75, 78–80; as freedom from labor, 66–67, 69–78; liberal / leftist views of work and, 75–78, 80–82; recreation spending in the U.S. and, 67; shorter-hours movement and, 8, 66–67, 85, 107, 111, 183; and white middle-class housewives, 146–49
Levin, Howard S., *Office Work and Automation,* 50–51
Levinson, Marc, 107
Levitt, William, 136
Lewis, John L., 92–93
liberal feminism, 144, 145–49, 153, 154, 157, 159
Liberty Mutual Insurance, 60
Lincoln, Abraham, 8
Long, Russell, 155
Lynd, Alice, 161
Lynd, Staughton, 161

Maccoby, Michael, 175
Management Information Systems (MIS), 50–51

Shannon, Claude, 43–44, 47–48, 50
Shepard, Alan, 64, 88
Sheppard, Harold L., *Where Have All the Robots Gone?* (with N. Herrick), 161
shorter-hours movement, 8, 85; four-day workweek and, 66–67, 183; thirty-five-hour workweek, 107, 111
Shriver, Sargent, 100–101
Silvey, Ted F., 34
Sinclair, Upton, *The Jungle*, 103
Sisterhood is Powerful, 148
slave labor: in ancient Greece, 72, 74, 77, 78; antebellum defense of, 74, 76, 78; aristocratic understanding of freedom in slave societies, 72–74, 76; automation discourse in defense of, 66, 76–78; "cheerful robots" (Mills) and, 12, 81, 82, 160; democracy and, 72–73, 77; machines as, 77, 130; robots as household slaves, 142–45
Slichter, Sumner, 103
Social Gospel, 134
social reproduction, 138–42, 145, 153, 156–57
Social Security, 10, 62, 76–77
Solanas, Valerie, *SCUM Manifesto*, 7, 151–52
Sorenson, Ted, 93, 109
Soviet Union (former): cybernetics movement, 111; *Sputnik* (1957 satellite launch), 64, 65–66, 85
space exploration: first Earth orbit (1961), 64; moon flights, 64–65, 74, 88, 168–69; in quest for freedom, 64–66, 85–88; science fiction and, 85–86, 87; Soviet *Sputnik* launch (1957) and, 64, 65–66, 85
speedup and labor degradation: at Amazon fulfillment centers, 189–90; in the automobile industry, 4–7, 13, 15–17, 27–38, 41–42, 122–23, 170–78; in coal mining, 91–93; in the containerization of dock work, 107–9; with digital computers in clerical work, 49–50, 59–63, 190; domestic labor and, 136–49, 158–59; equipment breakdowns and, 27–28, 37, 60; job classification changes and, 32–33, 94–96, 104, 106, 108–9; mandatory overtime and, 33, 173, 177–78; in the meatpacking industry, 103–4; new machinery and, 35–38, 50, 59–63, 91–96, 103, 104, 106, 108; physical demands and dangers of, 37–38, 60–61, 92, 93, 172–73, 177–78, 190; racism and, 34, 120–21, 122–23; on railroads, 94–96; retraining programs and job degradation, 99–100; time studies in, 27, 35–36, 49–50

Sputnik (Soviet satellite), 64, 65–66, 85
stagflation, 162
Stevenson, Adlai, 91, 141
Strasser, Susan, 141
Strauss, Dave, 130
strikes: airline mechanics (1966), 169; Chrysler unofficial actions (1960–65), 177; Ford Motor Buffalo Stamping plant (1950), 15–16; General Motors Lordstown (Ohio) Vega plant (1972), 169–76; General Motors Norwood (Ohio) plant (1972), 176–77; "generation gap" thesis for, 174–78; New York garment workers (1909), 8; sanitation workers (Memphis, 1968), 134–35, 184; strike wave (1946), 10, 18, 160; strike wave (1964), 166, 177; strike wave (1970), 160, 163–64; strike wave (1973), 178; strike wave (1979), 161; United Farm Workers boycott, 169
Student Nonviolent Coordinating Committee (SNCC), 128
Students for a Democratic Society (SDS), 116, 127–35; Economic Research and Action Project (ERAP), 128–32; "Port Authority Statement" (1967), 132–33, 134; Port Huron Statement (1962), 128–34
Sugrue, Thomas, 1
Sullivan, R. H., 20
surveillance capitalism, 189–90, 192
Swados, Harvey, 81, 174

Taft-Hartley Act (1947), 76–77, 178
Tate, Allen, 79
Taylor, Frederick Winslow: *The Principles of Scientific Management*, 9; Taylorism / scientific management and, 9, 20, 21, 35–36, 138, 182–83, 189–90
technological determinism: bargaining table vs., 10; challenges to, 4, 191–92; nature of, 4; in solving problems of capitalism, 4, 191
technological unemployment (Keynes), 9, 28–29, 93, 115–16, 117, 130–31
Tepperman, Jean, 57
Terrano, Angela, 31
Theobald, Robert, 77, 111, 142; and the Ad Hoc Commission on the Triple Revolution (October Group, 1963), 116–17, 130, 153–54; *Free Men and Free Markets*, 118
Tillmon, Johnnie, 155–57
totalitarianism, 82–83, 84
transfer machines, 16–17, 26, 46
Travellers Insurance Company, 59, 60–61
Triple Revolution (1964 pamphlet), 114–16, 127.

work ethic, 81, 131–32, 155, 156, 183–85
Work in America (1973), 165–66, 170, 182, 185
Work Incentive Program (WIN, 1967), 154
World War II: atomic bombs and, 10, 43, 44, 50; research and technological developments during, 42–44, 69
Wright, Frank Lloyd, 144

Yates, Richard, 145
youth culture: antiwar movement and, 161, 162, 167–68, 178; counterculture and, 166–67; "generation gap" thesis of autoworker strikes, 174–78; rebellion of the 1960s and, 129, 169, 174; Students for a Democratic Society (SDS) and, 116, 127–35

Zimpel, Lloyd, *Man Against Work,* 175–76

JASON RESNIKOFF is a lecturer in the
Department of History at Columbia University.

The Working Class in American History

Worker City, Company Town: Iron and Cotton-Worker Protest in Troy and Cohoes, New York, 1855–84   *Daniel J. Walkowitz*

Life, Work, and Rebellion in the Coal Fields: The Southern West Virginia Miners, 1880–1922   *David Alan Corbin*

Women and American Socialism, 1870–1920   *Mari Jo Buhle*

Lives of Their Own: Blacks, Italians, and Poles in Pittsburgh, 1900–1960   *John Bodnar, Roger Simon, and Michael P. Weber*

Working-Class America: Essays on Labor, Community, and American Society   *Edited by Michael H. Frisch and Daniel J. Walkowitz*

Eugene V. Debs: Citizen and Socialist   *Nick Salvatore*

American Labor and Immigration History, 1877–1920s: Recent European Research   *Edited by Dirk Hoerder*

Workingmen's Democracy: The Knights of Labor and American Politics   *Leon Fink*

The Electrical Workers: A History of Labor at General Electric and Westinghouse, 1923–60   *Ronald W. Schatz*

The Mechanics of Baltimore: Workers and Politics in the Age of Revolution, 1763–1812   *Charles G. Steffen*

The Practice of Solidarity: American Hat Finishers in the Nineteenth Century   *David Bensman*

The Labor History Reader   *Edited by Daniel J. Leab*

Solidarity and Fragmentation: Working People and Class Consciousness in Detroit, 1875–1900   *Richard Oestreicher*

Counter Cultures: Saleswomen, Managers, and Customers in American Department Stores, 1890–1940   *Susan Porter Benson*

The New England Working Class and the New Labor History   *Edited by Herbert G. Gutman and Donald H. Bell*

Labor Leaders in America   *Edited by Melvyn Dubofsky and Warren Van Tine*

Barons of Labor: The San Francisco Building Trades and Union Power in the Progressive Era   *Michael Kazin*

Gender at Work: The Dynamics of Job Segregation by Sex during World War II   *Ruth Milkman*

Once a Cigar Maker: Men, Women, and Work Culture in American Cigar Factories, 1900–1919   *Patricia A. Cooper*

A Generation of Boomers: The Pattern of Railroad Labor Conflict in Nineteenth-Century America   *Shelton Stromquist*

Work and Community in the Jungle: Chicago's Packinghouse Workers, 1894–1922   *James R. Barrett*

Workers, Managers, and Welfare Capitalism: The Shoeworkers and Tanners of Endicott Johnson, 1890–1950   *Gerald Zahavi*

Men, Women, and Work: Class, Gender, and Protest in the New England Shoe Industry, 1780–1910   *Mary Blewett*

The University of Illinois Press
is a founding member of the
Association of University Presses.

———————————————————

Composed in 10.75/13 Adobe Minion Pro
with Avenir display
by Jim Proefrock
at the University of Illinois Press
Manufactured by Sheridan Books, Inc.

University of Illinois Press
1325 South Oak Street
Champaign, IL 61820-6903
www.press.uillinois.edu